Standard COBOL:
A Problem-Solving
Approach

Standard COBOL:
A Problem-Solving Approach

Marilyn Z. Smith   *University of Southwestern Louisiana*

Houghton Mifflin Company · Boston
Atlanta
Dallas
Geneva, Illinois
Hopewell, New Jersey
Palo Alto
London

To Brian

Printed in the United States of America

Library of Congress Catalog Card Number: 73–10230

ISBN: 0-395-17091-5

Preface

This textbook is unique in that it offers a problem-solving approach to COBOL programming. Its emphasis is on learning how to develop and solve problems on the computer. Enough essential elements of COBOL are introduced to enable students to write complete programs by the second week of the course. Other topics are presented gradually and the student progresses from elementary to advanced programs.

This textbook is student-oriented, jargon free, and requires no previous computer experience. To aid the student its features include:

1. Standard (ANS) COBOL

2. Problem-solving techniques through the use of flowcharts

3. Skeleton outlines for COBOL programs

4. Suggested programs and exercises

The COBOL programming language has many dialects which have developed as manufacturers added their own options to make programming easier. Standard COBOL contains the basic elements which are common to all dialects. It is defined by the American National Standards Institute and is often referred to as ANS COBOL. Standard COBOL is machine independent and is supported by the major computer manufacturers. Therefore, the student learning standard COBOL will have no trouble applying his knowledge. Even though the text is written to teach standard COBOL, it includes in Chapter 12 specifics for various computers. Space is included in reference Appendix B so that the student may check the various options which are available at his computing center.

In addition to covering fundamentals of standard COBOL, this text provides a methodical approach to problem-solving. In numerous examples of increasing difficulty the problem is discussed; a method for solving it is selected; a flowchart of the method is constructed; and finally the program is written. The student is shown the gradual development from problem to computer program solution, with each step carefully explained.

To help the student write programs, this text includes the skeleton outline of a COBOL program. The outline shows all required and optional parts in the order in which they must appear in the program. Thus the student does not need to memorize the structure of a COBOL program, but can refer to the outline. Also, the skeleton outline bridges the gap between an elementary text and a reference manual because the outline is written in the same notation as reference manuals.

Throughout the text are numerous program suggestions and exercises. No answers are included so that the teacher may either assign the exercises as homework or discuss them in class in an atmosphere of creativity and ingenuity.

A problem may have several solutions and the author did not wish to imply that one way is more correct than another.

Other features of the text include an appendix on use of the card punch and drum control card, a chapter on writing reports including use of the Report Writer, and a chapter on the SORT verb. The text also discusses various ways to use subscripted data-names and the PERFORM command.

The author would like to thank the following individuals who reviewed this book in its early stages of development: Professor Hames Cress, Kent State University; Professor George E. Cusson, Springfield Technical Community College; Professor Roger Hamilton, Morningside College; Professor Edward H. Rategan, College of San Mateo; and Professor Arjan T. Sadhwani, University of Akron.

Marilyn Z. Smith

Acknowledgment

Contents

Chapter 1

Computer Concepts

1.1 Introduction

This chapter discusses important computer concepts which are fundamental to the study of a computer language such as COBOL. If the student has completed an introductory computer course, he may choose either to omit this chapter or to use it as a quick review. Section 1.2 covers the basic components of a computer: input and output devices, Central Processing Unit, and memory. Section 1.3 discusses computer languages and the way man can communicate with the machine. The student should become familiar with the list of special terms that is included at the end of the chapter.

1.2 Basic Design of a Computer

Computers are in wide use today because of their speed, accuracy, and versatility. The speed of the computer enables it to process huge amounts of information and produce accurate reports in a fraction of the time a person would take. Computers were originally designed to help with mathematical calculations, but people soon realized that a computer could be helpful in the business world for doing payrolls, ledgers, inventories, and other tasks where it is necessary to process a large amount of data. Whether people use a computer for scientific or commercial applications, there are some common elements in every task: the computer receives some information, works on it, and produces some results. These three steps are evident in the design of a computer. Each machine has a part that accepts data, a part that processes the data, and a part that gives out the results. The part that processes the data consists of a memory area and a processing area. These four parts of a computer are shown schematically in Figure 1.1.

Figure 1.1   Basic Design of a Computer

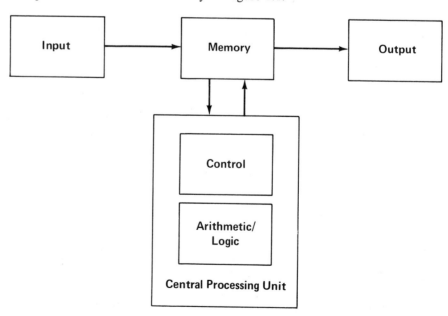

Source: Laura G. Cooper and Marilyn Z. Smith, *Standard FORTRAN: A Problem-Solving Approach* (Boston: Houghton Mifflin Co., 1973), Figure 2.1, p. 16.

The four basic parts of a computer are:

1. input devices
2. memory
3. central processing unit (CPU)
4. output devices

An *input device* is a machine which accepts the input and reads it into the computer. *Input* is any information going into the computer. It includes the data on which the computer will work and the instructions which tell the computer what to do with the data.

Presently, manufacturers have not produced computers to which we can talk, so we must record our data and instructions on punched cards (see Figure 1.9), magnetic tape, or some other medium which the computer will accept. The recorded information is transmitted to the computer by an appropriate input device. The input device which can "read" the holes on a punched card is a card reader, as shown in Figure 1.2. If a card reader transmits its input over telephone lines, we call it a terminal. Other machines

Figure 1.2   Card Reader

Courtesy IBM

which may be connected via telephone lines are the teletype and cathode ray tube (CRT) (see Figure 1.3). Terminals have the advantage that they do not need to be located near the computer in order to work. However, they are slow machines compared to other input devices. A tape drive, such as the one in Figure 1.4, can sense information recorded on a magnetic tape. The optical scanner can read the print made by a special typewriter. The disk in Figure 1.5 consists of many large flat circular surfaces similar in appearance to phonograph records. The surfaces contain tracks on which data can be recorded magnetically. Above the surfaces are heads which can read the magnetized areas on the disk. The disk is extremely fast—much faster than a tape drive or a card reader—but it is also more expensive. Therefore, most installations use cards or tape for input and reserve the disk for special priority projects.

Figure 1.3   CRT Terminal

Courtesy IBM

Figure 1.4   Tape Drive

Courtesy IBM

Figure 1.5   Disk

Courtesy IBM

As the computer receives the input, it is placed in the *memory* unit. Another name for the memory unit is *storage* unit, because this is the place where the computer stores data and instructions. We may picture memory as a series of post office boxes. Each box has a different number so that we can distinguish one from another; but unlike a post office we may place only *one* character in each box. An individual "box" in the computer's memory is called a *location* and its number is called an *address*. Pictorially, we may represent memory as in Figure 1.6. Location 352 contains the letter S and location 360 the number 6.

Figure 1.6 Representation of a Computer's Memory Locations

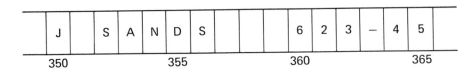

	J		S	A	N	D	S				6	2	3	–	4	5
350				355						360					365	

Actually a computer's memory is not a series of boxes but a series of magnetic cores which can be magnetized in two directions. Thus a core magnetized in a clockwise direction could represent the number zero and a core magnetized in a counterclockwise direction could represent a one. To form other numbers or characters we would need several cores. For example, the letter Y might be 011001 and the letter Z 011010. Most computers use from seven to nine cores to make up a character.

Once the data and instructions are in memory, the *central processing unit* (CPU) works on the input and executes the commands given to it. The *control portion of the CPU coordinates the processing of input*. It saves the input in the computer's memory, gives the commands to be executed to the arithmetic and logic section, and transfers all information to be written to the output section. The *arithmetic and logic* section can perform addition, sub-

Figure 1.7 Line Printer

Courtesy IBM

traction, multiplication, and division. It also can compute the answers to questions such as: Is current balance above 200 dollars? Do these people live at the same address?

An *output device* is a machine which transfers the output from the computer's memory to some medium such as paper or magnetic tape. *Output* is any information coming out of a computer. It may be something which was read in, such as a person's name, or something computed like a salary. One of the more common output devices is the line printer which writes on continuous paper forms. (See Figures 1.7 and 1.8.) The tape drive which can read input from a magnetic tape can also write information on a tape. The disk can write on its surfaces as well as read from them. Both the tape drive and the disk are faster than the printer, but the printer can produce reports which people can read. Normally tape and disk are used to save records which could be summarized and printed at a later time.

Figure 1.8   Printed Output from a Computer

```
XXXXXXXXXXXXXXXXXXXXXXXXXXXXXXXXXXXXXXXXXXXXXXXXXXXXXXXXXXXXXXXXXXXXXXXXXXXXX
XXXXXXXXXXXXXXXXXXXXXXXXXXXXXXXXXXXXXXXXXXXXXXXXXXXXXXXXXXXXXXXXXXXXXXXXXXXXX
XX                                                                         XX
XX                          ABC  COMPANY  INC.                             XX
XX                                                                         XX
XX                          ANYTOWN, USA.                                  XX
XX                                    12345                                XX
XX                                                                         XX
XX              XXXXXXXXXXXXXXXXXXXXXXXXXXXXXXXXXXXXXXXXXXXXXXXXXXX         XX
XX   1ST. BANK     X    DATE    X EMPLOYEE * X DEPT. XXXXXXXXX  CHECK *  X  XX
XX      OF         X            X            X       XXXXXXXXX          X  XX
XX   AMERICA       X 10-22-72 X    43281     X   456  XXXXXXXXX  0000004  X  XX
XX                 X            X            X       XXXXXXXXX          X  XX
XX              XXXXXXXXXXXXXXXXXXXXXXXXXXXXXXXXXXXXXXXXXXXXXXXXXXX         XX
XX                                                   X AMOUNT    X         XX
XX   PAY TO THE                                      X          X         XX
XX   ORDER OF    SEEFELDT,CATHY C.                   X  $*482.33 X         XX
XX                                                   XXXXXXXXXXXXXX        XX
XX                                       JOHN SMITH                        XX
XX                                                                         XX
XX                                       TREASURER                         XX
XX                                                                         XX
XXXXXXXXXXXXXXXXXXXXXXXXXXXXXXXXXXXXXXXXXXXXXXXXXXXXXXXXXXXXXXXXXXXXXXXXXXXXX
XX                                                                         XX
*******************************DETATCH AND SAVE****************************
XX                                                                         XX
XXXXXXXXXXXXXXXXXXXXXXXXXXXXXXXXXXXXXXXXXXXXXXXXXXXXXXXXXXXXXXXXXXXXXXXXXXXXX
XX                                                                         XX
XX   XXXXXXXXXXXXXXXXXXXXXXXXXXXXXXXXXXXXXXXXXXXXXXXX   XXXXXXXXXX  XX
XX   X      HOURS      X      EARNINGS      X        X   X  GROSS  X  XX
XX   X REG.    OVTM  X   REG.    OVTM   X FED W/H X   FICA    X   X   PAY   X  XX
XX   X                 X                    X        X        X   X        X  XX
XX   X 40.00    20.00 X $400.00 $300.00 X  $181.27 X  $*36.40 X   X $700.00 X  XX
XX   X                 X                    X        X        X   X        X  XX
XX   XXXXXXXXXXXXXXXXXXXXXXXXXXXXXXXXXXXXXXXXXXXXXXXX   XXXXXXXXXX  XX
XX                                                                         XX
XX                                                                         XX
XX   XXXXXXXXXXXXXXXXXXXXXXXXXXXXXXXXXXXXXXXXXXXXXXXX   XXXXXXXXXX  XX
XX   X             X EMPLOYEE X         X HOURLY X    SOCIAL      X   X  NET   X  XX
XX   X   DATE     X   NO.    X DEPT. X  RATE  X   SECURITY     X   X  PAY   X  XX
XX   X             X          X         X        X              X   X        X  XX
XX   X 10-22-72 X   43281   X   456   X 10.00 X  945-32-7895  X   X $482.33 X  XX
XX   X             X          X         X        X              X   X        X  XX
XX   XXXXXXXXXXXXXXXXXXXXXXXXXXXXXXXXXXXXXXXXXXXXXXXX   XXXXXXXXXX  XX
XX                                                                         XX
XXXXXXXXXXXXXXXXXXXXXXXXXXXXXXXXXXXXXXXXXXXXXXXXXXXXXXXXXXXXXXXXXXXXXXXXXXXXX
XXXXXXXXXXXXXXXXXXXXXXXXXXXXXXXXXXXXXXXXXXXXXXXXXXXXXXXXXXXXXXXXXXXXXXXXXXXXX
```

Terminals such as the teletype or CRT are output devices as well as input devices. Also, the computer can punch cards with its own card punch. One advantage of having the computer punch cards for output is that the cards may be used later as input.

The punched card is widely used because it is relatively inexpensive and easy to handle, provided there is not a large amount of input or output. Herman Hollerith developed the punched card during the 1880's, and therefore the cards are sometimes referred to as Hollerith cards. Notice the row of small numbers across the very bottom of the card in Figure 1.9. These numbers identify each of the 80 columns of the card. In each column we may punch only one character. Rows 0 through 9 are printed on the card; row 11 is the row immediately above the 0 row; row 12 is immediately above row 11 at the top of the card. The number 0 in column one is formed by a punch in the zero row; the number 1 in column two is formed by a punch in the one row; and so on for all the numbers. The letters in the alphabet are formed by two punches in one column. The letters A–I are a combination of the 12 punch (a punch in the 12 row) and one of the numbers from 1 to 9. For example, the letter A is a 12 punch and a 1 punch. The letters J–R are formed by an 11 punch and one of the numbers 1–9; the letters S–Z are composed of a 0 punch and one of the numbers 2–9. The special characters such as the + — $. ( ) / are a combination of one, two, or three punches in a column. The important idea to remember is not which punches make up which characters, but that punches in special locations on the card represent characters which the card reader can sense. The printing across the top of the card identifies the information punched on it, thus making it easy for people to read.

Figure 1.9   Punched Card

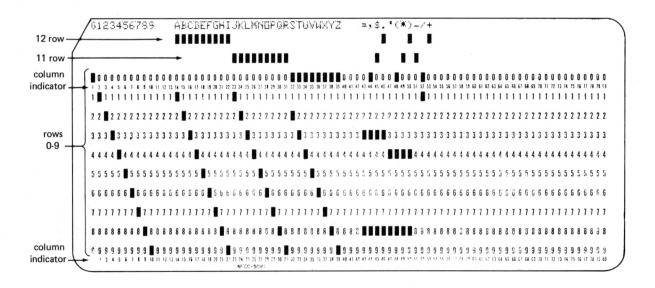

Companies with a lot of information to be stored often use magnetic tape, since it is a more durable form of data storage than punched cards. Characters are recorded on the tape by magnetizing specific areas. One example of a scheme for coding characters on tape is shown in Figure 1.10, where each dot represents a magnetized area.

Figure 1.10   Character Coding on a
Magnetic Tape

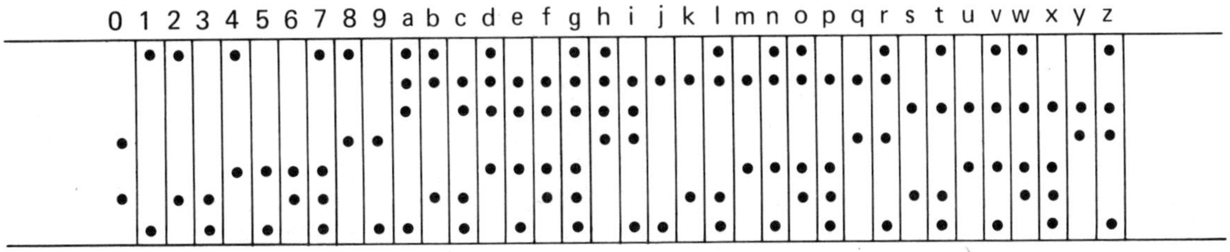

Source: Laura G. Cooper and Marilyn Z. Smith, *Standard FORTRAN: A Problem-Solving Approach* (Boston: Houghton Mifflin Co., 1973), Figure 2.3, p. 17.

1.3 Communicating with a Computer

People use computers to help them solve problems which are either too large or too boring to solve by hand. For example, a company with over 3,000 employees would probably have a computer compute and write its payroll checks. Several people could easily write all the checks, but the job would be rather long and tedious, and a computer does not get bored doing the same thing repeatedly. However, in order to have the computer process the payroll checks one must give it explicit instructions to follow. The set of instructions which a computer follows in order to complete a task is called a *program*, and the person who writes the instructions is a *programmer*. People frequently use programs in their activities even though they might not call them such. For example, an instruction booklet telling how to assemble a tool shed is a program. A person following the instructions should be able to put the shed together if there were no missing pieces and if the instructions were correct. Incorrect instructions could make it impossible to assemble the shed just as an incorrect or incomplete program could make a computer "print the wrong answer." Unless a computer has a defective part it will compute exactly what it is told using the formulas it is given.

Each computer has a basic set of instructions which it can understand. This set is called a *machine language*. The code for each instruction is usually a number, such as 21 for add, 22 for subtract. A person could learn machine language, but it is easier to learn a language that has some words or symbols in it; this type of language is termed a *symbolic language*. A symbolic language may also be a *problem-oriented language* because it is suited to solve a particular type of problem. For example, COBOL is a symbolic language. It uses words like ADD and SUBTRACT for commands. It is also a problem-oriented language because it was designed to solve business problems. COBOL is an acronym for *Common Business Oriented Language*.

Supervised by the Conference on Data Systems Languages (CODASYL) a group of experts developed the first version of COBOL in 1959. Their purpose in designing the language was to make one which would be similar to English and applicable to most computers. Installations which get newer and better models of computers to replace their old ones often have to put forth a great deal of time and effort to convert their old programs so that they will work on the new machine. If the program is in machine language, it will need to be rewritten completely, because each computer has its own machine language. Designing a language which is compatible for most computers can eliminate unnecessary reprogramming. It also means that people in different computer installations can share programs more easily and can eliminate duplication of work.

The first formal report defining COBOL was published in 1960; this version is known as COBOL-60. Improvements have been made to the language in the 1961 and 1965 versions of COBOL-61 and COBOL-65 respectively. This text will discuss the current, most recent version of COBOL as defined by the American National Standards Institute in 1968. ANS COBOL, or standard COBOL as it is usually called, contains several levels. Low level COBOL and high level COBOL contain the same basic instructions. The difference between them is that high level COBOL requires a large computer because it includes numerous options not available in low level COBOL. In this text we will attempt to discuss only those commands common to the majority of computers and will point out anything which may not be applicable to a smaller computer. Consult the Appendices and your installation's computer reference manual for details.

Since a computer can understand only its particular machine language, the commands written in COBOL must be translated into machine language. If we wanted to translate a French text into English so that we could read it, we would use a French-English dictionary. But to translate COBOL to machine language, we can use a special program to do our work. This program which does the translation is called a *compiler*. Therefore, any computer which has a COBOL compiler can process COBOL programs. Besides translating the language, a compiler checks each part to see if it is grammatically correct. If any mistakes in grammar (syntax) have been made, the compiler will print messages pointing them out so that we may correct them. When the COBOL statements are free from errors, the compiler will generate correct statements in machine language.

The next step after compilation is *execution*; that is, the computer performs all the actions specified in the machine language commands it has been given. After a program is executed we should check the results to see if they are correct. If they are, then our program worked. If not, then some of the instructions are incorrect and we must find them, correct them, compile the new program and execute it. When we try the program on the computer we say that we are *running the program*; this involves the two distinct steps of compilation and execution.

Special Terms

1. input	*12. location*
2. output	*13. address*
3. memory	*14. program*
4. storage	*15. programmer*
5. Central Processing Unit	*16. machine language*
6. input device	*17. symbolic language*
7. output device	*18. problem-oriented language*
8. tape drive	*19. compiler*
9. card reader	*20. syntax*
10. disk	*21. execution*
11. punched card	*22. running the program*

Chapter 2

Problem-Solving Procedure

2.1 Introduction

This chapter discusses the procedure which is a basis for solving problems on the computer. It is also a successful method when used with other computer languages and is not limited to COBOL. Section 2.2 presents the elements of the problem-solving procedure; section 2.3 shows how to apply the procedure to a simple problem. An important part of the procedure is designing a flowchart—a pictorial way of representing the problem's solution. The remainder of the chapter (section 2.4) concentrates on flowcharting rules and the solution to a second problem. The chapter concludes with exercises designed to give the student practice in developing his own flowcharts and a list of special terms.

2.2 Elements of the Procedure

Our purpose in learning a computer language is to be able to give commands to the computer to make the machine work for us. Studying the rules of the language is not enough; we must know how to put together the parts of the language in order to utilize the computer effectively. In this text we will discuss the rules of the COBOL language and a basic technique for solving problems. The seven steps of this problem-solving procedure are:

1. state the problem
2. select a method to solve the problem
3. flowchart the method
4. convert the processing steps of the flowchart into computer language commands
5. compile the program
6. execute the program
7. document the program

The organization of the text provides for learning in stages. We will study a sample problem, solve it by writing a computer program, and learn the new elements of COBOL presented in the program. The problems will proceed from simple to more complex ones so that the student can write simple but complete programs from the beginning and gradually increase his proficiency and knowledge of COBOL. First we will discuss the basic problem-solving procedure and then begin to apply it to a sample problem.

1. State the Problem

One of the most important steps in trying to solve a problem is being able to understand exactly what the problem is. We should know what information is given (the input) and what results are to be obtained (the output). If any calculations are involved, we should have them clearly in mind.

In preparing a problem for computer solution, many people use visual aids to help them plan their input and output. If the data will be punched on a card, someone must decide in what columns to put the information. A computer cannot look at a card and see that there is a name "somewhere" on the card; it must be told exactly which columns contain the name. The card in Figure 2.1 has been divided into four areas for a name, an address, an account number, and a current balance. The lines were drawn on the card to emphasize the specific use of each part of the card.

Figure 2.1   Sample Layout of an Input Card

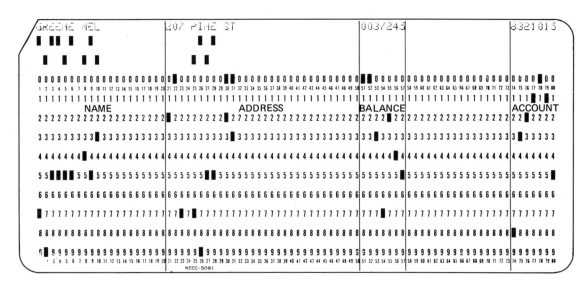

Programmers frequently use print charts to plan the layout and appearance of their printouts. The output should always be neatly spaced and clearly labeled to explain the numbers and/or words printed. See Figure 2.2 as an illustration. There is one box on the page for each column on the line.

2. Select a Method to Solve the Problem

Once we understand what we must accomplish, the next step is to decide how to do it. There may be several ways in which we can solve our problem and we must choose one. Depending upon the circumstances we may want the simplest one, or the fastest one, or the shortest one. Sometimes we may not be free to make a decision because there is only one method available. Other problems cannot be solved on a computer because no one has devised a way.

After we have chosen a method to use, we must change it into a step-by-step process which a computer can follow. This means giving instructions in a logical sequence. If there are decisions to make, we must tell the computer what to do if the answer is yes and what to do otherwise. You might say that we are making a recipe for the computer. Our method must tell what ingredients to use (the input) and the order in which to combine them. After everything is put together and has been processed, we have our finished product (the output). If we leave out an important step in the recipe or make a mistake in one step, we cannot expect the computer to produce the desired results.

3. Flowchart the Method

As we develop the step-by-step procedure for the computer we will construct a *flowchart*. A flowchart is a diagram which shows from start to finish all the processing steps necessary to solve the problem. In other words, a

Figure 2.2 Print Chart

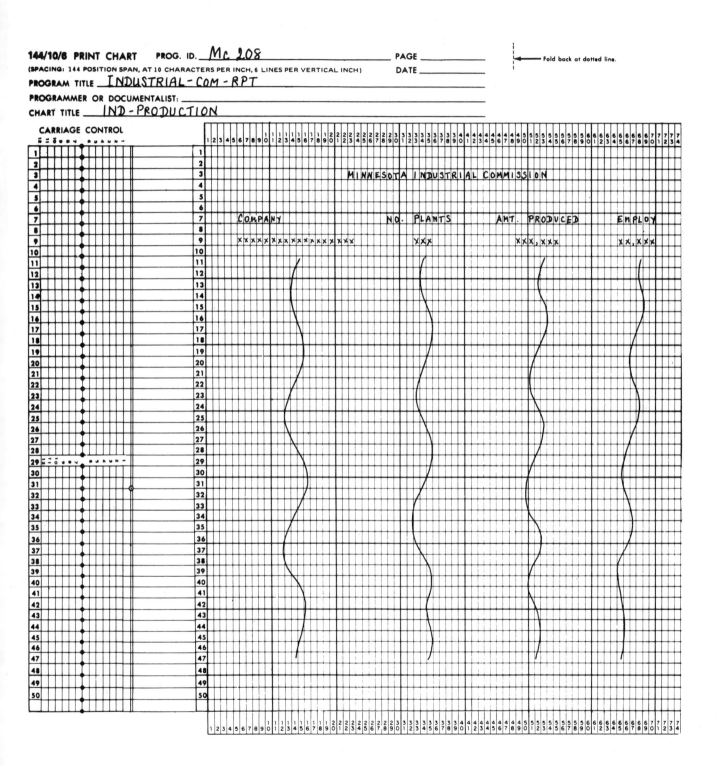

flowchart is a pictorial representation of the method. After constructing a flowchart, we should make up some data and use it to go through each step of the flowchart to see if our method works. If it doesn't, we can correct the flowchart before wasting any computer time. Rules for designing flowcharts will be discussed in section 2.4.

4. Convert the Flowchart Processing Steps into Computer Language Commands

In this text we will be writing in the ANS COBOL language.

5. Compile the Program

After a program is written we must submit it in some form to the compiler, which is stored in the computer. Usually this means punching the program on cards or typing it in at the keyboard of a terminal. Then we have the compiler process the program. The compiler checks the program for syntax errors and translates it, if possible, to machine language. Also most compilers usually list translated programs and any error messages at the printer. If error messages are printed, we must correct these grammatical errors and recompile the program so that we can get a correct version of the program in machine language. Remember, the compiler does not check the logic or method of our program to see if we are giving sensible instructions to the computer. It merely looks at the program to see if all the statements follow the rules of the COBOL language.

6. Execute the Program

When there are no grammatical errors in the program, we may ask the computer to execute the compiled (machine language) instructions. That is, we submit the machine language program and the data it processes to the computer. If we tell the computer to read a person's name from a card or a magnetic tape, we must also give it the card or tape to read. If an instruction says write a name and a salary on paper check forms, the computer will do it. During execution the computer follows the instructions in the order in which we have given them.

When the computer finishes executing the program, we should *always* check the results to see if they are correct. Some people mistakenly believe that anything the computer does is correct. But if a program said, "Charge everyone $300 for an electricity bill," the computer would do so. If a computer "makes mistakes," there is probably an error somewhere in the program. The ability to correct errors in programs is so important that we have devoted an entire chapter (Chapter 7) to the subject.

7. Document the Program

After a program is working we should add comments to explain what the program is about, what it uses for input, and what it outputs. These comments are called *documentation* and should explain in general terms the steps of the program. If others are going to use a program, they must have good documentation which will tell them what to do—how to arrange the input, whether it should be on card or tape, and so on.

Documentation is extremely helpful when it becomes necessary to modify a program. Knowing what the programmer intended makes it easier to understand and then change the program. Occasionally a programmer may forget the details of his own program if he hasn't looked at it for some time. With good documentation, however, he can quickly refresh his memory.

2.3 Solving a Problem

In this section we will begin to solve a problem using the procedure discussed above. We will design a flowchart and test it; in Chapter 3 we will write the COBOL program to accomplish the processing shown in the flowchart. Different flowchart symbols and their uses will be discussed in section 2.4.

1. State the Problem

We are given a deck of punched cards and wish to have them listed on a piece of paper. This problem often arises when we want to identify a "strange" deck of cards or to check the cards for errors before submitting them to the computer. (It's easier to read a listing than it is to read one card at a time.) Or, we might want to send a copy of a program to someone, and a printed copy takes less postage than a deck of cards.

The input will be a deck of 80-column cards and the output will be centered on printer paper showing everything exactly the way it is on the cards.

2. Select a Method to Solve the Problem

We may want to begin by drawing a picture of the way the output is supposed to look, as illustrated below.

It will be line after line showing exactly what is punched on each card. The first line will correspond to the first card; the second line, the second card, and so on.

How can we get a card printed? If we were sitting at a typewriter and were asked to type on a piece of paper everything which appears on the cards, we would have to read what is on the first card, type the information, read what is on the second card, type that one, and continue reading and typing until all the cards have been read. This is the method which we will use in the flowchart.

3. Flowchart the Method

How do we begin the flowchart? We give it a place to start. We do this by using an oval and writing the word "start" inside.

Since we eventually want to write the information which is punched on a

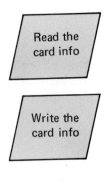

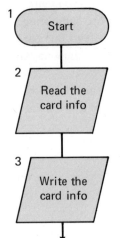

card, we must tell the computer to read the card. We indicate this processing step by using the input/output symbol. This rhombus says "read all the information on *one* card."

Once the computer reads a card, we may instruct it to write what it has read. Again we use the input/output symbol. This symbol is giving the command "write *one* line."

If we connect all three symbols, our flowchart says read then print the information from the first card.

In order to get the second card read and written we would need to add boxes 4 and 5 to the above flowchart.

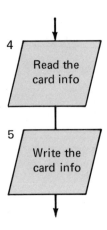

Figure 2.3   Initial Flowchart to List
a Deck of Cards

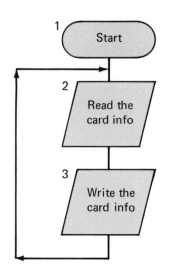

How long would our flowchart be if we had 1000 cards to write? It would be very long if we continue in this manner. What we need is a way of saying "repeat the reading and writing until all cards have been written." The repetition may be accomplished by drawing a line from the bottom of box 3 to the top of box 2 as in Figure 2.3. In this flowchart we no longer need boxes 4 and 5. Boxes 2 and 3 are said to be in a *loop* because their commands will be repeated many times.

Let us examine the flowchart in Figure 2.3 and go over its commands step by step.

Box 1.   Start
Box 2.   Read one card
Box 3.   Write what was on the card
Box 2.   Read another card
Box 3.   Write what was on that card
Box 2.   Read a card
Box 3.   Write what was on that card
.
.
.

When will these commands ever stop? Our flowchart has no stop instruction and no way out of the loop. This is an example of a *never-ending loop*.

If we were following this flowchart at a typewriter and came to the end of the deck, we would stop automatically. But a computer is not that smart; it would keep looking for more cards to read.

You might think that we could tell the computer "stop when you reach the last card," but a computer cannot distinguish the last card that easily. If we place at the end of the data deck a special card, then we can tell the computer to stop after it reads this card. The end card contains special punches and is different for each computer. (The IBM 360 end card has a /* punched in columns 1 and 2.) The test for the end card has been included in the flowchart in Figure 2.4.

Figure 2.4 Complete Flowchart to List a Deck of Cards

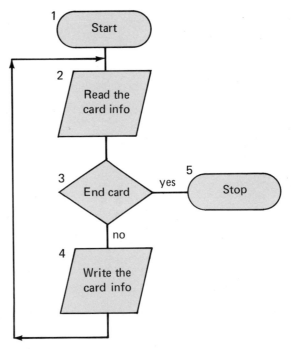

Why was the test for the end of the deck (box 3) made between boxes 2 and 4? The test appears in this position for two reasons: so that this special card signaling the end will not be printed, and because the computer must read the card before it can answer a question about it.

Now that we have finished the flowchart we must make up some sample data and go through our flowchart step by step to see if it is correct. For this problem it doesn't matter how many cards we pick or what the cards say, because each card should be written. Therefore, let's use the following three data cards plus the /* one which we use as the end card.

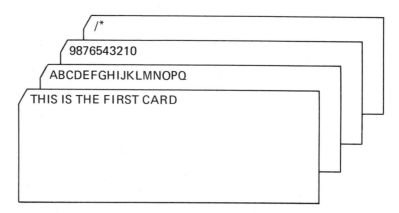

Let us now trace through the flowchart using the sample data. A *trace* is a tabular method for analyzing a flowchart. It has a column for each different element in the flowchart—one for numbering the steps, one for the flowchart box number currently being considered, one labeled "card info" where we write the information read from the card, one for the end test, and one for output. Actually, each time there is output it should be written on one line, but then our trace would need more room.

Step no.	Flowchart box no.	Card info	Test: end?	Output
1	2	THIS IS THE FIRST CARD		
2	3		no	
3	4			THIS IS THE FIRST CARD
4	2	ABCDEFGHIJK LMNOPQ		
5	3		no	
6	4			ABCDEFGHIJK LMNOPQ
7	2	9876543210		
8	3		no	
9	4			9876543210
10	2	/*		
11	3		yes	
STOP	5			

The trace follows all the commands in the flowchart in the order in which they are given. The first command of the flowchart is to read card info. This information comes from the first data card and we write it in the column headed "Card info." The second step asks the question: have we just read the end card? The answer is no, so we write that in the "Test" column. Since we had a no answer in box 3, we proceed to box 4 of the flowchart where we are told to write card info. Referring to the card info column, we copy the words THIS IS THE FIRST CARD directly into the "Output" column. Then our flowchart leads us from box 4 to box 2 where we read another card. This means that we have something new to put into the card info column. At this point we could cross off THIS IS THE FIRST CARD because it is the old value of card info. It may seem strange, but a computer works in the following way: it remembers only the information from one card at a time unless it is told to save the information. When it reads the second card, it forgets what was on the first card. Therefore, crossing through the data from the first card when we reach step 4 would be similar to the computer's forgetting it.

Our flowchart seems to be correct because it has in its OUTPUT column the information from three cards we wanted read, and that is the desired result of the processing represented in the flowchart. Our next step in solving the problem would be to convert the flowchart processing steps into COBOL instructions. Since flowcharting is such an important part of writing programs, we will postpone writing the program until the next chapter and will discuss flowcharting symbols and rules next.

2.4 Flowchart Rules

By custom, certain flowchart symbols represent specific commands. If programmers consistently use the same symbols, then it is easy to study another person's flowchart. Remember that the flowchart is a pictorial way of explaining the method a person is using to solve a problem, and it is much easier to comprehend the method from reading a flowchart than from reading the detailed computer language program. In this text we will discuss the flowchart symbols recommended by the American National Standards Institute and followed by most programmers.

Flowchart Symbols and Their Uses

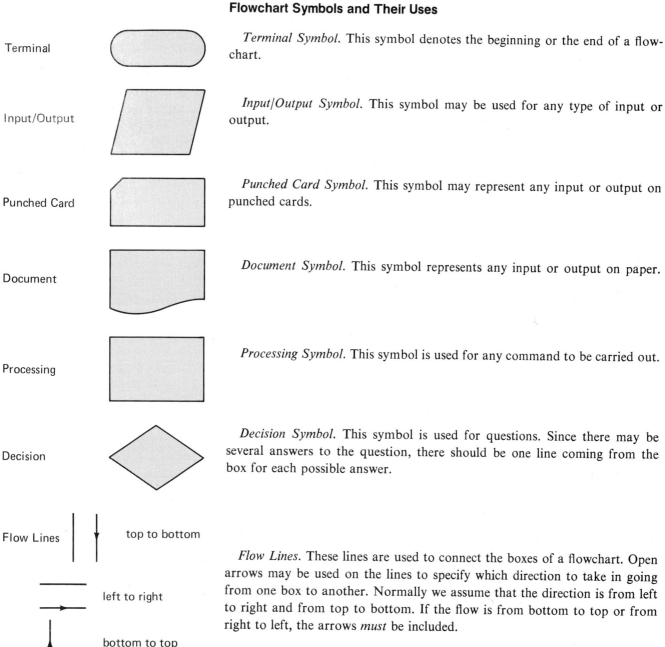

Terminal Symbol. This symbol denotes the beginning or the end of a flowchart.

Input/Output Symbol. This symbol may be used for any type of input or output.

Punched Card Symbol. This symbol may represent any input or output on punched cards.

Document Symbol. This symbol represents any input or output on paper.

Processing Symbol. This symbol is used for any command to be carried out.

Decision Symbol. This symbol is used for questions. Since there may be several answers to the question, there should be one line coming from the box for each possible answer.

Flow Lines. These lines are used to connect the boxes of a flowchart. Open arrows may be used on the lines to specify which direction to take in going from one box to another. Normally we assume that the direction is from left to right and from top to bottom. If the flow is from bottom to top or from right to left, the arrows *must* be included.

Connector

Connector Symbol. When it is not physically possible to join one part of a flowchart to another, the connector symbol is used. A number or letter is placed inside the circle to show which parts of the flowchart are being joined, as shown in the example below.

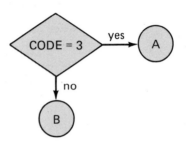

Preparation

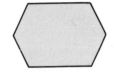

Preparation Symbol. This symbol may be used in the flowchart to indicate actions necessary to solve the problem but which are not involved directly in program processing to produce the output.

Predefined Process

Predefined Process Symbol. This symbol is used to summarize a process which is given in detail in a separate flowchart.

Annotation

Annotation Symbol. This symbol is used for comments which explain what the flowchart is doing.

Rules for Designing Flowcharts

1. Every flowchart must have a starting point and a way to stop.
2. Lines or connector symbols must join every box in the flowchart to another one. There must be no loose ends.
3. Lines in a flowchart should not cross. A connector should be used instead.
4. The answers and paths to take after encountering a decision box should be clearly marked.
5. Words, sentences, or symbols may be used inside the flowchart boxes.
6. The arrow (←) is frequently used when calculating a value. For example, the processing box at the left says that SALARY is calculated by multiplying RATE and HRS.
7. After a flowchart is completed, it should be tested with some sample input to see if the logic of the flowchart is correct.

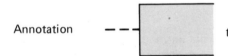

Flowchart designs and the use of these symbols will be discussed throughout the text as we solve sample problems. Being able to construct a flowchart improves with practice. Therefore, let us consider another problem and flowchart a solution.

Step 1: State the Problem

A large company with over 2000 employees has just completed its weekly payroll. They store the payroll data on tape and want to compute their current bank balance. The first number is the bank balance before the checks were written. Each of the remaining values on the tape is an amount paid to an employee. The output should be the final balance after all employees are paid.

Step 2: Select a Method to Solve the Problem

In order to compute the current balance we will need to subtract the amount of each employee's check from the bank balance. This means we start with the beginning balance, subtract one check from it and obtain a new balance, then subtract another check from the new balance and obtain another new balance. We will continue subtracting one check at a time until we have processed all checks. The last balance computed will be the current balance.

Step 3: Flowchart the Method

We start by reading the bank balance before any checks were written. Notice that we use the same input/output symbol whether we read from cards or tape.

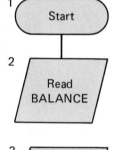

We then read the amount of a check.

Now we may compute a new balance by subtracting the check from the balance. This may be done as shown in either box 4a or 4b at the left.

4a

Subtract
CHECK from
BALANCE

or

4b

BALANCE ← BALANCE − CHECK

Exactly how are we supposed to read the command in box 4b? First, let us look at the part of the formula on the right-hand side of the arrow (BALANCE − CHECK). This says that we should subtract the amount of the check from the balance. The arrow tells us what we should do with the number just computed. It points to the name BALANCE, which means the number computed is the new value of BALANCE. Perhaps using some numbers will make this easier to understand. Let

    BALANCE = 200000
    CHECK   =   750

Then

    BALANCE ← BALANCE − CHECK

means that:

    BALANCE = 200000   199250
    CHECK   =   750

The old value of BALANCE (200000) has been crossed off and has been replaced by the new value (199250). The amount of CHECK has not changed.

The arrow (←) may be interpreted in either of the following ways:

1. is computed from
2. is replaced by

Normally we look at the items to the right of the arrow to see what is being computed and then to the left of the arrow to see where this value goes.

Returning to our flowchart we find that we have processed only one check. How can we make our flowchart repeat the reading and subtracting of checks from the balance until all checks have been subtracted? By putting a loop in our flowchart similar to the loop in Figure 2.4. This loop and a way to stop it has been included in the final flowchart of Figure 2.5.

Figure 2.5 Flowchart to Find
Current Balance

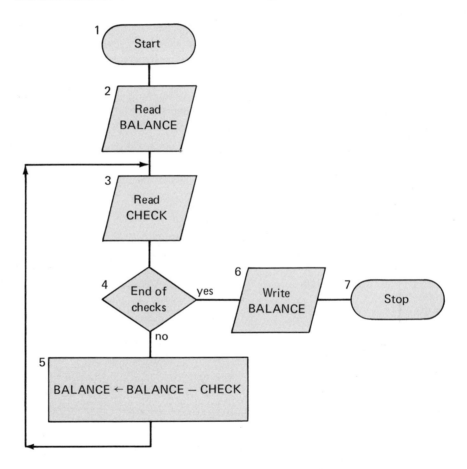

Exercises

1. Use the following tape to do a trace of the flowchart in Figure 2.5. The lines are drawn to show the separation of the tape into records. Each time the tape is read only one record is processed.

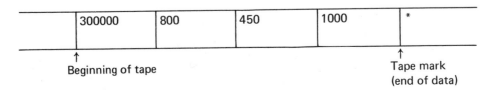

The column headings for the trace should be as follows.

Step no.	Flowchart box no.	Balance	Check	Test: end?	Output

2. The payroll department of a large company has one card for each of its employees. This card contains the following information:

   name
   hourly rate of pay
   number of hours worked.

   Write a flowchart to show the steps to write a check for each employee.

3. The payroll department of a large company has one card for each of its employees. This card contains

   name
   hourly rate of pay
   number of hours worked.

   Write a flowchart which will write a check for each employee and pay him double time for any hours worked over 40. Not all employees may have worked over 40 hours, so the flowchart should check to see whether or not to pay overtime.
   Check these values in the flowchart to see if the correct salaries will be computed.

JOHN TATE	$3.00	50	(SALARY = $180.00)
SUE SLOAN	$2.00	30	(SALARY = $ 60.00)

4. Write a flowchart which will compute the current balance for the Ace Construction Company. The information to use is on cards. The first card contains

   previous balance

   Each of the other cards contains

   amount and code

   The code is either CR for a credit (to be added to the balance) or a DB for a debit (to be subtracted from the balance).

5. Write a flowchart which will determine the total gross receipts at the Uptown Department Store. Each transaction is on a separate card which contains the amount of the sale. The problem is to add these sales amounts and find the total gross receipts.

6. Use the numbers 80, 65, 92, 40, 10, 30 and do a trace of the flowchart on the following page. The > symbol in box 6 means greater than. What is the flowchart doing?

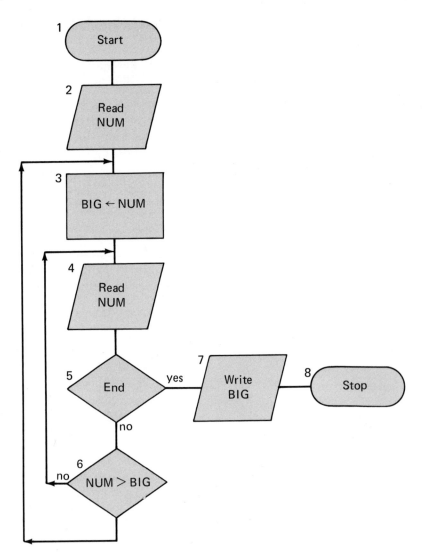

Special Terms

1. *documentation*
2. *flowchart*
3. *loop*
4. *never-ending loop*
5. *trace*

Chapter 3

Writing and Running a COBOL Program

3.1 Introduction

In this chapter we begin our study of the COBOL language. Section 3.2 discusses fundamentals of COBOL: the four divisions of a program, reserved words, programmer supplied names, and literals. In section 3.3 we examine a COBOL program which lists a deck of cards. This completes the problem begun and flowcharted in Chapter 2. After a program is written it must be tested on a computer; section 3.4 discusses punching a COBOL program on cards, punctuation rules, and documenting the program. The final section of the chapter (3.5) is more technical. It gives the general outline which every program must follow and is helpful when writing programs.

3.2 Fundamentals of COBOL

The COBOL language closely resembles English. All its commands are complete sentences; and the sentences are combined into paragraphs. A programmer may write a command such as

> SUBTRACT FICA AND INCOME-TAX FROM GROSS-SALAR
> GIVING NET-PAY

and it isn't too hard to figure out the meaning. The choice of words like FICA, INCOME-TAX, GROSS-SALARY, and NET-PAY is left to the programmer. The other words in the sentence are part of the COBOL language and must be used according to the rules. Before examining a complete program, let us study some fundamentals in order to understand the program better.

Four Divisions of a COBOL Program

Every COBOL program contains four divisions which help the programmer organize his work. They must be included in the order listed below.

IDENTIFICATION DIVISION. This division names the program. It can give other information such as the author's name, date written, security, and general remarks explaining the program.

ENVIRONMENT DIVISION. This division includes specifics about the computer on which the program will run. It names the input and output devices the program will use. The details in this division will vary from one computer to another; refer to section 12.4 for more specific information.

DATA DIVISION. This division is divided into sections in which the programmer describes and classifies all the data of the program. One section (WORKING-STORAGE) is for computed values and constants; another section (FILE) is for describing the large collections of data which are input and output.

PROCEDURE DIVISION. This division contains all the commands which the computer will execute; it is the one which corresponds to the processing steps shown on the flowchart. Like an English composition, the sentences form paragraphs. The paragraphs are named and may be combined into sections.

Every program has the same basic structure. It has headings and subheadings to separate the program into its four divisions. Some parts are necessary and must be included in the proper order and spelled correctly. Other parts are optional and may be omitted if not needed. Still other parts are supplied by the programmer. To help write programs with the correct form we will introduce in section 3.5 a skeleton outline of a COBOL program. Filling in the missing parts of the outline will enable us to write a complete program.

Programmer Supplied Names

As we mentioned previously, some words in the program are supplied by the programmer. These include paragraph and section names as well as names for data items. The names must obey the following rules.

Rules for Programmer Supplied Names

1. A name may be composed of the digits 0-9, the letters A-Z, and the hyphen (-).
2. It may be from 1 to 30 characters in length.
3. It may contain no blanks. For example, SUMONE and SUM-ONE are allowable names, but SUM ONE is not.
4. A hyphen may not be the first or last character of a name. Hyphens may not be used consecutively. For example, INCOME--TAX is not a legal name.
5. All names except paragraph and section names must begin with a letter. Paragraph and section names may be numeric. For example, 001, 002, 003, and 03 are allowable paragraph names. The names 003 and 03, which are numerically the same, are interpreted as different names by the COBOL compiler because they do not contain exactly the same characters.

   It should be mentioned that in high level COBOL a name need not begin with a letter; however, every name, except paragraph and section names, must contain at least one letter.
6. In low level COBOL each name in the DATA DIVISION must be unique. The high level COBOL compilers do not make this restriction. (See section 10.8 on qualification.)
7. A name may not be one of the COBOL reserved words in Appendix A.

Reserved Words

The reserved COBOL words have special meaning to the COBOL compiler and therefore may not be used as programmer supplied names. For example, SUM is a COBOL reserved word, but we may change it into SUM-SALARY and it is no longer a reserved word. Since most of the reserved words do not contain hyphens, we are safe in creating names containing hyphens. They probably are not reserved words. To be certain refer to Appendix A for a complete list of the COBOL reserved words.

Literals

Another item frequently used in a program is the literal. Whenever we wish to use titles or column headings in our output, we need some way of telling the computer exactly what the title is. A *literal* is not the name of something, but an actual value. It may be numeric (all numbers) or non-numeric (any kind of characters). For example, 30.75 is a numeric literal and 'ABC MANUFACTURING CO.' is a non-numeric literal.

A *non-numeric literal* is enclosed in single quotation marks (') and may contain a maximum of 120 characters. Any characters, even COBOL reserved words, may be part of a non-numeric literal. (The quote mark is sometimes referred to as a literal mark.)

A *numeric literal* is a number which is not enclosed in quote marks. It may be written with a leftmost plus (+) or minus (−) sign. A numeric literal with no sign is positive. It may contain a decimal point, but the decimal point may not be the rightmost character. The maximum size of a numeric literal is 18 digits.

Example

numeric literals	non-numeric literals
+7	'SUM = '
−312	'ERROR'
.004	'3.17'

3.3 A COBOL Program to List a Deck of Cards

Program 3.1 contains the COBOL commands to solve the problem discussed in section 2.3. It will list any deck of cards no matter what they contain. The PROCEDURE DIVISION corresponds to the flowchart in Figure 2.4. Study the program to see how the flowchart blocks become COBOL commands. There are some commands which are not indicated in the flowchart, but must be included in the program.

In this section we will explain briefly the parts of the program. Section 3.4 will give details about preparing the program and running it on the computer. Section 3.5 contains the skeleton outline of a COBOL program which will aid the student in writing his own programs. The reader may wish to compare the outline in Table 3.1 with sample Program 3.1 to see which parts are necessary and which are supplied.

IDENTIFICATION DIVISION

The only necessary part is PROGRAM-ID. The name LIST-A-DECK-OF-CARDS is the program-name and was supplied by the programmer. It conforms to the rules for programmer supplied names in section 3.2.

ENVIRONMENT DIVISION

Throughout this text we will be writing programs for the IBM 360 computer. If a program is written for another computer, most of the changes would be in the ENVIRONMENT DIVISION. For example, SOURCE-COMPUTER would be IBM-1130 for the IBM 1130 computer. Consult your instructor to learn the exact ENVIRONMENT DIVISION phrases to use at your computer installation.

Since our program will read cards and will write lines, we must include the INPUT-OUTPUT SECTION in our program. In it we give names to the card and printer files and specify that our program uses the card reader and line printer. A *file* is defined to be a collection of records. Each card in the deck is a record; therefore, the entire deck is a file. Similarly, each line we print is a record, and all our printed output is a file. Each computer installation has its own particular name for the "input-or-output-device." Be sure to find out which name to use in your own programs. Throughout this text we will use the name SYS005-UR-2540R-S for the card reader and SYS006-UR-1403-S for the printer. In this particular program the names CARD-FILE and WRITE-OUT were chosen by the author for the input card file and the printed output file. These names also obey the rules in section 3.2.

Program 3.1   A Program to List a
               Card Deck

COBOL Program Sheet

Sequence			COBOL Statement
001010		IDENTIFICATION DIVISION.
001020		PROGRAM-ID. LIST-A-DECK-OF-CARDS.
001030		ENVIRONMENT DIVISION.
001040		CONFIGURATION SECTION.
001050		SOURCE-COMPUTER. IBM-360.
001060		OBJECT-COMPUTER. IBM-360.
001070		INPUT-OUTPUT SECTION.
001080		FILE-CONTROL.
001090		SELECT CARD-FILE ASSIGN TO SYS005-UR-2540R-S.
001100		SELECT WRITE-OUT ASSIGN TO SYS006-UR-1403-S.
001110		DATA DIVISION.
001120		FILE SECTION.
001130		FD CARD-FILE DATA RECORD CARD-INFO LABEL RECORDS OMITTED.
001140		01 CARD-INFO PICTURE X(80).
001150		FD WRITE-OUT DATA RECORD CARD-LINE LABEL RECORDS OMITTED.
001160		01 CARD-LINE.
001170		04 FILLER PICTURE X(26).
001180		04 CENTR PICTURE X(80).
001190		04 FILLER PICTURE X(26).
001200		PROCEDURE DIVISION.

System

Punching Instructions   Sheet 1 of 2

Program LIST-A-DECK-OF-CARDS

Graphic

Card Form #

Identification 73 80

Programmer   Date   Punch

COBOL Program Sheet

System		Punching Instructions		Sheet 2 of 2
Program LIST-A-DECK-OF-CARDS		Graphic		Identification
Programmer	Date	Punch	Card Form #	73 80

Sequence (PAGE) (SERIAL)	CONT.	A	B — COBOL Statement
002010		GET-READY. OPEN INPUT CARD-FILE.
002020			OPEN OUTPUT WRITE-OUT.
002030			MOVE SPACE TO CARD-LINE.
002040		READ-WRITE. READ CARD-FILE AT END GO TO FINISH-UP.
002050			MOVE CARD-INFO TO CENTR.
002060			WRITE CARD-LINE AFTER ADVANCING 1 LINES.
002070			GO TO READ-WRITE.
002080		FINISH-UP. CLOSE CARD-FILE.
002090			CLOSE WRITE-OUT.
002100			STOP RUN.

DATA DIVISION

CARD-FILE is the name of the collection of cards (file-name) and CARD-INFO is the name given to one card (record-name). The 01 is a *level number*; the number 01 tells the computer that CARD-INFO is a record. The phrase PICTURE X(80) tells the computer that CARD-INFO is 80 columns long and that there will be alphanumeric characters on the card. *Alphanumeric* characters include letters of the alphabet, numbers, and other special characters such as the $, ( ) . In this description we are telling the computer to reserve an area in memory; the 80 means 80 characters and the X tells what kind of information will go into the area. That is, the symbol X stands for *alphanumeric* information. If the card contained only alphabetic letters or spaces, we would use PICTURE A(80); the symbol A means *alphabetic*. (More complex PICTUREs are discussed in Chapter 4.) When the computer reads the card it will transfer the characters from the card into this particular area in memory; the name of the area is CARD-INFO. Pictorially this is

CARD-INFO

CARD-LINE is the programmer supplied name for one printed line. It is a record-name and has the level number 01. In the middle of CARD-LINE we want to put the 80 characters from the card. This means that in a line 132 characters wide we will have two margins of 26 characters each: $(132 - 80)/2 = 26$. Therefore, our line has three parts: a margin, an area to print the card, and a margin. When we describe CARD-LINE we must tell the computer about the three parts of the line. Our description is done in an outline form. Beneath the 01 CARD-LINE we use a larger level number to show that the 01 is divided into parts; each part has the same level number. This level number may be anything from 02 through 10,[1] but in this program we use 04. Since we will not be placing any information in the margins, we will name them FILLER. (The special name FILLER tells the COBOL compiler that the area will not be referenced.) We use the name CENTR for the center of CARD-LINE where the information from the card will go. The description of CARD-LINE says that the first 26 characters are FILLER, the next 80 are named CENTR, and the last 26 are FILLER. Altogether CARD-LINE is 132 characters long $(26 + 80 + 26 = 132)$. Pictorially in memory we have

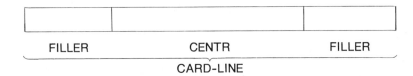

PROCEDURE DIVISION

GET-READY is the name of the first paragraph. Unlike English, a COBOL paragraph begins at the left-hand margin and all other lines are indented. A COBOL program which reads or writes any files must get the files ready before any reading or writing can take place. Readying the files was not mentioned in the flowchart, but it is a necessary part of the program. The OPEN command instructs the computer to get the files ready; the word INPUT says that CARD-FILE will be *read* by the program; the word OUTPUT says that WRITE-OUT will be *written* by the program.

The next command (MOVE SPACE TO CARD-LINE) puts blanks in the memory area named CARD-LINE. With each new program the computer's memory does not start out blank; usually it contains something left over from previously run programs. Therefore, we include this instruction to make sure our margins will be blank. SPACE is a special COBOL word which means one or more blanks. Since CARD-LINE is 132 characters long, 132 blanks will be placed in the area.

The READ-WRITE paragraph corresponds to the loop formed by boxes 2-4 in the flowchart. The READ statement commands the computer to:

1. Read one record (one card) from the CARD-FILE.
2. If the card just read is the special end card, then go to the paragraph named FINISH-UP.
3. If the card just read is not the end card, do not go to the paragraph named FINISH-UP, but continue on to the sentence following the READ.

---

[1] The high level COBOL compilers allow level numbers to range from 02 through 49.

When a card is read, everything on the card is placed into the computer's memory in the area named CARD-INFO. In order to write what was on the card we transfer all the information from the CARD-INFO area into the area named CARD-LINE so that it may be printed. We center the information by placing it in the part called CENTR. The command

WRITE CARD-LINE AFTER ADVANCING 1 LINES

will write whatever is in the memory area CARD-LINE and will single space the printing. If we had said AFTER ADVANCING 2 LINES the printing would be double spaced.

The GO TO statement forms a loop by telling the computer to return to the beginning of paragraph READ-WRITE and read another card. Notice that there is no box in the flowchart which says "go to." The line connecting boxes 4 and 2 becomes the GO TO command in the program.

The final paragraph is named FINISH-UP because that is the name used in the READ statement. In this paragraph we close any files which were opened and then tell the computer to stop.

3.4 Running a COBOL Program

After a program is written someone must punch its commands on cards so that they may be submitted to the computer. Sometimes the programmer punches his own cards; sometimes not. If someone other than the programmer will do the punching, it is important to write everything clearly and distinguish the zero from the letter O, the one from the letter I, and the two from the Z. At some places the custom is to slash the letter O making it Ø; at other places they slash the zero and leave the O unslashed. Learn the convention at your installation and use it. In this text only if it is unclear what is intended, we will slash the zeros.

Certain areas of the punched card are reserved for specific parts of a COBOL program. COBOL statements must be punched between columns 8 and 72; some statements must begin in column 8 (the division headings) and some in column 12 (all lines of a paragraph except the first). If a statement is too long to put on one card, it may be continued starting in column 12 of the next. Columns 1-6 may be used to number the cards; columns 73-80 to identify the program with an abbreviation of the program's name.

Programmers often write their programs on coding sheets. Each line of the sheet represents one card of the program deck, and each box represents one column. Column 8 (the A margin) and column 12 (the B margin) are clearly marked for the programmer. Since a COBOL statement may not extend past column 72, the coding sheet ends at column 72. Refer to Program 3.1 which was written on a coding sheet.

Summary of Card Columns and Their Use in COBOL

Columns	Use
1–6	Sequence number—this is optional. It may be used by the programmer to number his cards. These numbers are checked by the compiler to see if they are in ascending order. For example, if the first card in a program deck is

Columns	Use
	numbered 100, the second one may be 110, or any number larger than 100. It does not have to be numbered 101.
	The sequence number on a coding sheet is partially filled in. The first three digits are reserved for the page number and the second three for the line number. Normally lines are numbered in steps of 10: 010, 020, 030, and so on. Then if it becomes necessary to add a line between 020 and 030, it could be numbered 025. A sequence number 001020 would be the second line on page 1 of the coding sheet, and 003010 would be the first line on page 3.
7	Used to continue a non-numeric literal which cannot be completely written on one card.
	If a literal is divided between one card and the next, there must be a hyphen in column 7 and a literal mark (') in column 12 of the second card to continue the literal. There is also a literal mark at the beginning and end of the literal.
8	Starts a DIVISION name SECTION name paragraph name File Description (FD) Record description (level number 01) level number 77
	The DIVISION and SECTION names are followed by a period, and the remainder of the line is blank.
	A paragraph name is followed by a period and at least one blank before the text begins.
	The level number must be followed by at least one blank and the data name.
12–72	Contains record description data name first sentence of a paragraph continuation of a data description continuation of a sentence
	The first sentence begins in column 12 or after. Spaces may be used freely to make the program more readable; it is not necessary to type up to column 72.
73–80	Identification—optional. This area may contain either letters or numbers. Sometimes this area is used to number the cards in a deck.

Punctuation Rules

1. When a period follows a word, it must be placed immediately after the last letter of the word. That is, no space(s) may appear between the word and the period. A space must be used after the period.
2. A space must be included before and after the $+ - *$ or $/$ symbols.
3. Every level number must be followed by a space.

Cards are punched on a machine called a card punch or a key punch. Instructions for its use are given in Appendix C. The deck of cards on which the program is punched is called the COBOL *source deck*. In addition to the program cards there must be certain *control cards* to tell the computer what to do with the source deck (compile it, execute it) and *data cards* which the program works with. Since control cards vary from one computer installation to another, we will not discuss any specifics about them. Generally the cards are arranged in the order shown in Figure 3.1.

Figure 3.1 Arrangement of Card
Deck

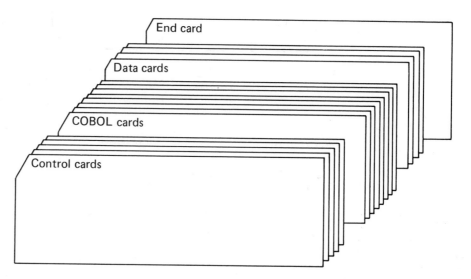

After the cards are submitted to the computer and we receive some output we must check it to see if the results are correct. If they aren't, we must find the error, correct it, and resubmit the program. Seldom do programs work correctly the first time. When the results are correct, we may document the program.

Documentation within the program may be done in the REMARKS section of the IDENTIFICATION DIVISION and in NOTE statements of the PROCEDURE DIVISION. We will add the following REMARKS section to Program 3.1 for its documentation. See Chapter 10 for more details on documentation.

```
001021 REMARKS. THIS PROGRAM LISTS A DECK OF CARDS.
001022        FOR INPUT WE MAY HAVE A DECK OF ANY 80
001023        COLUMN CARDS. THE OUTPUT WILL SINGLE SPACE
001024        AND CENTER THE LISTING ON PRINTER PAPER.
001025        THERE IS NO TITLE.
```

Exercise

Punch Program 3.1 on cards, supply some data and the necessary control cards, and run it on the computer.

3.5 Skeleton Outline of a COBOL Program

The skeleton outline of a COBOL program is very helpful as a reference for the form of a COBOL program. A programmer could memorize all the necessary headings, but referring to the skeleton outline probably would be simpler. A special notation of underlining, capitalization, brackets, braces, and so on is used in the skeleton outline. We should memorize the notation because it will tell us what we must include and what we may omit in our program. Reference manuals supplied by computer manufacturers are written in this notation. Therefore, whenever we need to see how a certain part of COBOL applies to a particular machine, we will have a head start toward understanding the technical reference manual.

The skeleton outline given in Table 3.1 includes only the basic parts needed in elementary programs. For a complete outline refer to Appendix B.

Table 3.1   Skeleton Outline of a
            COBOL Program

```
IDENTIFICATION DIVISION.
PROGRAM-ID.  program-name.
[AUTHOR.  sentence . . .]
[INSTALLATION.  sentence . . .]
[DATE-WRITTEN.  sentence . . .]
[SECURITY.  sentence . . .]
[REMARKS.  sentence . . .]
ENVIRONMENT DIVISION.
CONFIGURATION SECTION.
SOURCE-COMPUTER.  {IBM-360        }.
                  {computer-name  }
OBJECT-COMPUTER.  {IBM-360        }.
                  {computer-name  }
[SPECIAL-NAMES.  forms-control IS mnemonic-name . . .].
[INPUT-OUTPUT SECTION.]
 FILE-CONTROL.
    SELECT  file-name ASSIGN TO input-or-output device.*
                 .
                 .
                 .

DATA DIVISION.
 FILE SECTION.
 FD  file-name DATA {RECORD IS    } record-name [record-name . . .]
                    {RECORDS ARE  }
        LABEL RECORDS ARE OMITTED.
 01  record-name.
            description of record
                 .
                 .

[WORKING-STORAGE SECTION.]
[REPORT SECTION.]
PROCEDURE DIVISION.
[section-name SECTION.]
paragraph-name.  sentence. . . .
[paragraph-name.  sentence. . . .]
 [section-name SECTION.]                ] . . .
 [paragraph-name.  sentence . . .] . . .]
```

*On the IBM 360 computer the device name is of the general form:
                          SYSnnn-UR-device-S
where nnn   is a number from 000 through 221
       device is 2540R for the IBM 2540 card reader
               2501   for the IBM 2501 card reader
               1403   for the IBM 1403 printer
               2540P for the IBM 2540 printer

Notation Rules

1. Anything underlined must be included unless it is in brackets. This means that the header IDENTIFICATION DIVISION must be part of every COBOL program (see Table 3.1).

2. Any item in brackets, [ ], is optional. Therefore, any underlined words which are in brackets do not have to be included unless the option is used. For example, in Table 3.1, if there is no special security involved with the program, the heading SECURITY may be omitted.

3. From all the items in braces, { }, one and only one must be included in the program. For example, see the line which begins SOURCE-COM-PUTER. This phrase tells which computer compiles the program. Throughout this text all programs in the examples will be written for the IBM 360

computer. However, with a few changes, mainly in the ENVIRONMENT DIVISION, they could be used on any other computer with a COBOL compiler. (Consult Table 12.1 for more details.) The SOURCE-COM-PUTER phrase would be written

SOURCE-COMPUTER.   IBM-360.

for the IBM 360 computer and would be written

SOURCE-COMPUTER.   6500.

for the Control Data 6500 computer.

4. Any capitalized word which is not underlined may be included to make the program more readable. For example, in the FILE SECTION, we may write LABEL RECORDS ARE OMITTED or just LABEL RECORDS OMITTED. All capitalized words in the skeleton are reserved COBOL words and have special meaning to the COBOL compiler.[2] They must be spelled exactly the way they are written. For example, PROGRAM-ID cannot be written PROGRAM ID. It must contain a hyphen.

5. Any word not capitalized is to be supplied by the programmer. For example,

PROGRAM-ID.   program-name.

A name must be invented for the program. There are several rules to follow when making up names and these rules are given in section 3.2.

6. The ellipsis marks (. . .) indicate that the preceding word or phrase may be repeated as desired by the programmer. For example,

[REMARKS.   sentence . . .]

in the outline says that REMARKS may contain one or more sentences.

Exercises

1. Certain words in the following program segment have been omitted. In their place is a description of the kind of word which should go there. Replace the omitted words with appropriate ones.

```
IDENTIFICATION DIVISION.
PROGRAM-ID.   program-name.
ENVIRONMENT DIVISION.
CONFIGURATION SECTION.
SOURCE-COMPUTER.   computer-name.
OBJECT-COMPUTER.   computer-name.
INPUT-OUTPUT SECTION.
FILE-CONTROL.
     SELECT I ASSIGN TO input-device.
     SELECT O ASSIGN TO output-device.

DATA DIVISION.
FILE SECTION.
```

---

[2] This pertains only to capitalized words in COBOL skeleton outlines. When a program is written, it is customary to write it entirely in capital letters.

```
FD   I DATA RECORD record-name LABEL RECORDS OMITTED.
01   MAN.
     03  NAME        PICTURE X(30).
     03  FILLER      PICTURE X(10).
     03  ADRES       PICTURE X(20).
     03  FONE        PICTURE X(8).
     03  FILLER      PICTURE X(12).
FD   file-name DATA RECORD LIGN      LABEL RECORDS OMITTED.
01   record-name      PICTURE X(132).
```

2. Are all the paragraphs in the following PROCEDURE DIVISION necessary? Circle all the unnecessary names which should be omitted.

```
PROCEDURE DIVISION.
INIT.   OPEN INPUT FRENCH-CLASS.
READY.   OPEN OUTPUT TEST-RESULTS.
BLANKOUT.   MOVE SPACE TO RESULTS.
NEWPERSON.   READ FRENCH-CLASS AT END GO TO FINISH.
GRTW.   MOVE SNAME TO RNAME.
WRITE-IT.   WRITE RESULTS.
REPEAT.   GO TO NEWPERSON.
FINISH.   CLOSE FRENCH-CLASS TEST-RESULTS.
STOP-IT.   STOP RUN.
```

3. Tell exactly what each of the commands in the PROCEDURE DIVISION of exercise 2 does.

Special Terms

1. *file*
2. *skeleton outline*
3. *IDENTIFICATION DIVISION*
4. *ENVIRONMENT DIVISION*
5. *DATA DIVISION*
6. *PROCEDURE DIVISION*
7. *level number*
8. *alphanumeric*
9. *A margin*
10. *B margin*
11. *source deck*
12. *control cards*
13. *data cards*
14. *data-name*
15. *literal*
16. *numeric literal*
17. *non-numeric literal*
18. *figurative constant*

Chapter 4

Describing Input and Output

4.1 Introduction

After studying all or part of this chapter, the student should write his first programs. The essential sections are 4.2 and 4.6. Section 4.2 covers basic methods of describing data; section 4.6 summarizes basic PROCEDURE DIVISION commands for reading, writing, and moving data. If the student wishes to put titles or column headings on his printout, he should study section 4.3. Following that section are elementary program assignments. Section 4.4 discusses punching data cards; section 4.5 is on editing—making the output more meaningful by adding dollar signs, decimal points, etc. All types of editing characters are discussed here, but the reader may decide to concentrate on the more common ones ($, . Z) now and study the others later. Programs involving editing appear at the conclusion of the chapter.

4.2 Describing Data

In the DATA DIVISION a programmer names any piece of information he wishes to use in the program. He tells how many characters long each item is so that the compiler may reserve space in memory for the data. Also, the programmer categorizes the data and shows any relationship among items. For example, if a card contains a name, a department, and a phone number, these items are related because they come from the same card.

The DATA DIVISION contains three sections to categorize the data and show its use in the program. These sections, if included in a program, must be in the order shown below.

1. FILE SECTION—for describing files
2. WORKING-STORAGE SECTION—for saving anything which is not on a file (computed values, constants, other information)
3. REPORT SECTION—for describing output of the Report Writer[1]

In each of these sections data is described in basically the same way, except that the WORKING-STORAGE and REPORT sections may assign values to memory areas.

Before stating the rules of data description, we will discuss some basic concepts. A *field* is a unit of information. It is consecutive columns (on a card, tape, printer line, or other device) which contain one piece of data. For example, if a person's name is punched in columns 1–20 of a card, we say that the name field is 20 columns long. A collection of fields pertaining to the same subject is a *record*. In COBOL one card or one printed line is a record. A collection of records is a *file*. A collection of fields in a COBOL program is considered a *group*. A record is a group, but not all groups are called records, because a record designates a special subdivision of a file. Examples of files are a card deck, a printed report, or a collection of data on a magnetic tape. If a single card is not big enough to hold all the information of one record, it is possible to divide the data between two cards. Logically

[1] Not available on all computers.

we would say that the file contains records which are two cards long. COBOL, however, would consider it a file containing two records—each one card long. Individual items on the cards are fields. Figure 4.1 illustrates a card file. The entire collection of cards is the file; each card is a record; and on each card are three fields: name, address, and phone number.

Figure 4.1 Fields and Records in a Card File

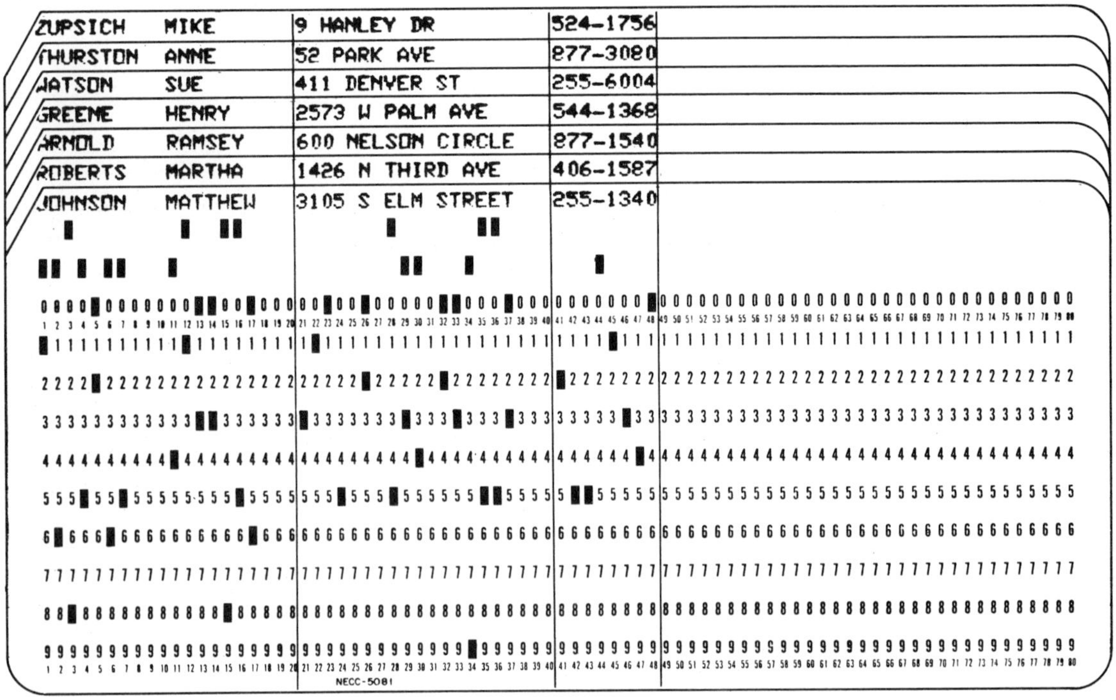

In the FILE SECTION we describe the fields belonging to the records of a file. Any item which is not part of a file is described in the WORKING-STORAGE SECTION.

Rules for Describing Data

1. Any data used in a COBOL program must be described according to size and class.

   Size is the number of characters contained in an item. *Class* tells whether the value of an item is numeric, alphabetic, or alphanumeric. The PICTURE clause describes the class of an item by using the following notation:

9	numeric
A	alphabetic
X	alphanumeric

   The number of times the 9 (or the A or the X) appears in the PICTURE clause tells the size of the item. No more than 30 characters may be in a PICTURE string. For example,

   PICTURE 99999

   specifies that the data item is a 5-digit number and

PICTURE XXXXXX

says that the item contains 6 alphanumeric characters. Instead of writing the symbol repeatedly in the PICTURE or when describing items more than 30 characters long, we may write the symbol and follow it by a number enclosed in parentheses. This number tells the size of the data item. For example, the above PICTUREs could have been written

PICTURE 9(5)
PICTURE X(6)

Using parentheses in a PICTURE makes it easy to determine the size of an item.

2. The fields belonging to a record are described in outline form to show their relationship to and position in the record. A record has the level number 01. The fields in a record may have any level number from 02 through 10.[2] For example, if a card contains a name, an address, and a phone number, then the description of the card will show that these pieces of data all come from the same card. If the card is punched in the following form:

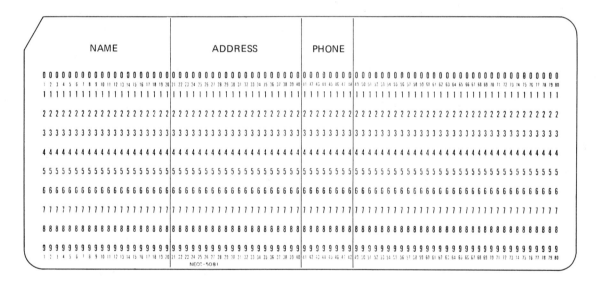

then it could be described in a COBOL program by the following.

```
01   INFO.
     03   NAME       PICTURE A(20).
     03   ADRES      PICTURE X(20).
     03   FONE       PICTURE X(8).
     03   FILLER     PICTURE X(32).
```

The data-names NAME, ADRES, FONE, and FILLER have the same level number to show that the card is divided into these four parts. The FILLER was included so that all 80 columns of the card would be described, even though the last 32 columns will not be used by the program. Let us describe another card which is punched in the following manner.

---

[2] In high level COBOL, the level numbers may be from 02 through 49.

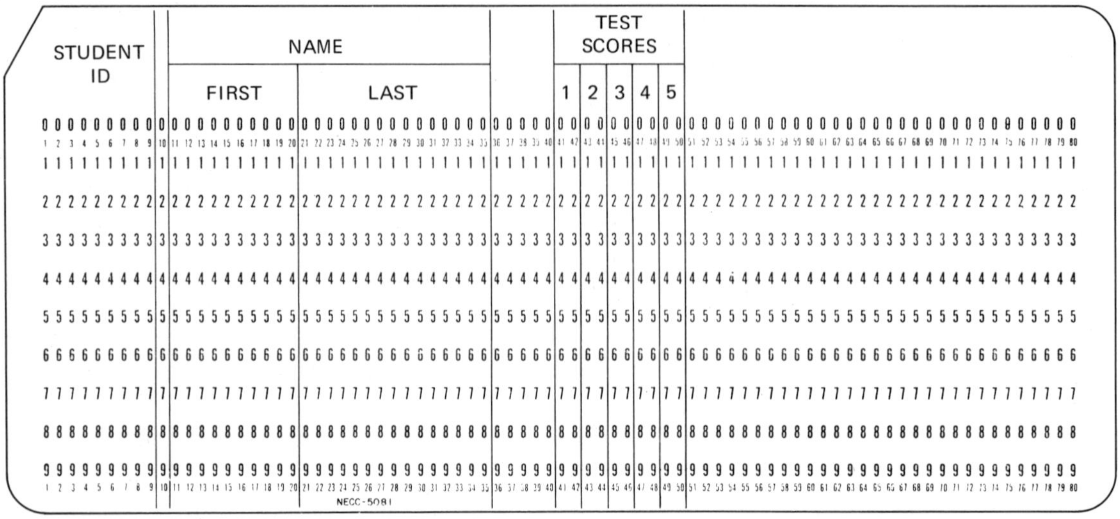

We could say that the card contains three different kinds of information:

student ID
name
test scores.

The name is composed of a first name and a last name; and the test scores are 5 separate numbers. In COBOL the card could be described by the commands shown in Figure 4.2.

Figure 4.2

```
01    STUDENT-INFO.
      04    STUDENT-ID        PICTURE 9(9).
      04    FILLER            PICTURE X.
      04    NAME.
            06    FIRST-NAME  PICTURE A(10).
            06    LAST-NAME   PICTURE A(15).
      04    FILLER            PICTURE X(5).
      04    TEST-SCORES.
            07    SCORE1      PICTURE 99.
            07    SCORE2      PICTURE 99.
            07    SCORE3      PICTURE 99.
            07    SCORE4      PICTURE 99.
            07    SCORE5      PICTURE 99.
      04    FILLER            PICTURE X(30).
```

Since STUDENT-ID is the first name mentioned under STUDENT-INFO, the PICTURE 9(9) tells not only that it occupies nine spaces, but that it is in the first 9 columns on the card. Some of the columns on the card were not used, but they must be described anyway. We use the name FILLER for these columns. The FILLER which follows STUDENT-ID shows that column 10 is not being used. If this FILLER line were omitted, the compiler would think that FIRST-NAME was in columns 10–19 (the next 10 columns following STUDENT-ID). We should be able to look at descriptions and figure out in which columns the data is punched.

Does it matter that NAME is subdivided into two items at the 06 level while TEST-SCORES is broken into items at the 07 level? No, it doesn't. Since FIRST-NAME and LAST-NAME are parts of NAME, their level number may be anything greater than the 04 level of NAME (but not greater than 10). Similarly SCORE1, SCORE2, SCORE3, SCORE4, and SCORE5 may have any level number greater than 04. The 06 and 07 level entries are indented to show that they are part of the 04 entries. This indentation is not necessary, but it makes the description more readable.

3. Name only the data which a program needs so that the compiler will have fewer names to keep track of.

If our program were going to use only the student ID and name from the card described in Figure 4.2, then we should name only those two pieces of data and make all the rest FILLER.

```
01   STUDENT-INFO.
     04   STUDENT-ID      PICTURE 9(9).
     04   FILLER          PICTURE X.
     04   NAME            PICTURE A(25).
     04   FILLER          PICTURE X(45).
```

Not using FIRST-NAME and LAST-NAME, we are saying that we will use the whole name exactly as it is punched on the card.

4. Any data-name immediately followed by names with a higher level number is a *group*. Any data-name which is part of a group and is not followed by a name with a higher level number is an *elementary item*.

For example, STUDENT-INFO, NAME, and TEST-SCORES in Figure 4.2 are all group items; STUDENT-ID, FIRST-NAME, LAST-NAME, SCORE1, SCORE2, SCORE3, SCORE4, and SCORE5 are elementary items. The areas FIRST-NAME and LAST-NAME belong to the group called NAME. Pictorially, NAME is the area enclosed by the double line

```
┌──────────────────────────────────────┐
│  FIRST-NAME          LAST-NAME        │
└──────────────────────────────────────┘
                NAME
```

and contains two parts. To refer to the entire name we use the word NAME; to refer to only the last name we use the word LAST-NAME.

5. The level number 77 is used for an *independent item*—a data-name which is not related to other data-names in the program and is not part of a group but can be used by all groups or files. This level number may appear only in the WORKING-STORAGE SECTION. If there are both 77 level items and 01 level items in WORKING-STORAGE, all 77 level names must be written before any 01 level item.

For example,

```
WORKING-STORAGE SECTION.
77      TOTAL-SALARY    PICTURE 9(6).
77      NUM-EMPLOY      PICTURE 999.
01      SAVE-INFO.
        03   ENAME       PICTURE A(20).
        03   ESAL        PICTURE 999.
        03   EDEPT       PICTURE XX.
```

6. The VALUE phrase gives an initial value to an elementary or independent item in WORKING-STORAGE.

The general form of the VALUE phrase is

VALUE IS literal

If the item has a numeric PICTURE, the literal must be a numeric literal. For example, the description

77   STANDARD-DEDUCT   PICTURE 999   VALUE 625.

would cause memory to contain the following.

| 6 | 2 | 5 |
STANDARD-DEDUCT

7. The general form of a data entry is

$$\text{level-number} \quad \text{data-name} \quad \left[\begin{Bmatrix} \underline{\text{PICTURE}} \\ \underline{\text{PIC}} \end{Bmatrix} \quad \text{IS} \quad \text{picture-string} \right]$$

$$[\underline{\text{VALUE}} \text{ IS literal}].$$

where level-number   is 01 for records; 02–10 for fields; 77 for independent items

data-name   obeys the rules for programmer supplied names given in section 3.2. In the DATA DIVISION all names must be unique; the same name may not be used to describe two areas.[3]

Only elementary and independent items may contain the PICTURE phrase. Only elementary and independent items in WORKING-STORAGE may use the VALUE phrase.

File Section

For each file in the program there must be an <u>FD (File Description)</u> entry preceding the record description. The general form of the FD is

$$\text{FD} \quad \text{file-name } \underline{\text{DATA}} \begin{Bmatrix} \underline{\text{RECORD}} \text{ IS} \\ \underline{\text{RECORDS}} \text{ ARE} \end{Bmatrix} \text{record-name [record-name . . .]}$$

$$\underline{\text{LABEL}} \ \underline{\text{RECORDS}} \ \text{ARE} \ \underline{\text{OMITTED}}.$$

Only a magnetic tape or disk file may have an identifying label at the beginning of the file. This label gives such information as date created, name and number of tape, and so on. If our file is recorded on punched cards or on printer paper, we use the phrase LABEL RECORDS OMITTED, because there can be no label record on these media.

Each record in the file must be named and the record described beneath the FD. The level number for each record is 01.

For example, suppose we want to title our output. This means we would have two different kinds of lines: the title and the line containing the printed information. Therefore, our printer file would contain two records.

FD OUTFILE DATA RECORDS TITLELINE OUTLINE LABEL
      RECORDS OMITTED.
01   TITLELINE.

[3] High level COBOL does allow duplication of names. See the section on qualification in Chapter 10.

```
      03   FILLER      PICTURE  X(50).
      03   TITLE       PICTURE  X(32).
      03   FILLER      PICTURE  X(50).
01    OUTLINE.
         .
         .
         .
```

Some programmers prefix a name with one or two letters of the file-name to help them recognize to which file a name belongs. For example, we could use I-NAME and I-ADRES for the items in IN-FILE and O-NAME and O-ADRES in OUT-FILE.

Working-Storage Section

The WORKING-STORAGE SECTION may be used as a place to store any information needed later by the program or to make room for any values computed in the program.

We may store constants or titles in the WORKING-STORAGE SECTION. For example, suppose we want to describe values for SS-DEDUCT and STATE-TAX and the title PAYROLL. Then we would write

```
WORKING-STORAGE SECTION.
77    SS-DEDUCT     PICTURE V9999    VALUE .0585.
77    STATE-TAX     PICTURE V99      VALUE .05.
01    PAYROLL.
      04   FILLER    PICTURE X(60)    VALUE SPACE.
      04   FILLER    PICTURE X(13)    VALUE 'YEARLY REPORT'.
      04   FILLER    PICTURE X(59)    VALUE SPACE.
```

The V in the PICTURE of SS-DEDUCT and STATE-TAX is used to show where the decimal point should be. It will be explained in more detail in section 4.5.

If a program reads RATE and HOURS from a card and wants to compute SALARY, then RATE and HOURS would be described in the FILE SEC-TION. SALARY is computed, so it could be described in a level 77 item in WORKING-STORAGE.

```
77    SALARY    PICTURE 9999.
```

In order to print salary, we would need to set aside a place in our output area and move SALARY into it. If SALARY will not be used to compute anything else, then we are wasting the computer's memory. We do not need to set aside two areas for salary: one in WORKING-STORAGE (to place the value when it is computed) and one in the FILE SECTION (to hold the number for printing). We may do away with the level 77 entry and describe salary as part of the printer file.

```
FD    PRINT-FILE . . .
01    PRTLINE.
      03   FILLER    PICTURE  X(44).
      03   PNAME     PICTURE  A(30).
      03   FILLER    PICTURE  X(10).
      03   SALARY    PICTURE  9999.
      03   FILLER    PICTURE  X(44).
```

When the value of SALARY is computed in the PROCEDURE DIVISION, it will be placed in the output area PRTLINE. Then it may be written.

4.3 Writing Titles and Headings

How do we go about putting a title or column heading on an output page? In what section do we describe the title? Since it will be part of our output file, we may write the description in the FILE SECTION. Or, since we know what we want the title to be, we may describe it in the WORKING-STORAGE SECTION. Where we describe the title in the DATA DIVISION does make a difference in the way we get the computer to print it. Basically there are two ways to print a title and we will discuss both of them. In both examples, PRINT-FILE will be the file-name of the printer file.

Method 1. Describe the title in the WORKING-STORAGE SECTION and move it to the output file area for printing.

```
FILE SECTION.
FD    PRINT-FILE    DATA RECORD P-LINE LABEL RECORDS
      OMITTED.
01    P-LINE    PICTURE X(132).
            .
            .
            .
WORKING-STORAGE SECTION.
01    TITLELINE.
      03    FILLER    PICTURE X(59)    VALUE SPACE.
      03    FILLER    PICTURE X(15)    VALUE 'PROGRESS REPORT'.
      03    FILLER    PICTURE X(58)    VALUE SPACE.
```

TITLELINE is the name of the title described in the WORKING-STORAGE SECTION. We named none of the parts of the line because we will always be referring to the whole title. Our write area is P-LINE and if we want the title printed, we must give two commands.

```
MOVE TITLELINE TO P-LINE.
WRITE P-LINE AFTER TOP-OF-PAGE.
```

The computer can write only what is in the record area of PRINT-FILE, so we must move the title into that area and then we may have it printed. TOP-OF-PAGE would need to be described in SPECIAL-NAMES to get the line printed on a new page. The SPECIAL-NAMES entry is discussed later in this chapter.

Where do we describe the remainder of our output lines? They could be other 01 levels of PRINT-FILE. See an example of this below.

Method 2. Describe the title in the FILE SECTION and give it a value in the PROCEDURE DIVISION.

```
FILE SECTION.
FD    PRINT-FILE DATA RECORDS TITLELINE OUTPUT-LINE
      LABEL RECORDS OMITTED.
01    TITLELINE.
```

```
        03   FILLER    PICTURE  X(59).
        03   TITLE     PICTURE  X(15).
        03   FILLER    PICTURE  X(58).
01      OUTPUT-LINE.
        03   FILLER    PICTURE  X(10).
        03   NAME      PICTURE  X(20).
             .
             .
             .
```

Since we have put TITLELINE in the FILE SECTION, we cannot use the VALUE phrase. Instead, we must use MOVE commands in the PROCEDURE DIVISION to make the margins blank and to center "PROGRESS REPORT" in TITLELINE.

```
    MOVE SPACE TO TITLELINE.
    MOVE 'PROGRESS REPORT' TO TITLE.
```

The first MOVE will blank out the entire 132 characters of TITLELINE. In this description we *had* to name the middle 15 characters of TITLELINE so that we could tell the computer to put the title there. Now to get the title printed we say

    WRITE TITLELINE AFTER TOP-OF-PAGE.

Comparison of Methods 1 and 2

Method 1 may be easier for the programmer because it eliminates a lot of MOVE statements in the PROCEDURE DIVISION. (Imagine how many MOVEs you would need to put column headings on your output.) However, method 1 uses more room in the computer's memory. P-LINE is 132 characters long and TITLELINE is 132 characters, or a total of 264 characters. With method 2 we are using only 132 characters for TITLELINE. Even if OUTPUT-LINE is 132 characters long, the computer does not reserve an extra 132 characters in memory. *All 01 levels of the same file share the same area in memory.* PRINT-FILE has one memory area 132 characters long; it may be called TITLELINE or OUTPUT-LINE but both names refer to the same area.

TITLE

TITLELINE or OUTPUT-LINE

This means that if we wanted to print a title and column headings using method 2, we would have to

1. move the title into the output area
2. write the title
3. blank out the area
4. move the column headings into the output area
5. write the column headings
6. blank out the area

In small programs we may not have to be concerned with how many memory locations our program takes. But in large programs we may be forced to save space wherever possible just so that the program will fit in the computer's memory. Remember that method 1 may be easier, but method 2 uses less room in memory.

Exercises

1. If YX has a description of PICTURE 999, is YX numeric, alphabetic, or alphanumeric?

2. If E has PICTURE X(10) what is its size?

3. Suppose a data card contains the following information:

social security number	cols. 1–9
last name	11–20
first name	21–30
street address	31–40
city	41–50
state and zip code	51–80

Fill in the missing numbers of the card's description:

```
FD    MASTER-CARDS DATA RECORD NFO LABEL RECORDS
      OMITTED.
__    NFO.
      04    SOCIAL-SECURITY      PICTURE 9(9).
      __    FILLER               PICTURE X.
      __    NAME.
      __    LNAME                PICTURE A(10).
      __    FNAME                PICTURE A(10).
      __    ADRES.
      __    STREET               PICTURE X(10).
      __    CITY                 PICTURE X(10).
      06    STATE                PICTURE X(30).
```

4. Describe a card which contains the following information:

last name	cols. 1–10
first name	11–20
height (in inches)	21–22
weight	24–26
age	30–31
aptitude score	32–34

5. If QUALIFIED is a card file, in what columns on the data card will we find N, SA, C, ST, X?

```
FD    QUALIFIED DATA RECORD PROS LABEL RECORDS
      OMITTED.
01    PROS.
      05    N        PICTURE A(25).
      05    SA       PICTURE X(15).
      05    C        PICTURE 999.
      05    FILLER   PICTURE X(7).
```

```
05   ST           PICTURE 9(10).
05   X            PICTURE X(20).
```

6. If the following WORKING-STORAGE SECTION appeared in a program, which entries are the following: a) records, b) elementary items, and c) independent items?

```
WORKING-STORAGE SECTION.
77   SUMA            PICTURE 9999.
77   SUMA-EDITED PICTURE 99999.
01   PAGE-HEADINGS.
     04   FILLER    PICTURE X(30)   VALUE SPACE.
     04   COL1      PICTURE X(30).
     04   FILLER    PICTURE X(20)   VALUE SPACE.
     04   PAGE-N-NO.
          06   PAGE-WORD   PICTURE A(5)   VALUE 'PAGE'.
          06   PAGE-NO     PICTURE 99     VALUE 01.
```

7. Using both methods 1 and 2 show how a COBOL program could get column headings of NAME, ADDRESS, and PHONE NUMBER printed on a page. You may use any spacing desired for the heading line.

Programs

In order to write any of the following programs, the reader may wish to refer to section 4.5 which gives a summary of PROCEDURE DIVISION commands. None of the programs use editing which is discussed in the next section.

1. The personnel manager of the ORGANIC FOOD FARM has a card punched for each of the workers at the farm. The card contains the following information:

name	cols. 1–20
no. hours worked per day	21–22
no. days worked per week	31

The manager needs a printed report which will list for him the employees' names, the number of hours worked per day, and the number of days worked per week. The report should start on a new page, and have an appropriate title and column headings. The general form of the output should be as diagrammed below.

Title		
Name	Hours	Days
————	————	————
————	————	————
————	————	————

2. A programming instructor has collected one card from each of his students and wishes to have a class roll made from these cards. The cards were punched in the following form:

social security number	cols. 1–9	
last name	10–22	
first name	23–31	
middle initial	32	
address	34–50	
phone number	51–58	(hyphen in 54)
sex	70	

The output should be titled and should list the following on one line for each student in the class.

first name
middle initial
last name
address
phone number
social security number

3. The Itty Bitty Machine Company has just installed a computer which will run COBOL programs, and the payroll department would like to start using the machine. For each worker they have prepared one card which contains the following information:

social security number	cols. 1–9
name	11–27
number of hours worked	31–32
rate per hour (in dollars)	35

The payroll department wants to use this data to print a payroll sheet looking something like this:

```
            ITTY BITTY MACHINE CO. PAYROLL
      323001067        MARTIN SAM        30        2
           .               .             .         .
           .               .             .         .
           .               .             .         .
```

Use any spacing you like for the output. Make a flowchart to show the procedure your program will follow and write a program which will do the report for the payroll department.

4.4 Punching Data Cards

When punching data on a card, alphanumeric or alphabetic data is punched in the leftmost part of a field (*left-adjusted*). If the data does not completely fill up the area, extra columns are left blank. Numeric data is punched in the rightmost part of a field (*right-adjusted*) with zeros filling up any extra columns. For example, to punch the word SCREWDRIVER in columns 1–20, we would start in column 1, continue through column 11, and leave columns 12–20 blank. To punch the number 35 in columns 21–23, we would punch it as 035.

If a number contains decimal digits, a decimal point is *not* punched on the card. Instead, we tell the computer where the decimal point should go by using a V in the PICTURE. For more information see section 4.5.

If numbers are positive, we do not need to punch a + sign on the card.

No sign on a number tells the computer that it is positive. However, if we wish to punch a negative number on a card, then we punch the − sign and the right-most digit in the same column. (To do this use the multi-punch key on the card punch.) Similarly to give a sign to a positive number, multi-punch the + sign over the right-most digit. This is contrary to mathematical notation in which the sign precedes the number. However, when our program prints numbers, we may have it print the sign in front of the number as is usually done (see section 4.5).

Figure 4.3 shows the word SCREWDRIVER left-adjusted in columns 1–20, the number 35 right-adjusted in columns 21–23, the value 12.75 punched in columns 26–29, and a −11 punched in columns 31–32. The lines were drawn on the card to point out the fields.

Figure 4.3

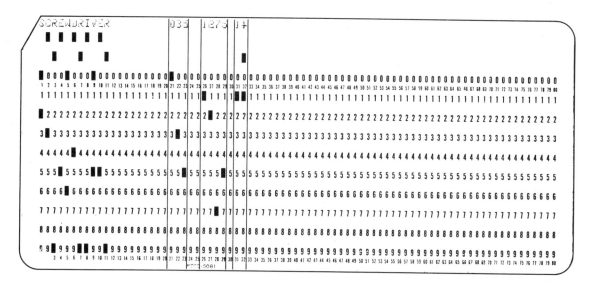

4.5 Editing Numbers

Until now data has been described very simply. An item is classed as alphanumeric, alphabetic, or numeric and its length is given in the PICTURE. The only numbers used have been whole numbers. In an actual problem we may have decimals or negative numbers. There may be numbers such as 436780 which we would like to print as $4,367.80. Variations in the PICTURE description will allow us to use decimals or make numbers more meaningful for output by adding dollar signs and decimal points.

Numeric Data

The following characters may be used in the PICTURE of a numeric item. Any number used in computation must have a numeric description.

9   reserves space for one numeric character.
V   shows the location of an assumed decimal point. There is no actual decimal point stored in the computer's memory and therefore the decimal point does not increase the size of the item. We may think of the assumed decimal point as an arrow (↑) pointing to the place where the actual decimal point should be. It is redundant to use the V as the rightmost character of the PICTURE. For example,

PICTURE 99V9

defines a three digit number with one decimal place. We may picture memory as the following:

The arrow shows that the decimal point is assumed to be before the last digit. The size of the item is 3 characters.

S   indicates an implied sign. It is the leftmost character in a PICTURE, but does not increase the size of the item. In memory the sign of the number will be placed in the same location as the rightmost digit of the number. This is the same way the number would be punched on a card. Pictorially, +267 would be stored in memory as

$$\boxed{2} \boxed{6} \boxed{\overset{+}{7}}$$

If there is no S in the PICTURE, an item will *always* be positive.

The following examples illustrate how data read from a card according to the specified PICTURE would be stored in memory and the value it would have. The numbers which have signs would have the sign (a + or −) multi-punched in the same column as the rightmost digit of the number. Notice what happens to a negative number placed in an area which has no S in the PICTURE.

PICTURE	Data	Stored	Value
9(4)	1234	1 2 3 4	1234
9V999	1234	1 2 3 4 ↑	1.234
S99	12	1 2	+12
S99	+12	1 +2	+12
S999	−123	1 2 −3	−123
999	−123	1 2 3	123
S9V999	+1234	1 2 3 +4 ↑	+1.234

If we want to give values to data items in WORKING-STORAGE, the VALUE phrase must reflect the PICTURE. For example,

```
77   X   PICTURE   999     VALUE   123.
77   Y   PICTURE   9V99    VALUE   6.34.
77   Z   PICTURE   S99V9   VALUE   +00.7.
```

will make   X = 123,   Y = 6.34,   and Z = +00.7. However,

```
77   RONG   PICTURE   99   VALUE   6.8.
```

will *not* make RONG = 6.8. Here RONG would equal 6 because the PIC-TURE says that RONG has no decimal digits. Neither will

    77   RONG   PICTURE   9V9   VALUE   68.

make RONG = 6.8. Here RONG would equal 8.0 because the PICTURE says there is one digit to the left of the decimal and one digit to the right. Only

    77   RONG   PICTURE   9V9   VALUE   6.8.

will set RONG = 6.8. Both the PICTURE and the VALUE phrase must show that RONG is to have a decimal digit.

Numeric Editing

Editing of numeric items includes the insertion of some characters and the elimination of others to make a number more meaningful for printout. For example, if X has a PICTURE of

PICTURE 9V99

and a value of

then printing X would show

   123

on the page. Assumed decimal points are necessary for computation but do not print. However, we may edit the value of X to get it printed as 1.23 with an actual decimal point. To do this we would need to set up another data item with a PICTURE which shows how X is to be printed. A data item such as the following would work.

    03   X-ED   PICTURE 9.99.

The description of X-ED would be part of the output file. In order to get X converted to a number with a decimal point we would say

   MOVE X TO X-ED.

The value of X-ED would be

| 1 | . | 2 | 3 |

X-ED

An actual decimal point has been inserted between the 1 and the 2, where the assumed decimal point was. Then if we printed X-ED we would have

1.23

written. Edited data may not be moved to a numeric or numeric edited area.

Let us consider the DATA and PROCEDURE divisions of a program (Program 4.1) which edits some of the numbers it reads and computes. The file CARD-FILE is on punched cards and PRINT-OUT is assigned to the printer.

Program 4.1

```
DATA DIVISION.
FILE SECTION.
FD      CARD-FILE DATA RECORD SALES-SLIP LABEL
        RECORDS OMITTED.
01      SALES-SLIP.
        03   NAME        PICTURE A(20).
        03   PRICE       PICTURE 9V99.
        03   NUM-SOLD    PICTURE 99.
        03   FILLER      PICTURE X(55).
FD      PRINT-OUT DATA RECORDS BLNK SALE LABEL
        RECORDS OMITTED.
01      BLNK            PICTURE X(132).
01      SALE.
        03   FILLER      PICTURE X(34).
        03   NME         PICTURE A(20).
        03   FILLER      PICTURE X(10).
        03   PR          PICTURE $9.99.
        03   FILLER      PICTURE X(10).
        03   NUM         PICTURE 99.
        03   FILLER      PICTURE X(10).
        03   TOT-SALE    PICTURE $999.99.
        03   FILLER      PICTURE X(34).
PROCEDURE DIVISION.
ST.     OPEN INPUT CARD-FILE. OPEN OUTPUT PRINT-OUT.
        MOVE SPACES TO BLNK.
LP.     READ CARD-FILE AT END GO TO STPIT.
        MOVE NAME TO NME.
        MOVE PRICE TO PR.
        MOVE NUM-SOLD TO NUM.
        MULTIPLY PRICE BY NUM-SOLD GIVING TOT-SALE.
        WRITE SALE AFTER ADVANCING 2 LINES. GO TO LP.
STPIT.  CLOSE CARD-FILE PRINT-OUT. STOP RUN.
```

If

PRICE = | 1 | 5 | 0 |
          ↑

NUM-SOLD = | 0 | 2 |

Then

MOVE PRICE TO PR.

will make

PR = | $ | 1 | . | 5 | 0 |

and the command

MULTIPLY PRICE BY NUM-SOLD GIVING TOT-SALE.

will make

TOT-SALE = | \$ | 0 | 0 | 3 | . | 0 | 0 |

The MULTIPLY computes the product of NUM-SOLD and PRICE and then edits the answer. When SALE is written, the contents of PR and TOT-SALE will appear with dollar sign and decimal point—just as they are stored in the computer's memory.

Normally whenever we wish to edit a number, the number has already been described somewhere in the DATA DIVISION. To edit it, we must describe in another PICTURE its appearance in printed form. Then, moving the number into the area with the edit PICTURE will prepare the number for printing. A number which is the result of a computation may also be edited.

Any data item which has been edited will contain characters which are not numbers; therefore, an edited item is an alphanumeric item and may *not* be used in computation. For example, if we wished to compute TAX as .04 times TOT-SALE in Program 4.1, then we may *not* compute TAX by saying

MULTIPLY TOT-SALE BY .04 GIVING TAX.   *incorrect*

If we wish to use the value of TOT-SALE and multiply it by .04, then we must include a description of it in WORKING-STORAGE which is entirely numeric, such as

77   TOT-SAL   PICTURE 999V99.

That is, we are setting aside *two areas*—one for editing the product of NUM-SOLD and PRICE and another for computing with it. The correct commands would be

MULTIPLY NUM-SOLD BY PRICE GIVING TOT-SAL.
MOVE TOT-SAL TO TOT-SALE.
MULTIPLY TOT-SAL BY .04 GIVING TAX.

Also, we would need to describe TAX in the SALE record so that it could be printed. What would the PICTURE of TAX be?

The following characters may be used in an editing PICTURE:

9   Z   *   \$ +   −   .   ,   CR   DB   0   B

The character 9 has been discussed previously under numeric data. The other characters will be explained below. The Z and * are called *replacement characters* because they are used only to replace leading zeros. The \$ + − . , CR DB 0 and B are *insertion characters* because they are added to the data to make the numbers more meaningful.

Z Character. The Z is a zero suppression character. Each Z in a PICTURE will replace one leading zero with a blank. Zero suppression stops when the first non-zero character is reached. Z's may be used in a PICTURE with the decimal point, comma, zero, or B. The b's in the following example denote blank spaces.

Example

Data	Editing Picture	Edited Result
00214	ZZ999	bb214
37642	ZZ999	37642
00010	ZZ999	bb010
00010	ZZZZZ	bbb10
007↑95	ZZZ.99	bb7.95

Asterisk (*) *Character.* The asterisk (*) is for check protection. It replaces leading zeros with asterisks and is frequently used on checks to keep people from altering the amount printed. Like the Z editing character, it may be used with the decimal point, comma, zero, or B; check protection stops with the first non-zero character.

Example

Data	Editing PICTURE	Edited Result
00612	**999	**612
00078	**999	**078
00060	*****	***60
37604	****9	37604
007↑51	***.99	**7.51

Dollar Sign ($) *Character.* The dollar sign ($) is the leftmost character in the PICTURE when it is used. It is included in the size of the edited item.

Example

Data	Editing PICTURE	Edited Result
321	$999	$321
108	$ZZZ	$108
006	$ZZZ	$bb6
006	$999	$006
006	$***	$**6
1↑50	$9.99	$1.50

Plus (+) *Character.* The plus sign (+) may be used as the first or last character of a PICTURE, but not both. It will be printed if the data is positive. A negative sign (−) will be written if the data is negative. Data with no implied sign in the PICTURE is always positive.

Example

Data	Editing PICTURE	Edited Result
763	+999	+763
021	+999	+021
8̄12	+999	−812
7̇0̇2	999+	702+
611	$999+	$611+

Minus (−) *Character.* The minus sign (−) may also be used as the first or last character of a PICTURE, but not both. Either the plus sign or the minus sign may be used, but both of them may not appear in a PICTURE. If the data is positive, no sign will be written. If the data is negative, a minus sign will be printed.

Example

Data	Editing PICTURE	Edited Result
803	−999	b803
$\overset{+}{803}$	−999	b803
$\overset{-}{803}$	−999	−803
210	999−	210−
050	−ZZZ	bb50

Decimal Point (.) *and Comma* (,) *Characters.* The decimal point and/or comma will be inserted among the digits as they appear in the PICTURE. They increase the size of the data item. There may be only one decimal point in a picture, and it may not be the rightmost character. The ↑ in the following example shows the location of an implied decimal point in the data item to be edited. If the edited number is not large enough, a blank will be inserted instead of a comma.

Example

Data	Editing PICTURE	Edited Result
468↑081	999.999	468.081
7286↑04	$9,999.99	$7,286.04
8871↑10	Z,ZZZ.99	8,871.10
0000↑031	Z,ZZZ.999	bbbbb.031

CR and DB Characters. The credit (CR) or debit (DB) characters if used, must be at the rightmost end of a PICTURE. It will print if the data being edited is negative. If the data is positive or unsigned, blanks will appear instead of the letters CR or DB. Only one of the two symbols CR or DB may be used in a PICTURE.

Example

Data	Editing PICTURE	Edited Result
$\overset{-}{4610}$	9999CR	4610CR
3217	9999CR	3217bb
$\overset{+}{1108}$	9999DB	1108bb
$\overset{-}{1108}$	9999DB	1108DB

Zero (0) *Character.* The zero (0) will insert a zero character in the specified position of the edited item.

Example

Data	Editing PICTURE	Edited Result
1234	99099	12034
7618	$9999.00	$7618.00
0009	ZZZ900	bbb900

B Character. The letter B puts a blank space in the specified location of the edited item. It is often used to separate a social security number for printing or to separate a number from either CR or DB.

Example

Data	Editing PICTURE	Edited Result
323408439	999B99B9999	323b40b8439
62178	9(5)BBCR	62178bbCR
30014	9(5)BBDB	30014bbbb

Zero Suppression with $ + or −. Zero suppression is also accomplished with any one of these "floating" characters:

$
+
−

Leading zeros are made blank and one of these characters appears in front of the first non-zero digit. There must be *one more* character in the PICTURE than the number of digits on which we wish to suppress zeros. For example, to suppress leading zeros in an area 5 digits long, the editing PICTURE must contain $(6) or +(6) or −(6). Five of the characters provide space for the five digits; the sixth is for the extra character inserted ($ + or −).

Example

Data	Editing PICTURE	Edited Result
0276	$$$$$	b$276
37091	$$$$$$	$37091
0004	++++9	bbb+4
0316	—————	b−316
0002	—————	bbbb2

Rules for PICTURE Editing

1. Only one of the characters Z * $ + or − may be used in a single PICTURE for zero suppression. If either the Z or * is used for zero suppression, the $ + or − may be used as an insertion character.
2. If either the + or − is used as an insertion character, it may be either the leftmost or rightmost character in the PICTURE. Both the + and − may not be included in the same PICTURE.
3. The $ must always be the leftmost character in the PICTURE.

4. A leftmost plus sign or a leftmost minus sign and a dollar sign may not be included in the same PICTURE. However, a dollar sign and either a + or − may appear in a PICTURE if the + or − is the rightmost character.
5. The character 9 may not be specified to the left of a zero suppression character.
6. These symbols may appear only once: V, S, decimal point, CR, and DB.
7. The decimal point may not be the rightmost character in a PICTURE.
8. The maximum number of digits which may be edited is 18.

Exercises

1. If X has a PICTURE of 999V99 is X numeric, alphabetic, or alphanumeric?

2. If X and CHOP are described by the following:

   ```
   77   X       PICTURE   9V999   VALUE   3.692.
   77   CHOP    PICTURE   9.9.
   ```

   What will be the values of X and CHOP after the following is executed?

   MOVE X TO CHOP.

3. If PEN has a PICTURE 9.999 is PEN numeric, alphabetic, or alphanumeric?

4. What is the size and class of the following data items?

   ```
   77   MAX     PICTURE   999.
   77   STAT    PICTURE   A(25).
   77   NUM     PICTURE   999V9(4).
   77   AG      PICTURE   $99,999.99.
   77   BL      PICTURE   XXXXXX.
   ```

5. Complete the following so that CON will have a value of 3.14.

   ```
   77   CON     PICTURE
   ```

6. What is the largest number which can be stored in MAX, where MAX is described by

   ```
   77   MAX     PICTURE   $9(5).99.
   ```

7. Refer to the following descriptions and draw a picture of the contents of A, B, C, and D in memory after the MOVE is executed. Use a b to denote a blank space.

   ```
   77   ONE   PICTURE 9(5)V99      VALUE 00010.75.
   77   A     PICTURE 9(5).99.
   77   B     PICTURE Z(5).99.
   77   C     PICTURE $*(5).99.
   77   D     PICTURE ZZ,ZZZ.99.
               MOVE ONE TO A B C D.
   ```

8. Refer to the following descriptions and draw a picture of the contents of

X, Y, Z, and Q after the MOVEs are executed. Use a b to denote a blank space.

```
77   NUM   PICTURE S999      VALUE +122.
77   CON   PICTURE S9V9      VALUE −7.8.
77   X     PICTURE +999.
77   Y     PICTURE −999.
77   Z     PICTURE 9.9BCR.
77   Q     PICTURE 9.9 −.
                MOVE NUM TO X Y.
                MOVE CON TO Z Q.
```

9. If in memory we have

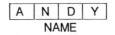

NAME

what will be the contents of NAME, X, and Y after the following command?

MOVE NAME TO X Y.

X and Y are described in the following manner.

X PIC X(5).
Y PIC XXX.

4.6 Summary of PROCEDURE DIVISION Commands

In this section we will discuss simplified versions of the COBOL commands used in the first program. Most COBOL statements have numerous options, some of which are normally used only by advanced programmers in complex programs. Therefore, in an effort to simplify the material for the beginning programmer, we will state the commands in their most commonly used forms. These commands are organized according to their use: Input/Output, Data Movement, and Control (Logic). Before we begin the discussion of the commands let us consider the organization of the PROCEDURE DIVISION.

All commands are complete sentences, and the sentences are combined into paragraphs. Sometimes it is necessary to begin a new paragraph because we need a way to reference a particular command. Other paragraphs are formed to group the commands and show the effect they have on the entire program. For example, it may be logical but not necessary to have paragraphs named PRINT-HEADINGS or SUMMARY-ROUTINE, because these names give the reader an idea of the type of work being done in the paragraph. If the program is a long one, we may wish to combine paragraphs into sections for easy reference or for logical reasons. The general outline of the PROCEDURE DIVISION is:

PROCEDURE DIVISION.
[section-name SECTION.]
paragraph-name. command.
        .
        .
        .

paragraph-name. command.
        .
        .
        .

[section-name <u>SECTION</u>.]
paragraph-name. command.
.
.
.

Rules for the PROCEDURE DIVISION

1. Paragraph-names and section-names must follow the rules given in section 3.2 for programmer supplied names.
2. All SECTION headings are optional, but there must be at least one paragraph in the program.
3. Every command must be contained in some paragraph.
4. A section header begins with the section-name in column 8 (the A margin), followed by the word SECTION and terminated with a period. The remainder of the line is blank.
5. A paragraph begins with the paragraph-name in column 8 (the A margin). Following the paragraph-name is a period. The first command may be on the same line as the paragraph-name as long as there is at least one space between the period and the beginning of the command. The remainder of the line containing the paragraph-name may be blank; if so, the first command would begin in column 12 (the B margin) of the next line. Succeeding lines in the paragraph begin in column 12.

For example, the following is a rough outline of a PROCEDURE DIVISION divided into sections and paragraphs.

```
PROCEDURE DIVISION.
INITIALIZATION SECTION.
OPEN-FILES. OPEN INPUT MASTER-FILE CHANGE-FILE.
    OPEN OUTPUT NEW-MASTER.
DATA-INIT. MOVE ZERO TO GROSS-SUM NET-SUM.
    MOVE 1 TO I J K.
HEADING-ROUTINE.
        .
        .
        .
READ-INCOME-TAX-TABLE.
        .
        .
        .
UPDATE-FILE SECTION.
READ-MASTER.    . . .
READ-CHANGE.    . . .
ADD-TO-FILE.    . . .
DELETE-FROM-FILE.    . . .
        .
        .
        .
SUMMARY SECTION.
        .
        .
        .
```

Input/Output

OPEN. The OPEN command readies files so that the computer may read or write them. A file to be read must be opened as an INPUT file. A file to be written must be opened as an OUTPUT file.

A file which is already open cannot be opened again. However, a file which is open may be closed and then opened again.

Form: OPEN $\left\{ \begin{matrix} \underline{\text{INPUT}} \\ \underline{\text{OUTPUT}} \end{matrix} \right\}$ file-name [file-name . . .] .

Example

If we want to read the SS-DATA file and write the files PUNCH-CARD and SS-REPORT, we open them by saying

```
OPEN INPUT SS-DATA.
OPEN OUTPUT PUNCH-CARD.
OPEN OUTPUT SS-REPORT.
```

or we may combine the two OPEN OUTPUTs into just one sentence.

```
OPEN INPUT SS-DATA.
OPEN OUTPUT PUNCH-CARD SS-REPORT.
```

CLOSE. The CLOSE statement terminates the processing of files. Any file which has been opened must be closed before the program stops.

Form: <u>CLOSE</u> file-name [file-name . . .] .

Example

To close two files named EMPLOYEE-INFO and TAX-DATA we could say

```
CLOSE EMPLOYEE-INFO.
CLOSE TAX-DATA.
```

or we could close both files with one command.

```
CLOSE EMPLOYEE-INFO TAX-DATA.
```

READ. When the READ command is executed, only one record from the file named is read. The word RECORD may be included in the READ statement to emphasize this fact. The contents of that record are transferred from cards, tape, or whatever medium the file was written on into the computer's memory. If the file is on punched cards, the AT END part of the READ statement checks the card just read to see if it is the special "end" card which is placed at the end of the card deck. If the computer has just read the "end" card, it then executes the statement (or statements) following the AT END phrase. If the computer has not encountered the "end" card, it does not execute those statements.

Form: <u>READ</u> file-name RECORD AT <u>END</u> any-statement . . . .

Example

In the FILE SECTION we have the following file described.

```
FD    MEMBERS DATA RECORD PERSON LABEL RECORDS
      OMITTED.
01    PERSON.
      03    NAME          PICTURE A(20).
      03    ADRES         PICTURE X(20).
      03    OTHER-INFO    PICTURE X(40).
```

A portion of the cards in this file is shown below.

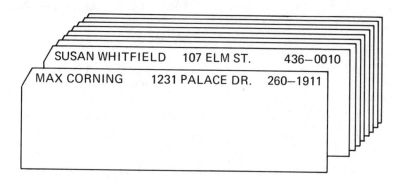

When the computer executes the following command

READ MEMBERS AT END GO TO FNSH.

it places all the information on the first card into the memory area named
PERSON. Pictorially, memory contains

MAX CORNING	1231 PALACE DR.	260-1911

PERSON

The second time the computer executes a command which says to read **MEM-
BERS**, it reads the second card in the deck. The data on that card replaces the
contents of PERSON. So now memory contains the following information.

SUSAN WHITFIELD	107 ELM ST.	436-0010

PERSON

All the data from the first card has been lost. The computer cannot reread a
card, so a program must use the first card's data before it reads a second card.

Example

The flowchart segment below shows that when the computer encounters
the "end" card it should close two files and then stop.

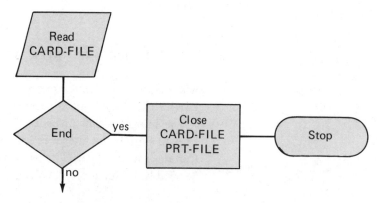

In COBOL we could write the instructions in any of the following ways:

Method 1.

P01.   READ CARD-FILE AT END GO TO P02.

.

.

.

P02.   CLOSE CARD-FILE PRT-FILE. STOP RUN.

Method 2.

P01.   READ CARD-FILE AT END CLOSE CARD-FILE PRT-FILE
STOP RUN.

The second method eliminates one paragraph and one GO TO statement. To make the computer do everything (close the files and stop) when it comes to the "end" card, we place a period only after the word RUN. What if there had been a period after the word PRT-FILE in the second method? The computer would interpret that paragraph as two separate commands and after it had read one card it would go on to the next sentence and stop. It would not have closed any files, nor would it have read any more data.

WRITE. This command writes the contents from one record in memory on a printer file. The record must be the name of a 01 level item of a file described in the FILE SECTION. The file must be open for output before anything can be written on it.

Form: $\underline{\text{WRITE}}$ record-name $\begin{Bmatrix} \text{BEFORE} \\ \text{AFTER} \end{Bmatrix}$ ADVANCING $\begin{Bmatrix} \text{integer LINES} \\ \text{mnemonic-name} \end{Bmatrix}$.

The word BEFORE used in the WRITE statement means that the record will be written and then so many lines will be skipped. The word AFTER means that the lines will be skipped and then the record will be written.

Example

The command

WRITE PRT-LINE BEFORE ADVANCING 5 LINES.

will write the contents of PRT-LINE and then will advance 5 lines down the page. This leaves space between what was written and what will be written next.

The command

WRITE PRT-LINE AFTER ADVANCING 5 LINES.

will advance the printer's paper 5 lines before writing the contents of PRT-LINE. This leaves space between the previous line written and PRT-LINE.

The integer which precedes the word LINES tells the printer how many lines to skip. If the integer is 1, 2, 3, . . . then 1, 2, 3, . . . lines will be skipped. Certain values of the integer have different effects on specific computers. See Table 4.1 for more detailed information.

Table 4.1

Describing Input and Output **61**

Computer	Value of Integer	Effect
IBM 360	must be positive and less than 100	skip number of lines specified
	zero	goes to new page
CDC 6000 Series	negative or greater than 66	goes to new page

Instead of specifying a certain number of lines to skip we may use the "mnemonic-name" in the WRITE statement. The mnemonic-name is a programmer supplied name which is defined under the heading SPECIAL-NAMES in the ENVIRONMENT DIVISION. The general form of the SPECIAL-NAMES line is

SPECIAL-NAMES. forms-control IS mnemonic-name.

Paper on an IBM printer is divided into 12 areas called channels. Channel 1 is at the top of the page and channel 12 is at the bottom. The other channels are equally spaced in between. The forms-control names for these channels are C01, C02, C03, . . . , C12. For example, to get a line written at the top of the page on an IBM 360, we would include

SPECIAL-NAMES. C01 IS TOP-OF-PAGE.

and the command would be

WRITE PRINT-LINE AFTER TOP-OF-PAGE.

Data Movement

MOVE. The MOVE command is used to transfer data from one area in memory to another.

Form: MOVE $\begin{Bmatrix} \text{data-name} \\ \text{literal} \end{Bmatrix}$ TO data-name [data-name . . .] .

In the DATA DIVISION a programmer names and describes different areas of memory. He sets up areas for input, areas for output, and areas for computed values. The name given to each area is called a *data-name*. For example, in Program 3.1 CARD-INFO is a data-name.

The result of a MOVE command depends upon the PICTURE of the area where the data goes. During a MOVE operation there are two things to remember:

1. Data moved from an alphanumeric area to an alphanumeric area is always left-adjusted. Extra spaces are made blank.
2. Data moved from a numeric area to a numeric area is placed according to the decimal point. Any extra spaces are filled with zeros.

A statement such as

MOVE X TO Y.

will always leave the contents of X unchanged. The original contents of Y will be erased and will be replaced by the contents of X. The result will be two copies of the characters in X.

Rules for the MOVE Command

1. Data may be moved from an alphabetic area to an alphanumeric area, but not vice versa.
2. Numeric data may not be moved to an alphabetic area.
3. Numeric-edited data may be moved only to an alphanumeric area.
4. Numeric or alphabetic data moved to an alphanumeric area will be left-adjusted with blank fill.
5. In moves to alphanumeric areas where the receiving area is too short, extra characters will be truncated.
6. Alphabetic data moved to an alphabetic area follows the same rule as alphanumeric items. (See rules 4 and 5.)
7. In numeric moves if there is not a large enough receiving area, digits may be truncated before or after the decimal point.
8. In numeric moves in which the receiving area is too large, zeros will be added to fill up the remaining places.
9. Data may be moved from one place in storage to another regardless of the level number, provided the move is valid as determined by rules 1–4.
10. Data may be moved freely between the FILE SECTION and WORKING-STORAGE SECTION, provided the move is valid.
11. A move involving a group treats the group as an alphanumeric area. It ignores the PICTUREs of the elementary items.

Below are examples of what happens to the contents of memory when the following statement is executed. The contents of X always remain the same.

MOVE X TO Z.

X		Z	
PICTURE	Contents	PICTURE	Contents
X(4)	A B C D	X(4)	A B C D
X(4)	C O L D	X(5)	C O L D
X(4)	H O T .	X(3)	H O T
A(4)	J O H N	A(4)	J O H N
A(3)	M O O	A(4)	M O O
A(4)	M O O D	A(3)	M O O
9(4)	4 3 6 8	9(4)	4 3 6 8
9(3)	6 1 8	9(4)	0 6 1 8
9(3)	8 9 1	99	9 1

If we want to make MAXINC (an item described in the FILE SECTION or WORKING-STORAGE SECTION) equal to 5000, then we can do it by saying

MOVE 5000 TO MAXINC.

If in addition we wish to set MAXTOT equal to 5000, the command is

MOVE 5000 TO MAXTOT.

or we may replace both MOVEs with the following statement:

MOVE 5000 TO MAXINC MAXTOT.

If we want to put the word "yes" in CHECKER, this MOVE command accomplishes it.

MOVE 'YES' TO CHECKER.

CHECKER must have an alphabetic (A) or alphanumeric (X) PICTURE.

Figurative Constants. In COBOL there are certain words which always have the same value; these are called *figurative constants*, a complete list of which is discussed in section 10.6. Two of these constants are SPACE and ZERO.

SPACE has a value of one or more blank characters. It may be used to blank out or erase an area. For example, an area named CARD-LINE may be blanked out by saying

MOVE SPACE TO CARD-LINE.

No matter how many characters long CARD-LINE is, it will contain all blanks. SPACE may not be moved to a numeric area. However, SPACE may be moved to a group which contains a numeric area, because a move involving a group ignores the PICTUREs of the group's elementary items.

The name ZERO is either the number zero or a string of zero characters. If we wish to make SUMA equal zero, SUMB equal zero, and SUMC equal zero, we may say

MOVE ZERO TO SUMA SUMB SUMC.

or we could use the numeric literal 0 and write

MOVE 0 TO SUMA SUMB SUMC.

The constant ZERO may not be moved to an alphabetic area.

Control (Logic)

When executing COBOL instructions, the computer proceeds from the first one to the second to the third . . . and from the first paragraph to the second. It does the commands in the order in which they are written unless the program says otherwise. It is the control portion of the computer which has the statements executed in sequence. A statement such as STOP RUN will make the computer stop; the computer will execute no more instructions after it executes the STOP RUN statement. A GO TO command tells the computer to proceed (branch) to another portion of the program and to begin executing the statements in sequence until another GO TO or a STOP RUN is encountered.

GO TO. Normally COBOL statements are executed in the same sequence in which they are written. The GO TO statement causes the computer to proceed from one part of the program to another. It changes the order in which the statements are executed.

Form: GO TO procedure-name.

The *procedure-name* is the name of a paragraph or a section in the PROCEDURE DIVISION.

Example

```
R-W-LOOP. READ CARD-FILE AT END GO TO CLOSE-UP.
    MOVE INFO TO RITE.
    WRITE OUTREC AFTER ADVANCING 2 LINES.
    GO TO R-W-LOOP.
CLOSE-UP.  . . .
```

After the computer has written OUTREC it will not proceed to paragraph CLOSE-UP, but will execute the READ statement next. When the computer reaches the end of CARD-FILE it will leave the paragraph R-W-LOOP and will go on to paragraph CLOSE-UP.

STOP RUN. This command causes the computer to stop execution of the program. The general form of this command is:

Form: STOP RUN.

There must be at least one STOP RUN statement in the program. However, a program may contain several STOP RUN statements.

Programs

1. The Itty Bitty Machine Company has its sales records punched on cards. Each card contains salesman's name, social security number, cost per machine, number of machines in a crate, and number of crates sold. The company's sales department would like a listing of employees, social security numbers, cost per machine, number of machines in a crate, and number of crates sold. As chief programmer it is your assignment to write a program which will make this listing.
   Input data is in the following format:

social security number	cols.	1–9
last name		10–22
first name		23–31
middle initial		33

address	34–50	
phone number	51–58	(hyphen in 54)
cost per machine	60–62	(assumed decimal between 60 and 61)
no. machines in a crate	64–65	
no. crates sold	67–70	

To produce the output, write and center an appropriate title at the top of a new page. Then list the following with one line for each person. Edit numbers wherever possible.

social security number
first name
last name
cost per machine
number of machines in a crate
number of crates sold

2. The personnel manager of the Organic Food Farm has a card punched for each of the workers at the farm. The card contains the following information:

name	cols. 1–20
no. hours worked per day	21–22
no. days worked per week	31
hourly rate of pay	36–38 (dec. pt. between 36 and 37)

The payroll department wishes to print a payroll listing of the employees' names, hours worked per day, number of days worked per week, hourly rates of pay, and weekly salaries. Edit the output wherever necessary.

Special Terms

1. *size*
2. *class*
3. *group*
4. *elementary item*
5. *independent item*
6. *editing*
7. *replacement character*
8. *insertion character*
9. *zero suppression*
10. *check protection*
11. *floating character*
12. *field*
13. *record*
14. *file*
15. *left-adjusted*
16. *right-adjusted*
17. *procedure-name*
18. *branch*

Chapter 5

Doing Arithmetic

5.1 Introduction

In this chapter we will study the COBOL arithmetic commands ADD, SUB-TRACT, MULTIPLY, and DIVIDE. First, in section 5.2 we see how they are applied in the solution of a problem. Secondly, in section 5.3 we study the rules for the statements. The final section (5.4) discusses a way to express arithmetic commands in an algebraic-like formula in the COMPUTE statement. Since COMPUTE is not available on all computers, that section may be omitted. Let us proceed to study an example.

5.2 An Elementary Arithmetic Problem

State the Problem

The payroll department of a company needs to compute the average salary earned by its employees. The payroll data is kept on cards with one card for each employee. The format of each card is presented below.

name	cols. 1–20	
social security number	21–29	
salary	31–37	xxxxx.xx

Select a Method to Solve the Problem

In order to compute the average salary we need to know the total salary of all the employees and the number of employees. To find the average, we divide total salary by the number of employees. How do we find out how many employees there are? If we were doing this by hand, we would count the cards. We would start at zero and as we looked at each card we would increase the count by one. When there were no more cards, our last count would tell us how many employees there were. How could we total the employees' salaries? As we were counting the cards, we could add the salary on the card currently being counted to our previous total and keep a running total of the salaries. When we had looked at all the cards, we would know the total of the employees' salaries.

Flowchart the Method

We begin the flowchart by looking at or reading a card. What information do we need from the card? Just the employee's salary. Now that a card has been read we need to count it—that is, increase our count by one. Also, we need to add the SALARY to the TOTAL salary. So far we have processed only one card. We need to repeat these three steps for all the cards. This can be done by joining the three boxes at the left together and forming a loop.

Read SALARY

Add 1 to COUNT

Add SALARY to TOTAL

Figure 5.1   Preliminary Flowchart to
Count Employees and
Total Salary

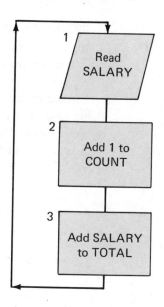

The flowchart in Figure 5.1 will repeatedly read many cards and will count them, but it has no way to stop. We need to add a box which will check for the special end card which is placed after the data cards. What should our flowchart do if we have read the end card? We should compute the average and write it. These additions have been made to Figure 5.2.

Figure 5.2   Preliminary Flowchart to
Compute Average
Salary

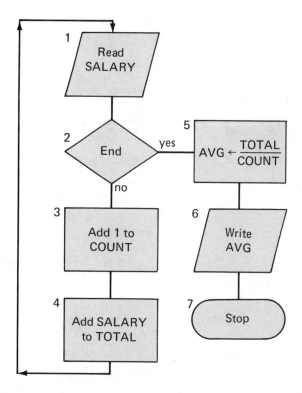

Let us look at our flowchart and pretend that we have just read the first employee's card, and his SALARY is $2000.00. Box 2 asks if we have just read the end card. Since we haven't, we proceed to add 1 to COUNT. What is the current value of COUNT? Initially it should be zero, but nothing in our flowchart says to make it zero. Therefore, we need to add this step to our flowchart. Box 4 instructs us to add SALARY to TOTAL. We know that

Figure 5.3 Final Flowchart to
Compute Average
Salary

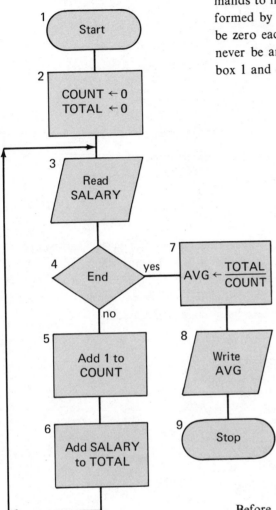

SALARY is $2000.00, but what value does TOTAL have? Since we are working on the first employee's data the TOTAL should be zero. Again, this step is not in our flowchart and should be added. Where should we add the commands to make COUNT and TOTAL zero? If we place them inside the loop formed by boxes 1 through 4 in Figure 5.2, then COUNT and TOTAL will be zero each time we go through the loop. This means that COUNT could never be anything larger than one. The commands should be placed before box 1 and outside the loop as in the final flowchart in Figure 5.3.

Before continuing further we should make up some numbers and trace through the flowchart in Figure 5.3 to see if it works.

Exercise

Use the following cards to trace through the flowchart in Figure 5.3.

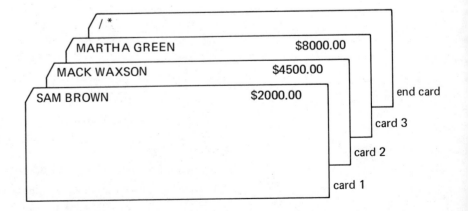

Convert the Flowchart into a Language the Computer Understands

In order to write the COBOL program for this problem, we should refer to the skeleton outline of a program in Table 3.1. We must include all necessary headings and any optional parts needed by this program. We begin by writing

```
IDENTIFICATION DIVISION.
PROGRAM-ID. AVERAGE-SALARY.
ENVIRONMENT DIVISION.
CONFIGURATION SECTION.
SOURCE-COMPUTER.    IBM-360.
OBJECT-COMPUTER.    IBM-360.
```

Do we need to have SPECIAL-NAMES? We could use it to write our output at the top of a new page. Therefore, we will include it.

```
SPECIAL-NAMES. C01 IS NEW-PAGE.
```

Will we need an INPUT-OUTPUT SECTION? We will need one if there are any files used by the program. Since our data is on cards and we will be writing an answer, we will have two files. Therefore, we add

```
INPUT-OUTPUT SECTION.
FILE-CONTROL.
     SELECT PAYROLL ASSIGN TO SYS005-UR-2540R-S.
     SELECT PAY-REPORT ASSIGN TO SYS006-UR-1403-S.
```

Then in the DATA DIVISION we need to describe our card file PAYROLL and our printer file PAY-REPORT. This can be done by referring to the format of the cards and deciding what our output should look like.

```
DATA DIVISION.
FILE SECTION.
FD    PAYROLL DATA RECORD EMPLOYEE LABEL RECORDS
      OMITTED.
01    EMPLOYEE.
      03   FILLER       PICTURE X(30).
      03   SALARY       PICTURE 9(5)V99.
      03   FILLER       PICTURE X(43).
FD    PAY-REPORT DATA RECORD ONE-LINE LABEL RECORDS
      OMITTED.
01    ONE-LINE         PICTURE X(132).
```

In saying that ONE-LINE contains 132 characters we have not yet specified exactly what different items will be printed on one line. We will do that in the WORKING-STORAGE section of the DATA DIVISION. We must also describe in WORKING-STORAGE anything that is being computed. This program computes TOTAL, COUNT, and AVG. Since AVG is going to be part of our output, we will describe it as part of a line to be printed. The numbers TOTAL and COUNT will be independent items, and thus will have the level number 77. How large should TOTAL and COUNT be? In other words, what are the largest possible values TOTAL and COUNT could have? To a great extent this depends upon the size of the company. If we estimate that there will be no more than 9999 employees and a total salary of less than 100 million, then we would describe TOTAL and COUNT in the following way.

```
WORKING-STORAGE SECTION.
77   COUNT   PICTURE 9999.
77   TOTAL   PICTURE 9(8)V99.
```

The PICTURE of TOTAL has an assumed decimal point for two reasons:

1. it is possible that the salaries will have some cents and will not be whole dollar amounts, and
2. TOTAL will be used to compute AVG and must have a numeric PICTURE; it must *not* have an actual decimal point in the PICTURE.

If we want our output to be something like the following

AVERAGE EMPLOYEE SALARY IS $7,324.85

then we would write the description of the output line as

```
01   COMPUTED.
     03   FILLER   PICTURE X(48)   VALUE SPACE.
     03   FILLER   PICTURE X(27)   VALUE
              'AVERAGE EMPLOYEE SALARY ISb'.
     03   AVG      PICTURE $ZZ,ZZZ.99.
     03   FILLER   PICTURE X(47)   VALUE SPACE.
```

We name only the area in which the value of AVG goes; using the word FILLER for the other parts of COMPUTED does *not* give them a name. The word FILLER tells the compiler that the programmer will never refer in any instruction to those areas of storage. However, we may give a value to the FILLER areas. The b at the end of the literal denotes a blank and is used to separate the word IS from the dollar sign of AVG. The PICTURE of AVG says that leading zeros will not be printed; there will be a dollar sign and decimal point; and, if the number is 1000 or more, a comma will be printed.

Have we described every data item we need in our program? So far it seems that we have. Therefore, let us write the PROCEDURE DIVISION and if we find that we need to include other things in the DATA DIVISION, we can go back and insert them later. As we write the instructions let us follow step by step the boxes of the flowchart in Figure 5.3.

As we begin the program we must open the files we will be reading and writing.

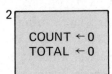

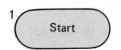

BEGIN. OPEN INPUT PAYROLL. OPEN OUTPUT PAY-REPORT.

We can make COUNT and TOTAL zero in one MOVE statement.

MOVE ZERO TO COUNT TOTAL.

Another way to make them zero when the program begins execution would be to use a VALUE phrase in WORKING-STORAGE.

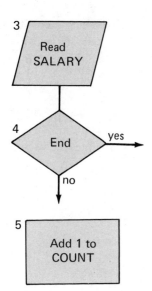

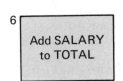

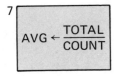

We need to put the READ command in a new paragraph, because the flowchart shows that we will be returning to it after executing the instruction in box 6. Remember that when we want to read the card which contains SALARY we do this by reading the file to which the card belongs.

READ-CARD. READ PAYROLL AT END GO TO COMPUTE-PRINT.

In COBOL the way to add one to the value of COUNT is to say

ADD 1 TO COUNT.

When the computer executes this command, it will add one to the current value of COUNT. This number becomes the new value of COUNT, and the old value is erased from memory. For example, if

$$\text{COUNT} = \boxed{0 \mid 0 \mid 2 \mid 0}$$

and we say

ADD 1 TO COUNT.

then

$$\text{COUNT} = \boxed{0 \mid 0 \mid 2 \mid 1}$$

This flowchart command is the same in COBOL.

ADD SALARY TO TOTAL.

When this ADD instruction is executed, the value of SALARY is added to the value of TOTAL. This computed sum becomes the new value of TOTAL; the old value is replaced by this new one. However, the value of SALARY remains the same.

After box 6 we want to return to box 3. In the program this is done by saying

GO TO READ-CARD.

To divide TOTAL by COUNT and place the answer in AVG we say

COMPUTE-PRINT. DIVIDE TOTAL BY COUNT GIVING AVG.

This will divide the value of TOTAL by the value of COUNT and will place the result into the place reserved in memory for AVG. Since the PICTURE of AVG contained editing characters, the value of AVG will be edited as it is placed in memory.

We need to put this DIVIDE statement in a new paragraph because flowchart box 4 told us to go to box 7 if we had read the "end" card. Looking back to see how we expressed box 4 in COBOL, we find that it says GO TO COMPUTE-PRINT when the "end" card has been read. Therefore we must name this paragraph COMPUTE-PRINT because we want to come here after reading the "end" card.

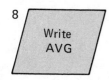

To write the value of AVG, we must write the line which contains it. Since all writing can be done only from the record ONE-LINE of the file PAY-REPORT, we must transfer the line to be printed into ONE-LINE before we may write it.

> MOVE COMPUTED TO ONE-LINE.
> WRITE ONE-LINE AFTER ADVANCING NEW-PAGE.

Before we conclude our instructions we must close the files we were using.

> CLOSE PAYROLL PAY-REPORT.

Then we may stop execution by saying

> STOP RUN.

The complete program follows.

```
IDENTIFICATION DIVISION.
PROGRAM-ID. AVERAGE-SALARY.
ENVIRONMENT DIVISION.
CONFIGURATION SECTION.
SOURCE-COMPUTER.    IBM-360.
OBJECT-COMPUTER.    IBM-360.
SPECIAL-NAMES. C0l IS NEW-PAGE.
INPUT-OUTPUT SECTION.
FILE-CONTROL.
     SELECT PAYROLL ASSIGN TO SYS005-UR-2540R-S.
     SELECT PAY-REPORT ASSIGN TO SYS006-UR-1403-S.
DATA DIVISION.
FILE SECTION.
FD   PAYROLL DATA RECORD EMPLOYEE LABEL RECORDS
     OMITTED.
01   EMPLOYEE.
     03   FILLER    PICTURE X(30).
     03   SALARY    PICTURE 9(5)V99.
     03   FILLER    PICTURE X(43).
FD   PAY-REPORT DATA RECORD ONE-LINE LABEL RECORDS
     OMITTED.
01   ONE-LINE      PICTURE X(132).
WORKING-STORAGE SECTION.
77   COUNT         PICTURE 9999.
77   TOTAL         PICTURE 9(8)V99.
01   COMPUTED.
     03   FILLER    PICTURE X(48)         VALUE SPACE.
     03   FILLER    PICTURE X(27)         VALUE
          'AVERAGE EMPLOYEE SALARY ISb'.
     03   AVG       PICTURE $ZZ,ZZZ.99.
     03   FILLER    PICTURE X(47)         VALUE SPACE.
PROCEDURE DIVISION.
BEGIN. OPEN INPUT PAYROLL. OPEN OUTPUT PAY-REPORT.
     MOVE ZERO TO COUNT TOTAL.
READ-CARD. READ PAYROLL AT END GO TO COMPUTE-PRINT.
     ADD 1 TO COUNT.
     ADD SALARY TO TOTAL.
     GO TO READ-CARD.
COMPUTE-PRINT. DIVIDE TOTAL BY COUNT GIVING AVG.
     MOVE COMPUTED TO ONE-LINE.
     WRITE ONE-LINE AFTER ADVANCING NEW-PAGE.
     CLOSE PAYROLL PAY-REPORT.
     STOP RUN.
```

5.3 The ADD, SUBTRACT, MULTIPLY, and DIVIDE Commands

In this section we will study the skeleton forms and rules of the four arithmetic commands in COBOL. Basically we should remember that there are two parts to any arithmetic:

1. the numbers used in the computation
2. the number computed (the result).

In COBOL there are certain rules for describing these two groups of numbers.

Rules for Data Used in Computation

1. Numeric literals or data-names may be used.
2. The data-names must be described with a numeric PICTURE (one containing only 9 V S).
3. The data-names must be elementary or independent items in the DATA DIVISION; the maximum size of each is 18 digits.
4. The result of the computation must be the name of an elementary or independent item in the DATA DIVISION.
5. The PICTURE of the result may be numeric or numeric-edited.

All COBOL arithmetic statements have two options—rounding the result to the desired number of decimal places or checking the size of the result to see if it is larger than the area reserved for it. For example, if the value 26.77 were computed and were to be placed in the location named MAX with a PICTURE of 99V9, then MAX would contain

and would *not* be correct. Using the SIZE ERROR option of an arithmetic statement, we can have the computer check the result of the computation to see if it can be placed in the designated area in memory. If it can, then the result will be stored in memory; if it cannot, then the result will not be stored in memory and the programmer may decide what should be done. He may wish the program to stop immediately, or he may want a message printed saying that an error has occurred. For example, suppose in memory we have

For another example, if 1068 were computed as the value of SUM-EMP whose PICTURE is 999, then SUM-EMP would be

then

MULTIPLY HRS BY NOPRO GIVING TOTPRO.

would make TOTPRO have the value

0	8	0
TOTPRO

when it should be 1080, but four digits cannot fit in a place large enough for three digits. The computer would continue processing the program and would never give a message saying that an error resulted when TOTPRO was computed. However, if we had said

> MULTIPLY HRS BY NOPRO GIVING TOTPRO ON SIZE ERROR
> DISPLAY 'TOTPRO IS INCORRECT'.

then the computer would print the message "TOTPRO IS INCORRECT" and TOTPRO would still be 000 (its original value before the multiplying was done). (See Chapter 10 for a discussion of the DISPLAY command; it is frequently used to write error messages such as this one.)

Both of the rounding and size error options may be specified in one arithmetic command, in which case the result is rounded before the size error is checked.

The ADD Statement

There are two forms of the ADD statement which are very similar.

Form 1: ADD $\begin{Bmatrix} \text{data-name} \\ \text{literal} \end{Bmatrix}$ $\begin{bmatrix} \begin{Bmatrix} \text{data-name} \\ \text{literal} \end{Bmatrix} \dots \end{bmatrix}$ <u>TO</u> data-name-n
[ROUNDED] [ON <u>SIZE ERROR</u> statement[1] . . .] .

Form 2: ADD $\begin{Bmatrix} \text{data-name} \\ \text{literal} \end{Bmatrix}$ $\begin{Bmatrix} \text{data-name} \\ \text{literal} \end{Bmatrix}$ . . . <u>GIVING</u> data-name-n
[ROUNDED] [ON <u>SIZE ERROR</u> statement[1] . . .] .

With form 1 the values of all the data-names and/or literals are summed and the result is the new value of "data-name-n" (the data-name after the word TO). The value of data-name-n which was used in the summing will be replaced by the computed sum. For example, if

0	8
MON

0	7
TUES

0	9
WED

then

ADD MON TUES TO WED.

will make

0	8
MON

0	7
TUES

2	4
WED

---

[1] Only the following statements may be used: ACCEPT, ADD,* ALTER, CLOSE, COMPUTE,* DISPLAY, DIVIDE,* EXAMINE, EXIT, GENERATE, GO TO, INITIATE, MOVE, MULTIPLY,* OPEN, PERFORM, RELEASE, SEEK, SET, SORT, STOP, SUBTRACT,* WRITE. (*Without the SIZE ERROR option.)

The values of MON and TUES are the same as they were before the addition took place. But WED is no longer 09; it is now 24. In order to keep the value of WED as 09, we must use form 2.

In form 2 the values of the data-names and/or literals preceding the word GIVING are added and the sum becomes the current value of "data-name-n". The former value of "data-name-n" is lost. For example, if

0	8		0	7		0	9		3	0
MON			TUES			WED			PART-A	

then

ADD MON TUES WED GIVING PART-A.

will make

0	8		0	7		0	9		2	4
MON			TUES			WED			PART-A	

Only the value of PART-A has changed.

Suppose we have described in the DATA DIVISION the items SCORE and TOTAL-SCORE. To add the number in SCORE to the number in TOTAL-SCORE and keep their sum in TOTAL-SCORE we could use form 2 and say

ADD SCORE TOTAL-SCORE GIVING TOTAL-SCORE.

But it would have been simpler to use form 1 and say

ADD SCORE TO TOTAL-SCORE.

Example 1

Compare the effect of the following two ADD statements. Suppose we are given

4	5		1	2
HOURS			HRSOVTIME	

then

ADD HOURS TO HRSOVTIME.

has the following effect.

4	5		5	7
HOURS			HRSOVTIME	

But

ADD HRSOVTIME TO HOURS.

will result in the following.

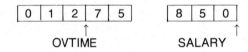

The sum replaces the value of the data-name written after the word TO.

Example 2

Notice the difference that the ROUNDED option makes on the sum computed in the following ADD statements.

If in memory we have

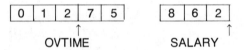

then the command

ADD OVTIME TO SALARY.

will result in the following:

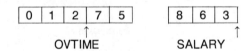

Whereas if the command had been

ADD OVTIME TO SALARY ROUNDED.

then the result would be

Example 3

If the PICTURE of SALARY in example 2 had been 999V99, then the value computed would be exact.

Suppose that we begin with

then the command

ADD OVTIME TO SALARY.

would result in the following

It would not make sense to use the ROUNDED option in this ADD statement because both the number computed and SALARY have two decimal places. There is no way to take a number with two decimal places and round it off so that it has two decimal places.

Example 4

Notice the different value computed when the word TO is changed to the word GIVING.

Suppose we have

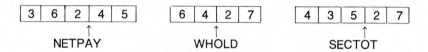

then the command

ADD NETPAY WHOLD TO SECTOT.

computes the new value for SECTOT as

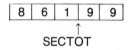

But the command

ADD NETPAY WHOLD GIVING SECTOT.

would make SECTOT have the value

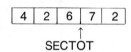

Which one of these two ADD statements is correct depends upon the intent of the programmer.

Example 5

The result of an addition may be edited.

Suppose we have

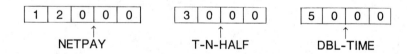

and GROSSPAY is described by PICTURE $9(5).99,
then

ADD NETPAY T-N-HALF DBL-TIME GIVING GROSSPAY.

will compute

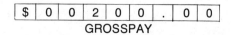

Example 6

Any time we wish to add a certain number to other items, the number must be a numeric literal.

If we wish to add a $25 bonus to everyone's NETPAY and store the answer in NETPAY, we could use one of the following statements:

Form 1: ADD 25 TO NETPAY.
Form 2: ADD 25 TO NETPAY GIVING NETPAY.

These two statements above are equivalent, but the first one is more efficient. We could *not* use the following statements.

ADD '$25' TO NETPAY. *not allowed*
ADD '25' TO NETPAY. *not allowed*

Both '$25' and '25' are non-numeric literals.

Example 7

Notice how the SIZE ERROR option keeps the result from being too large for its area in memory.

Suppose we have

SECT   DIV

and we execute the following

ADD SECT TO DIV ON SIZE ERROR GO TO SZ-ERROR.

Then DIV will be computed to be

DIV

If the value of SECT becomes

SECT

and we say

ADD SECT TO DIV ON SIZE ERROR GO TO SZ-ERROR.

then the total of 080 and 973 (1053) should become the new value of DIV. But since a 4-digit number cannot be placed in the area named DIV, the computer will go to the paragraph named SZ-ERROR and DIV will remain

DIV

The SUBTRACT Statement

Following are the two forms of the COBOL SUBTRACT command.

Form 1: <u>SUBTRACT</u> $\begin{Bmatrix} \text{data-name} \\ \text{literal} \end{Bmatrix}$ $\begin{bmatrix} \begin{Bmatrix} \text{data-name} \\ \text{literal} \end{Bmatrix} \end{bmatrix}$ . . . <u>FROM</u>

data-name-n [<u>ROUNDED</u>] [<u>ON SIZE ERROR</u> statement[2] . . .].

Form 2: <u>SUBTRACT</u> $\begin{Bmatrix} \text{data-name} \\ \text{literal} \end{Bmatrix}$ $\begin{bmatrix} \begin{Bmatrix} \text{data-name} \\ \text{literal} \end{Bmatrix} \end{bmatrix}$ . . . <u>FROM</u>

data-name-m <u>GIVING</u> data-name-n [<u>ROUNDED</u>] [<u>ON SIZE</u>

<u>ERROR</u> statement[2] . . .].

Form 1 will subtract the values of the data-names and/or literals preceding the word FROM from the value of "data-name-n" and the result will be the new value of "data-name-n." The former value of "data-name-n" is lost.

For example, if we had in memory

WHHOLD   GROSSPAY

and said

SUBTRACT WHHOLD FROM GROSSPAY.

the resulting values would be

WHHOLD   GROSSPAY

Only the value of "data-name-n" (or GROSSPAY in this example) changes. In order to save the previous value of GROSSPAY we would need to use form 2.

In form 2 the values of all the data-names and/or literals preceding the word FROM are subtracted from the value of "data-name-m" and the result replaces the former value of "data-name-n." Only the value of "data-name-n" changes. All other values remain the same.

Therefore, if

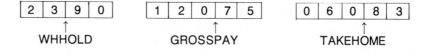

WHHOLD   GROSSPAY   TAKEHOME

and we say

SUBTRACT WHHOLD FROM GROSSPAY GIVING TAKEHOME.

then the resulting values of the data names are the following.

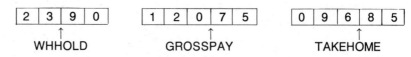

WHHOLD   GROSSPAY   TAKEHOME

[2] See footnote 1 on page 74.

Example 1

All literals used in the SUBTRACT statement must be numeric literals. To subtract 1 from the number in SCORE we could say

SUBTRACT 1 FROM SCORE.

but we could *not* write

SUBTRACT '1' FROM SCORE.   *not allowed*

since '1' is a non-numeric literal.

Example 2

It is possible to combine several SUBTRACT commands into one. Instead of writing

SUBTRACT FICA FROM GROS-PAY.
SUBTRACT PENSION FROM GROS-PAY.
SUBTRACT MISC-DEDUCT FROM GROS-PAY.

we could use the following and save the computer from unnecessary work.

SUBTRACT FICA PENSION MISC-DEDUCT FROM GROS-PAY.

Example 3

The PICTURE of the item where the result is placed "shapes" the answer. Suppose we have

then the result of the following

SUBTRACT B FROM A GIVING C.

may be a variety of answers depending upon the PICTURE describing C. The correct answer is

$$A - B = 16.3625 - 4.0032$$
$$= 12.3593$$

Consider the following PICTURES of C and the corresponding value.

C	PICTURE	99V9999	C =	1 2 3 5 9 3
C	PICTURE	99V999	C =	1 2 3 5 9
C	PICTURE	99V99	C =	1 2 3 5
C	PICTURE	99	C =	1 2

| C | PICTURE | 9 | | C = | | 2 |

| C | PICTURE | 9V999 | | C = | | 2 | 3 | 5 | 9 |

| C | PICTURE | V999 | | C = | | 3 | 5 | 9 |

Example 4

The rounding option may be applied to the result of a subtraction. If we have

| 1 | 6 | 3 | 6 | 2 | 5 | | 4 | 0 | 0 | 3 | 2 |

A   B

then the command

SUBTRACT B FROM A GIVING DIFF ROUNDED.

would cause the value of DIFF to be

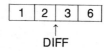

| 1 | 2 | 3 | 6 |

DIFF

if DIFF has a PICTURE of 99V99.

Example 5

The result of a subtraction may be edited.
Suppose we have

| 2 | 5 | 0 | 0 | | 2 | 7 | 0 | 8 | 6 |

DUES   SAL

and NETPAY has PICTURE $999.99 then

SUBTRACT DUES FROM SAL GIVING NETPAY.

would result in the following.

| $ | 2 | 4 | 5 | . | 8 | 6 |

NETPAY

Example 6

To compute a negative number, a sign must be used in the PICTURE of the result.
If we have

| 3 | 7 | 5 | | 3 | 0 | 3 |

CHEX   DEP

and instruct the computer to

SUBTRACT CHEX FROM DEP GIVING DIFF.

and DIFF has a PICTURE of S999 then its value is

0	7	2̄

DIFF

On the other hand, if TRAN has a PICTURE of −999 and we had said

SUBTRACT CHEX FROM DEP GIVING TRAN.

then the value of TRAN would be

−	0	7	2

TRAN

The difference between TRAN and DIFF is that TRAN is edited and DIFF is not. DIFF is a numeric item and may be used in computation, but the value of TRAN may be printed and would appear with a negative sign.

Example 7

The SIZE ERROR option may be used on a SUBTRACT command to make sure that enough room was allowed for the answer.

Suppose we had

4	2	6	3

CRED

0	1	5	0

DEB

7	8	7

BAL

and gave the command

SUBTRACT DEB FROM CRED GIVING BAL ON SIZE ERROR
DISPLAY 'INCREASE SIZE OF BAL'.

then when 150 is subtracted from 4263, the result is 4113, which cannot be placed in BAL. Therefore BAL would remain 787 and the computer would print the message

"INCREASE SIZE OF BAL"

The MULTIPLY Statement

Following are the two forms of the MULTIPLY command.

Form 1: MULTIPLY $\begin{Bmatrix} \text{data-name-1} \\ \text{literal} \end{Bmatrix}$ BY data-name-2 [ROUNDED]
[ON SIZE ERROR statement[3] . . .] .

Form 2: MULTIPLY $\begin{Bmatrix} \text{data-name} \\ \text{literal} \end{Bmatrix}$ BY $\begin{Bmatrix} \text{data-name} \\ \text{literal} \end{Bmatrix}$ GIVING data-name-3
[ROUNDED] [ON SIZE ERROR statement[3] . . .] .

[3] See footnote 1 on page 74.

In form 1 the value of data-name-1 or the literal (depending upon which one is used) is multiplied by the value of data-name-2 and the product becomes the new value of data-name-2. The former value of data-name-2 is destroyed. For example, if

NO-MADE

and we say

MULTIPLY 5 BY NO-MADE.

then NO-MADE becomes

NO-MADE

If we wish to keep the original value of NO-MADE, then we must use form 2 and write something like the following

MULTIPLY 5 BY NO-MADE GIVING WEEK-TOT.

This would make

In form 2 the product becomes the value of data-name-3.

Example 1

The result of a multiplication operation may be edited.
If we had

and MAN-HOURS was described by PICTURE ZZZ,ZZZ, then

MULTIPLY EMP BY NO-DAYS GIVING MAN-HOURS.

would compute 12500 and would edit the result in the following manner

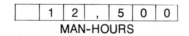

Example 2

Only two numbers may be multiplied together in one MULTIPLY statement.

If we wanted to compute an employee's overtime salary as 2 × RATE × HRS-OVER, then we would need to use two MULTIPLY statements. First we could say

MULTIPLY RATE BY 2 GIVING 2-RATE.

and then

> MULTIPLY 2-RATE BY HRS-OVER GIVING OV-SALARY.

First we told the computer to multiply the value of RATE by 2 and store the answer in 2-RATE. Then we take the value in 2-RATE and multiply it by the value of HRS-OVER. The final product is placed in OV-SALARY.

Example 3

The SIZE ERROR option may be used to check the size of a result before storing it.

If we had

8	6	9
OZ	JARS	TOT

and said

> MULTIPLY OZ BY JARS GIVING TOT ON SIZE ERROR DISPLAY
> 'INCREASE SIZE OF TOT' STOP RUN.

then the value of TOT would remain

9
TOT

and the computer would print the message "INCREASE SIZE OF TOT" and would then stop. In this example, we have commanded the computer to do two things if there is a size error.

However, if we had said

> MULTIPLY OZ BY JARS GIVING TOT.

then TOT would become

8
TOT

an incorrect value. TOT should be 48, but since there is no room saved for the 4, it is truncated. The computer will continue processing the program's instructions and will never inform the programmer of this error.

The DIVIDE Statement

Division may be done with either of the following forms. Division by zero causes a size error.

Form 1: DIVIDE $\begin{Bmatrix} \text{data-name-1} \\ \text{literal} \end{Bmatrix}$ INTO data-name-2 [ROUNDED]
[ON SIZE ERROR statement[4] . . .] .

Form 2: DIVIDE $\begin{Bmatrix} \text{data-name-1} \\ \text{literal-1} \end{Bmatrix} \begin{Bmatrix} \text{INTO} \\ \text{BY} \end{Bmatrix} \begin{Bmatrix} \text{data-name-2} \\ \text{literal-2} \end{Bmatrix}$ GIVING
data-name-3 [ROUNDED] [ON SIZE ERROR statement[4] . . .] .

[4] See footnote 1 on page 74.

In form 1 the value of data-name-1 or the literal (depending upon which one is used) will be divided into the value of data-name-2. The number computed will become the new value of data-name-2. The value of data-name-2 which was used in the computation is erased. For example, if POINTS = 300 and we say

DIVIDE 5 INTO POINTS.

then the new value of POINTS would be 60. If we wanted POINTS to remain 300, then we would have to use form 2 and place the result as the value of another data-name.

In form 2 the result becomes the new value of data-name-3. The values of data-names 1 and 2, if used in the division, do not change. If the word INTO is used, then the following quotient is computed:

$$\frac{\text{data-name-2 or literal-2}}{\text{data-name-1 or literal-1}}$$

On the other hand, if BY is used, then the quotient computed is the following:

$$\frac{\text{data-name-1 or literal-1}}{\text{data-name-2 or literal-2}}$$

Either of the following statements will produce the same results:

DIVIDE 5 INTO POINTS GIVING AVERAGE.
DIVIDE POINTS BY 5 GIVING AVERAGE.

If POINTS = 300, then AVERAGE will be 60 and POINTS will remain 300.

Example 1

Study how the following PICTUREs affect the result of a division.
Our command is

DIVIDE .361836 BY 4.37 GIVING CON.

If we have

CON PICTURE V9999	then	0 8 2 8
CON PICTURE V9(6)	then	0 8 2 8 0 0
CON PICTURE V999	then	0 8 2

Example 2

The result of a division may be ROUNDED.
If we said

DIVIDE .361836 BY 4.37 GIVING CON ROUNDED.

the actual number computed is

$$\frac{.361836}{4.37} = .0828$$

If CON is described by PICTURE V999 then we would have

0	8	3

↑
CON

Example 3

The SIZE ERROR option may be used to see if the result of a division will fit into the area where it is to be placed.

If we have

0	4		3

↑
A   B

then the command

DIVIDE A INTO B ON SIZE ERROR GO TO ERR-1.

will compute

$$\frac{3}{.04} = 75$$

But since the number 75 cannot be placed in B, B will remain

3

and the computer will go to the paragraph named ERR-1.

Exercises

Refer to the following WORKING-STORAGE SECTION to answer questions 1–21.

```
WORKING-STORAGE SECTION.
77   M     PICTURE 9(4).
77   N     PICTURE 9(4).
77   Q     PICTURE 999V9(4).
77   P     PICTURE S99.
77   MX    PICTURE $9(4).00.
```

1. If M = 0100, N = 0200, and P = +34, what will be their values after the instruction

ADD P M TO N.

2. If Q = 100.9364, M = 3000, N = 0600, what will be their values after the command

ADD M Q GIVING N ROUNDED.

3. If M = 5000, N = 0364, what will be the contents of Q after the instruction

ADD M N GIVING Q.

4. If M = 5000, N = 6378, what will be the contents of N after the operation

ADD M TO N ON SIZE ERROR GO TO ERR-N.

5. If M = 0826, N = 4010, what will be the contents of MX after the operation

ADD M N GIVING MX.

6. If M = 0060, N = 0720, what will be the contents of Q after the instruction

ADD M N GIVING Q.

7. If M = 0362, N = 0809, what will be their contents after the instruction

SUBTRACT M FROM N.

8. If M = 0300, P = +35, N = 0900, what will be the contents of N after the command

SUBTRACT M P FROM N.

9. If Q = 122.6388, M = 0462, what will be the value of M after the instruction

SUBTRACT Q FROM M ROUNDED.

10. If M = 0324, N = 0280, what will be the contents of P and N after the instruction

SUBTRACT M FROM N GIVING P.

11. If M = 0020, Q = 123.6877, what will be the contents of MX after the command

SUBTRACT M FROM Q GIVING MX.

12. If M = 0025, N = 0350, P = −33, what will be the contents of P after the command

SUBTRACT M FROM N GIVING P ON SIZE ERROR GO TO FIN.

13. If M = 0036, what will it equal after the instruction

MULTIPLY 2 BY M.

14. If N = 0023, what will N equal after the instruction

MULTIPLY 1.6 BY N ROUNDED.

15. If M = 2607, N = 4821, what will be the contents of N after the instruction

MULTIPLY M BY N ON SIZE ERROR GO TO 25.

16. If M = 2000, N = 6210, what will be the contents of M after the instruction

MULTIPLY N BY M.

17. If P = +90, what will be the contents of MX after the statement

MULTIPLY P BY 46 GIVING MX.

18. If M = 0373, what will be the contents of M after the command

DIVIDE 4 INTO M.

19. If M = 0373, what will be the contents of Q after the command

DIVIDE M BY 4 GIVING Q.

20. If N = 6341, what will be its contents after the command

DIVIDE 2 INTO N ROUNDED.

21. If N = 8187, P = −35, what will be the contents of N and P after the statement

DIVIDE 7 INTO N GIVING P ON SIZE ERROR GO TO D-PART.

Programs

1. The Payroll Department of the Hammer and Saw Construction Company needs a program which will compute the salary for each of its employees. All the pertinent information is kept on cards with one card for each worker. The format of the cards is as follows:

name	cols. 1–20	
social security number	22–30	
hours worked @ regular pay	32–33	
hours worked @ overtime pay	35–36	
rate of pay	41–43	x.xx

Each employee receives double-time or twice the normal rate of pay for any hours worked overtime.

The payroll printout should include the following:

worker's name
no. hours @ regular pay
no. hours @ overtime pay
rate of pay

regular pay
overtime pay
total pay (regular pay + overtime)

The report should be titled and should begin on a new page.

2. Using the cards given in program 1, write a program which will calculate the total number of workers, the total amount of money spent for regular salaries, overtime salaries, and the total salaries. Label these four numbers with an appropriate message.

3. A professor in a large lecture course needs a program which will process his class grades. He has an assistant who will prepare for each student in the class one card with the following information:

name	cols.	1–20
test 1 score		21–23
test 2 score		25–27
test 3 score		29–31
final exam		33–35

Each test was worth a maximum of 100 points. The final was also worth 100 points but should be counted double when figuring the student's average. The program should print student's names, their test scores, and their average (points earned divided by total points possible). Label the output and start the list on a new page.

4. Write a program which will calculate the profit from the sale of animals at McKenzie Farms. The data cards contain the following information:

purchase price	cols.	1–5	xxx.xx
sale price		6–10	xxx.xx
type of animal		11–20	

Your program should print the total purchase price of all the animals, the total sale price, and the profit from the sale. Be sure to label these totals.

5. The Midnight Bowling League wants a program which will compute a handicap for each of its members and will use that handicap to compute the total series. The data cards contain the following information:

name	cols.	1–20
average		21–23
points from game 1		25–27
points from game 2		29–31
points from game 3		33–35

Compute a person's handicap using the formula

$$\text{handicap} = (200 - \text{average}) \times .8$$

Compute the total series = total points + (handicap $\times$ 3).

Your program should print for each person: name, handicap, total points from the three games, and total series. Label the columns with appropriate headings.

6. Write a program which will approximate the annual percentage rate of a loan. Input to the program will be in the following form.

number of payments in one year (*m*)	cols. 1–2	
true dollar cost of loan (*l*)	5–10	xxxx.xx
net amount of loan (*p*)	15–20	xxxx.xx
number of payments made (*n*)	22–24	

The true dollar cost of the loan is all the money paid to the lender (including fees) minus the amount of money received from the lender. The formula for calculating the percentage rate *r* is

$$r = \frac{2ml}{p(n + 1)}$$

For output, print each of the input values as well as the computed value of *r*. Label each value.

5.4 The COMPUTE Statement[5]

Any arithmetic operation which can be done in an ADD, SUBTRACT, MULTIPLY, or DIVIDE statement can also be done with a COMPUTE command. Exponentiation (raising a number to a power, for example 2^3) may be accomplished with COMPUTE. In fact, several arithmetic operations may be combined in one COMPUTE statement. For example, to calculate TOT-SALE as AMOUNT plus 4% of AMOUNT for tax, we would write

COMPUTE TOT-SALE = AMOUNT + .04 * AMOUNT.

This is instructing the computer to multiply the value of AMOUNT by .04 and add it to the value of AMOUNT to compute the value of TOT-SALE. The asterisk (*) is the symbol used for multiply and the plus sign (+) is the symbol which denotes addition.

In a COMPUTE statement the following symbols are used to represent the corresponding arithmetic operations.

Symbol	Arithmetic Operation
+	addition
−	subtraction
*	multiplication
/	division
**	exponentiation

The general form of the COMPUTE statement is:

[5] The COMPUTE statement is a feature of high level COBOL. This section may be omitted if desired.

$$\text{COMPUTE data-name [ROUNDED]} = \begin{Bmatrix} \text{literal} \\ \text{arithmetic expression} \\ \text{data-name} \end{Bmatrix}$$

[ON SIZE ERROR statement[6] . . .] .

The simplest kinds of COMPUTE statements would be written in one of the following forms.

COMPUTE data-name = literal.
COMPUTE data-name-1 = data-name-2.

In these cases, the COMPUTE is working like a MOVE. For example, we could accomplish the same result by saying either of the following.

COMPUTE TOT = Ø.
MOVE Ø TO TOT.

Similarly, we could use either of the following and have the same result.

COMPUTE SAVE-ACCT = ACCOUNT.
MOVE ACCOUNT TO SAVE-ACCT.

More complex COMPUTE statements result when we use an arithmetic expression. An arithmetic expression is a combination of data-names, numeric literals, and arithmetic operation symbols. For example,

AMOUNT + .04 * AMOUNT

is an arithmetic expression.

Rules for Forming an Arithmetic Expression

1. A simple arithmetic expression contains data-names and numeric literals separated by arithmetic operation symbols. There must be at least one space before and after a symbol.
2. Two operation symbols may not be written one after another. The exponentiation symbol (**) is considered as one symbol with no space between the asterisks.
3. An arithmetic expression may start with a + or a − sign.
4. Other expressions may be formed by enclosing a simple arithmetic expression in parentheses. This expression in parentheses and/or other expressions in parentheses and/or data-names and/or numeric literals, all separated by an arithmetic operation symbol also form an arithmetic expression.

Some examples of arithmetic expressions are given below.

NETPAY + DBLTIME + TIME-N-HALF
GROSSPAY − SSDEDUCT − FICA
PRODUCTS / MAN-HOURS
(CUM-QUAL-PTS + CUR-QUAL-PTS) / (CUM-HRS + CUR-HRS)
2 * RATE * HRS
(DAY1 + DAY2 + DAY3 + DAY4 + DAY5) / 5

How does the computer evaluate arithmetic expressions? If there are no

[6] See footnote 1 on page 74.

parentheses in an expression, the computer proceeds from left to right evaluating the operations in the following order:

1. exponentiation
2. multiplication and division
3. addition and subtraction

If an expression contains both multiplication and division (or addition and subtraction), then the operations are performed from left to right. The following examples show step by step the way arithmetic expressions are evaluated.

Example 1

$$SUMM + DIFF ** 2$$

If SUMM = 10 and DIFF = 2, then the operation performed first is

$$DIFF ** 2$$

which is 2^2 equal to 4. Next four will be added to SUMM, or

$$4 + 10 = 14$$

The final result is 14.

Example 2

$$AVG * CNTY / TOTPOP$$

If AVG equals 355, CNTY equals 10, and TOTPOP equals 71, then first AVG and CNTY will be multiplied.

$$355 \times 10 = 3550$$

Next 3550 will be divided by 71.

$$3550 / 71 = 50$$

The final result is 50.

Example 3

$$GROSS - PENSION\text{-}FUND - INCOME\text{-}TAX$$

If GROSS equals 350.25, PENSION-FUND equals 22.00, and INCOME-TAX equals 35.00, then first, PENSION-FUND will be subtracted from GROSS.

$$350.25 - 22.00 = 328.25$$

Next the value of INCOME-TAX will be subtracted from 328.25.

$$328.25 - 35.00 = 293.25$$

The final result is 293.25.

If there are parentheses in an expression, the expression in the innermost set of parentheses is evaluated first according to the above rules. Sometimes parentheses are necessary so that an expression will be evaluated correctly. Notice the difference between the results in examples 4 and 5 and examples 6 and 7.

Example 4

$$(DAY1 + DAY2 + DAY3 + DAY4 + DAY5) / 5$$

If DAY1 equals 8, DAY2 equals 7, DAY3 equals 6, DAY4 equals 8, and DAY5 equals 8, then the parentheses instruct the computer to add DAY1, DAY2, DAY3, DAY4, and DAY5 first.

$$8 + 7 + 6 + 8 + 8 = 37$$

Then 37 will be divided by 5.

$$37 / 5 = 7.4$$

The final result is 7.4.

Example 5

$$DAY1 + DAY2 + DAY3 + DAY4 + DAY5 / 5$$

If DAY1, DAY2, DAY3, DAY4, and DAY5 have the same values as in example 4 above, then the first computation is to divide DAY5 by 5.

$$8 / 5 = 1.6$$

Then DAY1 will be added to DAY2,

$$8 + 7 = 15$$

15 will be added to DAY3.

$$15 + 6 = 21$$

21 will be added to DAY4.

$$21 + 8 = 29$$

Finally, 29 will be added to 1.6.

$$29 + 1.6 = 30.6$$

The final result is 30.6.

Example 6

$$CUM\text{-}QUAL\text{-}PTS / (PREV\text{-}HRS + HRS\text{-}THIS\text{-}SEM)$$

If CUM-QUAL-PTS equals 256, PREV-HRS equals 88, and HRS-THIS-SEM equals 12, then the computer will begin by adding PREV-HRS and HRS-THIS-SEM.

$$88 + 12 = 100$$

Then CUM-QUAL-PTS will be divided by 100

$$256 \ / \ 100 \ = \ 2.56.$$

The final result is 2.56.

Example 7

$$\text{CUM-QUAL-PTS} \ / \ \text{PREV-HRS} \ + \ \text{HRS-THIS-SEM}$$

If all items have the same values as in example 6 above, then the first number computed is CUM-QUAL-PTS divided by PREV-HRS.

$$256 \ / \ 88 \ = \ 2.99$$

Then 2.99 is added to HRS-THIS-SEM.

$$2.99 \ + \ 12 \ = \ 14.99$$

The final result is 14.99.

If we wish to divide the sum of DAY1, DAY2, DAY3, DAY4, and DAY5 by 5, then we must use parentheses in example 4. If we wish to divide CUM-QUAL-PTS by the sum of PREV-HRS and HRS-THIS-SEM, then we must use parentheses as in example 6.

An arithmetic expression in a COMPUTE statement tells the computer what to evaluate; the data-name following the word COMPUTE is the name in memory which receives the value computed. The ROUNDED and SIZE ERROR options may be used in a COMPUTE command.

Rules for the COMPUTE Statement

1. All data-names in the arithmetic expression must have numeric PIC-TUREs.
2. All literals used in the arithmetic expression must be numeric.
3. The data-name whose value is computed may have an edited PICTURE.
4. On some compilers[7] any intermediate result obtained when the arithmetic expression is evaluated must not be larger than the area reserved for the final result or an error will occur.

To illustrate rule 4, let us study the following example. If we have

```
  ┌───┐     ┌───┐     ┌───┬───┐
  │ 8 │     │ 6 │     │   │   │
  └───┘     └───┘     └───┴───┘
                            ↑
  HRS       DAYS       AVG
```

and the command

$$\text{COMPUTE AVG} \ = \ \text{HRS} \ * \ \text{DAYS} \ / \ 5.$$

Then when HRS is multiplied by DAYS, we should calculate $8 \times 6 = 48$, but 48 is too large for AVG. Therefore, 48 would be truncated to 8; then when 8 is divided by 5, the result would be 1.6. The correct result should be

[7] The IBM 360 compiler.

$\dfrac{48}{5}$ = 9.6. The PICTURE of AVG should be at least PICTURE 99V9 so that the result can be computed correctly.

Example 1

The result of a COMPUTE will be stored according to the PICTURE of the data-name where the result is to be placed.

If we have

REGULAR-PAY   OVERTIME

and the command

COMPUTE GROSS-SAL = REGULAR-PAY + OVERTIME.

If GROSS-SAL is described by PICTURE 9999V99, then it will contain

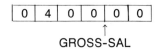

GROSS-SAL

But if GROSS-SAL is described by PICTURE $9(4).99, then it will contain

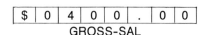

GROSS-SAL

Example 2

The ROUNDED option may be used in a COMPUTE. Notice the difference in the result when COMPUTE is used rather than a MOVE command.

If we have

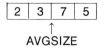

AVGSIZE

and SIZ has a PICTURE of 99, then saying

MOVE AVGSIZE TO SIZ.

will make SIZ have the value

$$\boxed{2\ \vert\ 3}$$

But if we had said

COMPUTE SIZ ROUNDED = AVGSIZE.

Then SIZ would be

$$\boxed{2\ \vert\ 4}$$

Example 3

The square root of a number may be found in a COMPUTE statement. Finding the square root is the same as raising a number to the ½ power (.5). Therefore if we wished to find the square root of NUM we would write

COMPUTE SQROOT = NUM ** .5.

Exercises

1. Convert the following formulas into COMPUTE commands.
   a. $A = P(1 + r)^t$
   b. SS = 5.2% of SAL
   c. $D = r \cdot t$
   d. DELTA = PNOW − PPREV
   e. P = 50 + 3·Q
   f. MID = (FIRST + LAST)/2

2. Evaluate the following arithmetic expressions assuming that ADIV = 40, BDIV = 30, NUM = 5, PRICE = 2.10, and QUAN = 10.
   a. NUM + PRICE * QUAN
   b. (ADIV + BDIV) / 2
   c. QUAN * 12 / NUM
   d. NUM ** 2
   e. ADIV / 4 − BDIV / 10

3. Explain the order in which the operations will be performed in the following arithmetic expressions.
   a. XTRA + MON * Q − RUINED
   b. (MAN + 1) * DAYS / 5
   c. QNT ** 2 + PR ** 2
   d. M / N * O

Programs

1. The Reliable Savings and Loan pays interest on its savings accounts at the rate of 5¼% per year compounded quarterly. The Standard Bank and Trust pays 5½% interest per year compounded yearly on its savings accounts.

   Write a program which will read an amount to deposit from a card. The number is punched in columns 1–7 and is in the form xxxxx.xx. The program should calculate the amount which would be accumulated at the end of each quarter in the savings account in the Reliable Savings and Loan and at the Standard Bank and Trust.

   The output should start on a new page and all columns printed should be clearly labeled. Write the quarter number and the amount accumulated in each account at the end of each quarter. Continue this report for a total of 5 years (20 quarters).

   The formula for the amount accumulated by compounding the interest is

$$A = P(1 + r)^t$$

where   *A*   is the amount accumulated

           P   is the original amount deposited

           r   is the interest rate for the period in which interest is compounded. (i.e., 5% compounded semi-annually would be a rate of 2½% per period)

           t   is the number of time periods interest has been compounded.

2. Write a program to compute the monthly payment necessary to amortize an amount *A* at a monthly interest rate *I* for a number of months *M*. The formula to compute the payment is:

$$P = \frac{I \cdot A (1 + I)^M}{(1 + I)^M - 1}$$

where   *P*   is the payment

           A   is the amount to be amortized

           I   is the monthly interest rate

           M   is the number of months

For input, your program may have one or more data cards in the following format:

```
amount              cols.  1–7     xxxxx.xx
interest/month             11–14   .xxxx
number of months           16–18
```

The output should print the amount to amortize, monthly interest rate, yearly interest rate, number of months, monthly payment, and total amount to be paid (number of months × monthly payment).

3. Write a program to compute the amount of money to invest at a yearly interest rate *I* in order to receive *D* dollars at the end of *N* years. The formula for amount to invest *A* is:

$$A = \frac{D}{(1 + I)^N}$$

Input to the program will be on cards with each card containing the following:

```
dollars desired     cols.  1–7     xxxxx.xx
interest rate              8–9     .xx
number of years            10–11
```

The output from the program should be the amount to invest, interest rate, number of years, and dollars received. Double space the output and label each column appropriately.

Chapter 6

Making Decisions

6.1 Introduction

This chapter introduces the IF statement in the sample problem solved in section 6.2. Rules of the statement and its more commonly used forms appear in section 6.3. Section 6.4 discusses options of the IF statement which are available with high level COBOL. These include compound tests, sign tests, condition-names, and negated tests. That section may be omitted if desired.

6.2 A Sample Program

Suppose we need to write a program to solve the following problem. The credit bureau wants a list printed of all the people in category 1A who are under 27 years of age. These people should not be allowed to buy on credit because they are poor risks. The bureau's files are on cards in the following format:

name	cols.	1–20
social security number		21–29
age		31–32
category		33–34
other information		35–80

As we study the problem we realize that we do not want to print all the people in the file, but only those who are in category 1A and who are under 27. If a person is in category 1A and is 28 say, then we would not want to write his name. Therefore, in order to process the cards we will need to read the name, the age, and the category. Then we may be able to determine whether or not to write the name. We begin our flowchart in Figure 6.1.

Figure 6.1 Beginning Flowchart to Print List for Credit Bureau

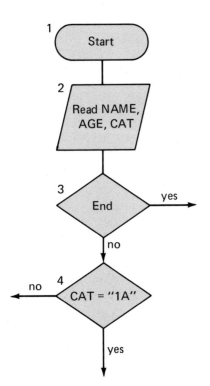

After we read a card and it is not the "end" card, then we ask if the category (CAT) is "1A". The quote marks were placed around the 1A in the flow chart to show that we wish to compare exactly those characters to the value of CAT. If CAT is "1A", then we should go on to see if the AGE is less than 27. The symbol < means less than and will be used in the flowchart in Figure 6.2. If CAT is not "1A", then we should form a loop back to box 2 so that

Figure 6.2 Continuing the
Flowchart for Credit
Bureau Listing

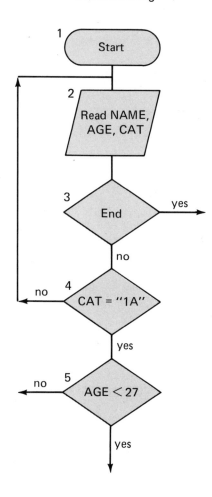

we may go on to the next person's card. Adding these parts to our flowchart in Figure 6.1, we have Figure 6.2.

If the AGE is less than 27, we know that this person is in category 1A, and we should write his name. After writing the name, we should loop back to box 2 and go on to read the next card. If the AGE is not less than 27, we should proceed to the next person's card. If there are no more cards, we should stop. These additions to the previous flowchart in Figure 6.2 are included in the final one in Figure 6.3.

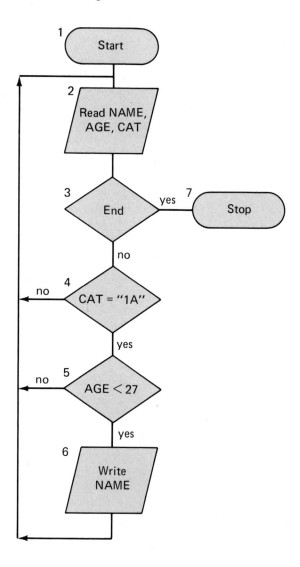

Figure 6.3 Final Flowchart to List
People Under 27 in
Credit Bureau
Category 1A

Now that the flowchart has been written, we should make up some names, ages, and categories to test our flowchart and see if it will do everything our problem wants. Once we are satisfied with the flowchart, our next step is to convert it into COBOL instructions.

Referring to the skeleton program outline in Table 3.1, we may write the following.

```
IDENTIFICATION DIVISION.
PROGRAM-ID. CREDIT-LIST.
ENVIRONMENT DIVISION.
CONFIGURATION SECTION.
SOURCE-COMPUTER.    IBM-360.
OBJECT-COMPUTER.    IBM-360.
SPECIAL-NAMES. C01 IS TOP-OF-PAGE.
INPUT-OUTPUT SECTION.
FILE-CONTROL.
     SELECT CFILE ASSIGN TO SYS005-UR-2540R-S.
     SELECT OFILE ASSIGN TO SYS006-UR-1403-S.
```

In order to write the DATA DIVISION, we need to see how the input cards are punched and describe them accordingly. Also, we need to decide what our output should look like. Let us title the listing "Persons in Category 1A under the Age of 27" and double space the listing of names.

```
DATA DIVISION.
FILE SECTION.
FD   CFILE DATA RECORD REG LABEL RECORDS OMITTED.
01   REG.
         03   C-NAME      PICTURE    A(20).
         03   FILLER      PICTURE    X(10).
         03   AGE         PICTURE    99.
         03   CAT         PICTURE    XX.
         03   FILLER      PICTURE    X(46).
FD   OFILE DATA RECORD PRTLINE LABEL RECORDS OMITTED.
01   PRTLINE             PICTURE    X(132).
WORKING-STORAGE SECTION.
01   NAME-LINE.
         03   FILLER      PICTURE    X(56)     VALUE SPACE.
         03   NL-NAME     PICTURE    A(20).
         03   FILLER      PICTURE    X(56)     VALUE SPACE.
01   TITLE.
         03   FILLER      PICTURE    X(45)     VALUE SPACE.
         03   FILLER      PICTURE    X(42)     VALUE
             'PERSONS IN CATEGORY 1A UNDER THE AGE OF 27'.
         03   FILLER      PICTURE    X(45)     VALUE SPACE.
```

Since we have placed NAME-LINE and TITLE in the WORKING-STORAGE SECTION, we could insert blanks where necessary and could also specify the title. Our output line PRTLINE has been described as merely an area 132 spaces long. This is method 2 of section 4.3.

Let us now proceed to convert the flowchart commands into COBOL language statements.

We begin the program by opening our files and writing the title. Our flowchart does not specify these two tasks, but they must be done before we read any cards or write any names. Since TITLE is not a part of OFILE, we must move it to the output area PRTLINE so that it may be written. The word

1 (Start)

TOP-OF-PAGE is a special name which we defined to be the way of writing a line at the top of a new page.

> PROCEDURE DIVISION.
> PRELIM. OPEN INPUT CFILE. OPEN OUTPUT OFILE.
> MOVE TITLE TO PRTLINE.
> WRITE PRTLINE AFTER TOP-OF-PAGE.

Since we need to read only the name, age, and category from the data card, those are the only items named in the record REG of CFILE. To read a card and check for the end we say

> RLOOP. READ CFILE AT END GO TO FIN.

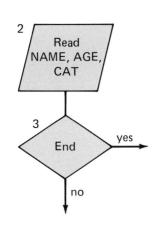

We have started a new paragraph because the flowchart tells us that we need to return to this step from either boxes 4, 5, or 6.

The test for the end card in box 3 is part of the READ statement. The test for a category of 1A must be done with an IF statement. If CAT is not "1A" we wish to return to box 2 (paragraph RLOOP in the program), otherwise we wish to go on to the next box in the flowchart. Therefore, we write

> IF CAT IS NOT EQUAL TO '1A' GO TO RLOOP.

The literal marks are necessary because we want to check the value of CAT to see if it is exactly the characters 1A. If CAT is not equal to "1A", then the computer will go to paragraph RLOOP. If CAT is "1A", the computer will proceed to the next sentence in the program. Even though this IF sentence does not parallel the flowchart test exactly, it will accomplish the same purpose.

In COBOL this test could be written in a manner similar to the previous one.

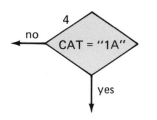

> IF AGE IS NOT LESS THAN 27 GO TO RLOOP.

If the age is less than 27, the computer proceeds to the next sentence in the program. If the age is not less than 27 (this means the age is 27 or greater), the computer proceeds to RLOOP to read another card. The numeric literal 27 was used in this IF statement because it is being compared to AGE, which has a numeric PICTURE.

In order to write the name we must move it to the proper place in NAME-LINE and then transfer the entire line to the output area so that it may be written. After writing the line we wish to return to box 2 (paragraph RLOOP).

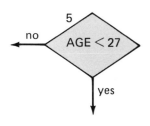

> MOVE C-NAME TO NL-NAME.
> MOVE NAME-LINE TO PRTLINE.
> WRITE PRTLINE AFTER ADVANCING 2 LINES.
> GO TO RLOOP.

We could have expressed boxes 5 and 6 in a different IF statement which follows.

> IF AGE IS LESS THAN 27 MOVE C-NAME TO NL-NAME
> MOVE NAME-LINE TO PRTLINE
> WRITE PRTLINE AFTER ADVANCING 2 LINES.
> GO TO RLOOP.

This IF statement asks the opposite question of the previous one. If the age is less than 27, the computer is instructed to do three things—move the name, move NAME-LINE, and write the line. All three commands are part of the IF statement because there is no period until after the word LINES. They were indented to point out to the reader that the IF statement contains all these parts. Since there is no GO TO in the IF statement, the computer will proceed to the next sentence in the program after writing the line. Therefore, whether or not the age is less than 27, the computer branches to paragraph RLOOP.

Before we stop the execution of the program, we must close our files. These commands must be placed in a new paragraph named FIN because that is the name we chose in the READ statement.

```
FIN. CLOSE CFILE OFILE.
     STOP RUN.
```

The complete program follows.

```
IDENTIFICATION DIVISION.
PROGRAM-ID. CREDIT-LIST.
ENVIRONMENT DIVISION.
CONFIGURATION SECTION.
SOURCE-COMPUTER.   IBM-360.
OBJECT-COMPUTER.   IBM-360.
SPECIAL-NAMES. C01 IS TOP-OF-PAGE.
INPUT-OUTPUT SECTION.
FILE-CONTROL.
     SELECT CFILE ASSIGN TO SYS005-UR-2540R-S.
     SELECT OFILE ASSIGN TO SYS006-UR-1403-S.
DATA DIVISION.
FILE SECTION.
FD   CFILE DATA RECORD REG LABEL RECORDS OMITTED.
01   REG.
        03   C-NAME    PICTURE   A(20).
        03   FILLER    PICTURE   X(10).
        03   AGE       PICTURE   99.
        03   CAT       PICTURE   XX.
        03   FILLER    PICTURE   X(46).
FD   OFILE DATA RECORD PRTLINE LABEL RECORDS OMITTED.
01   PRTLINE          PICTURE   X(132).
WORKING-STORAGE SECTION.
01     NAME-LINE.
        03   FILLER    PICTURE   X(56)     VALUE SPACE.
        03   NL-NAME   PICTURE   A(20).
        03   FILLER    PICTURE   X(56)     VALUE SPACE.
01     TITLE.
        03   FILLER    PICTURE   X(45)     VALUE SPACE.
        03   FILLER    PICTURE   X(42)     VALUE
             'PERSONS IN CATEGORY 1A UNDER THE AGE OF 27'.
        03   FILLER    PICTURE   X(45)     VALUE SPACE.
PROCEDURE DIVISION.
PRELIM. OPEN INPUT CFILE. OPEN OUTPUT OFILE.
        MOVE TITLE TO PRTLINE.
        WRITE PRTLINE AFTER TOP-OF-PAGE.
RLOOP. READ CFILE AT END GO TO FIN.
        IF CAT IS NOT EQUAL TO '1A' GO TO RLOOP.
        IF AGE IS NOT LESS THAN 27 GO TO RLOOP.
        MOVE C-NAME TO NL-NAME.
        MOVE NAME-LINE TO PRTLINE.
```

7 Stop

```
          WRITE PRTLINE AFTER ADVANCING 2 LINES.
          GO TO RLOOP.
     FIN. CLOSE CFILE OFILE.
          STOP RUN.
```

6.3 The IF Statement

Now that we have seen how the IF statement may be used to ask questions in a program, let us study the rules for forming an IF statement in COBOL. The form of the IF statement follows.

$$\underline{\text{IF}}\ \text{test}\ \begin{Bmatrix} \text{statement} \ldots \\ \underline{\text{NEXT SENTENCE}} \end{Bmatrix} \left[\begin{Bmatrix} \underline{\text{ELSE}}\ \text{statement} \ldots \\ \underline{\text{ELSE NEXT SENTENCE}} \end{Bmatrix} \right].$$

There are several kinds of tests which a programmer may make; these will be discussed in detail below. If the test is true when the IF is executed, then the computer will execute the statement or statements following the test. If the test is not true, then the computer will proceed to execute the statements following the word ELSE. If the ELSE part is omitted or if ELSE NEXT SENTENCE is used, the computer will go on to the sentence following the IF statement.

For example, in the program of section 6.2 we wrote

```
     IF CAT IS NOT EQUAL TO '1A' GO TO RLOOP.
     IF AGE IS NOT LESS THAN 27 GO TO RLOOP.
```

The tests in these two statements are

```
     CAT IS NOT EQUAL TO '1A'
```

and

```
     AGE IS NOT LESS THAN 27
```

If CAT happened to have the value 2A, then during execution when the computer determined that 2A was not equal to 1A (that is, the test is true), it would execute the GO TO RLOOP command and would not go on to the second IF statement. On the other hand, if CAT were 1A, then the computer would by-pass the GO TO RLOOP and would go on to the second IF statement. We could have written the statements as

```
     IF CAT IS NOT EQUAL TO '1A' GO TO RLOOP ELSE NEXT
        SENTENCE.
     IF AGE IS NOT LESS THAN 27 GO TO RLOOP ELSE NEXT
        SENTENCE.
```

but the ELSE NEXT SENTENCE is not necessary.

If we had said

```
     IF AGE IS LESS THAN 27 MOVE C-NAME TO NL-NAME
        MOVE NAME-LINE TO PRTLINE
        WRITE PRTLINE AFTER ADVANCING 2 LINES.
     GO TO RLOOP.
```

the test is

AGE IS LESS THAN 27

and there are three commands to be executed if the value of AGE is less than 27. If, for example, AGE = 24, then the computer asks: Is 24 less than 27? Since it is, the computer would move C-NAME, move NAME-LINE, and would write PRTLINE. From there it proceeds to the sentence following the IF—the GO TO RLOOP command. If AGE = 27, then the computer would ask: Is 27 less than 27? No, it is not; therefore, the computer would skip over the MOVEs and WRITE and would go on to the GO TO RLOOP sentence. In this example, whether or not the age is less than 27, the computer ends up going to the sentence following the IF statement. However, if a "GO TO" command is part of the IF statement, the computer may not get to the statement following the IF.

Relational Test

One of the most frequently used tests in an IF statement is the relational test whose form is

$$\begin{Bmatrix} \text{data-name} \\ \text{literal} \end{Bmatrix} \text{relation} \begin{Bmatrix} \text{data-name} \\ \text{literal} \end{Bmatrix}$$

The relation may be any of the following.

IS [NOT] GREATER THAN
IS [NOT] LESS THAN
IS [NOT] EQUAL TO

If we wished to ask the question: Is A less than or equal to 100, then we could write the following test.

A NOT GREATER THAN 100

The phrase NOT GREATER THAN means the same as less than or equal to ($\leq$). Similarly, the phrase NOT LESS THAN means the same as greater than or equal to ($\geq$).

Two literals may *not* be used in the relational test. An example of this would be to ask if 30 IS GREATER THAN 40. Since we already know the answer, there is no need to ask the computer this question.

The following are examples of relational tests which may be used in an IF statement.

AGE LESS THAN 27
SEX IS EQUAL TO 'F'
SEX NOT EQUAL TO 'M'
INCOME NOT GREATER 3200

Class Test

A data-name which is described as alphanumeric (PICTURE X) may contain numbers or letters or a combination of both. The class test which may be used in an IF statement instructs the computer to test the contents of a data-name to see if they are strictly numeric (all numbers) or alphabetic (all letters). For example, suppose we had two types of data cards—one which contained personal information about a student, and one which contained his quality points and cumulative hours. The deck should be arranged so that an information card precedes the grade card. However, since it is possible that some cards might be out of order, our program should check the order of the cards. The cards are described below.

```
FD    STUDENTS DATA RECORD INFO GRADES LABEL RECORDS
      OMITTED.
01    INFO.
      03   ST-ID     PICTURE   9(9).
      03   NAME      PICTURE   X(21).
      03   ADRES     PICTURE   X(15).
      03   FILLER    PICTURE   X(35).
01    GRADES.
      03   S-ID      PICTURE   9(9).
      03   QPTS      PICTURE   999V9.
      03   CUMHRS    PICTURE   999V9.
      03   FILLER    PICTURE   X(63).
```

Our program will read the first card and see if there is a name on the card as there should be. If there isn't, then we will transfer to paragraph NO-NAME which will print the card in error. In COBOL this would be written

```
READ STUDENTS END GO TO STP.
IF NAME IS NOT ALPHABETIC GO TO NO-NAME.
```

If the name were not alphabetic, then we have read one of the cards containing quality points and cumulative hours. Remember that the two records GRADES and INFO do not name two separate memory areas. They are two names for one area 80 columns long. Whenever a card is read, the data on the card is placed into the read area. The data-name QPTS references columns 10–13 of the area, and NAME references columns 10–30. If the NAME area is not alphabetic, it must be because there are numbers punched in columns 10–13 of the area.

The form of the test for the class of an item is the following.

$$\text{data-name IS [\underline{NOT}]} \begin{Bmatrix} \underline{\text{NUMERIC}} \\ \text{ALPHABETIC} \end{Bmatrix}$$

The NUMERIC test may not be used on a data-name described by an alphabetic PICTURE (A). The ALPHABETIC test may not be used on a data-name described with a numeric PICTURE (9).

Referring to the file description above, we could have the following tests

```
QPTS IS NUMERIC
CUMHRS NOT NUMERIC
NAME ALPHABETIC
```

Exercises

1. Following is part of a DATA DIVISION of a COBOL program. KARD is a card file and RIT is a printer file.

```
FD   KARD DATA RECORD CHANG LABEL RECORDS OMITTED.
01   CHANG.
     03   SCORE     PICTURE    999.
     03   FILLER    PICTURE    X(77).
FD   RIT DATA RECORD CHANCER LABEL RECORDS OMITTED.
01   CHANCER.
     03   FILLER    PICTURE    X(20).
     03   HIS       PICTURE    999.
     03   FILLER    PICTURE    X(109).
```

Use the flowchart below and write the PROCEDURE DIVISION of the program in COBOL. What is this flowchart doing?

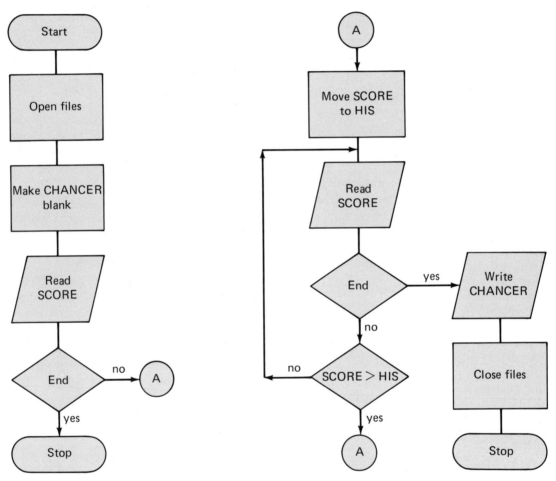

2. Convert the following flowchart segment into COBOL.

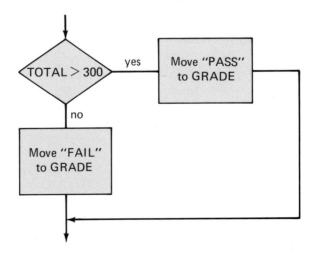

3. Convert the following flowchart segment into COBOL.

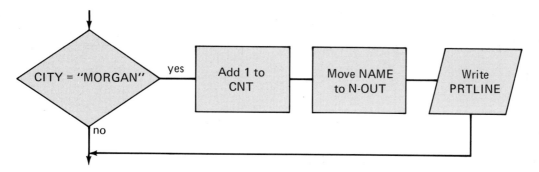

4. What will be printed by the following commands if GD = 85? if GD = 97? if GD = 60?

```
IF GD > 90 MOVE 'A' TO FINALG.
IF GD > 70 MOVE 'B' TO FINALG ELSE
    MOVE 'C' TO FINALG.
DISPLAY FINALG.
```

5. Do the statements in exercise 4 correctly express the commands in the following flowchart? If not, then correct them.

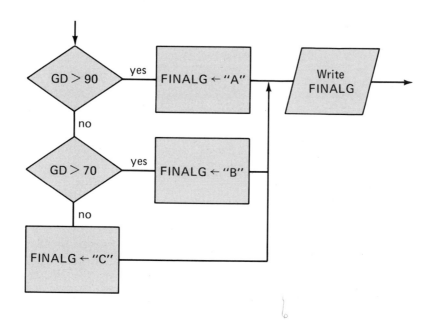

Programs

1. Fly-By-Night Airlines has currently received stewardess applications from girls all over the nation. Before any interviews are given, a girl must meet all of the following standards:

height	5' 0"–5' 5" (low ceilings on planes)
weight	95–120 pounds
age	18–25
aptitude test	80 or better

A letter will be written inviting any girl who meets these qualifications to a personal interview. There are two cards input for each applicant.

Card 1:	last name	cols.	1–10
	first name		11–20
	street address		21–30
	city		31–40
	state		41–50
	zip code		51–55
	1		80
Card 2:	last name	cols.	1–10
	first name		11–20
	height (in inches)		21–22
	weight		24–26
	age		27–28
	aptitude score		29–31
	2		80

The following letter will be output and sent to any girl who meets all the qualifications of the airline. The exact date of the interview will be typed in later.

```
            Fly-By-Night Airlines

              Boondocks, U.S.A.


Mary Anybody
1 Boardwalk
Seaside, N.J.   23108

Dear Miss Anybody:

      It is our pleasure to announce that
you have been chosen for an interview on
                  Please be prompt.

              Sincerely,

              Mark Goodham
```

2. Itty Bitty Machine Company's Payroll Department needs a program to process the company's payroll. Employees who work more than 40 hours a week should get overtime pay for any hours worked over 40. The rate for overtime work is 1½ times the normal rate. For example, a person who worked 50 hours in one week at $2 an hour should be paid

$$40 \times \$2 = \$80 \quad \text{regular salary}$$

plus

$$10 \times \$2 \times 1.5 = 10 \times 3 = \$30 \quad \text{overtime salary}$$

equals

$$\$80 + \$30 = \$110 \quad \text{gross salary.}$$

If an employee does not work more than 40 hours, he should not be paid overtime.

After computing gross salary, calculate the amount to deduct for social security: 5.85% of gross salary. Then calculate the amount to withhold for income tax: 15% of gross salary. Finally compute take home pay: gross salary − social security deduction − income tax.

The input data is in the following format:

social security number	cols. 1–9	
name	11–27	
hours worked	32–33	
rate (in dollars and cents)	35–37	x.xx

Output these items for each worker:

social security number
name
gross salary
amount of social security deduction
amount of income tax deduction
take home pay

Compute all amounts in dollars and cents and edit them. Design your own form of output. Be sure to start the payroll listing at the top of a new page. Put an appropriate title and column headings on the output.

3. The input will be a deck of income tax information cards. Each person will have one card in the following format:

social security number	cols. 1–9	
name	10–30	
wages	31–36	xxxx.xx
interest	38–43	xxxx.xx
dividends	45–50	xxxx.xx
tax withheld	52–57	xxxx.xx
no. exemptions	60	

Write a program to compute the following.

1. total income = wages + interest + dividends
   If total income is less than $5000.00 or greater than $10,000.00, this program cannot compute the income tax. For this person, write out only social security number, name, and a message to the effect that the person's income is not within the range of the program.
2. amount for exemptions = $675 × no. of exemptions
3. amount to compute tax on = total income − amount for exemptions
4. $\text{tax} = \dfrac{\text{amount to compute tax on}}{5}$
5. balance due = tax − tax withheld

The output should be a double-spaced printout of each person's social security number, name, and balance due. Edit the balance due with either a — or a CR to designate a refund.

4. The results of the quarter's eight exams in Large Lecture Course 101 have been punched on cards. Your job is to write a program which will take the information from the cards and use the following scale to assign the final grade for each student. The numbers in the scale are all percentiles.

90–100	A
80–89	B
70–79	C
60–69	D
0–59	F

Also compute the grade distribution—the number of A's, B's, C's, D's, and F's received.

The format of each card is

student number	cols.	1–9
last name		10–22
first name		23–31
first score		41–42
second score		43–44
third score		45–46
fourth score		47–48
fifth score		49–50
sixth score		51–52
seventh score		53–54
eighth score		55–56

The output should be single-spaced with an appropriate title. For each student, produce a printout containing student number, name, and final letter grade. Print the grade distribution on a separate page.

5. The efficiency experts are studying the workers at the Organic Food Farm and need the following report:

1. number of workers who work 30 hours a week or less and the average salary paid to those workers
2. number of workers who work more than 30 hours a week, but less than 50 hours, and the average salary paid to this group of workers
3. number of workers who work 50 hours or more per week and the average salary paid to this group

All numbers printed in the report should be labeled with an appropriate message.

The input data is on cards with one card for each employee. The format of the cards is as follows:

name	cols.	1–20
no. hours worked per day		21–22
no. days worked per week		31
rate		35–37 x.xx

6. The payroll department needs a program which will check its records for possible errors. All records are on cards in the following format:

social security number   cols. 1–9
name   10–30
rate   31–34   xx.xx
hours   35–36
sex   37

The program should check the card for the following items:

missing information (blank areas)
questionable rate of pay (greater than $15)
questionable hours (over 60)

Print any card which contains an error and print a message saying what is wrong with it. Tabulate and print the number of good records and the number of bad records.

7. Hurts Rent-A-Car service punches its rental records on cards and needs a program to process them. The cards contain the following information:

renter's name   cols. 1–20
type of car   21–27   (alphabetic)
number of days   28–29
car class   30   (numeric)

The program should produce a listing of renters, number of days, type of car, and rental charge. The fees are based on the following scale:

Class	Rate
1	$11.00/day
2	$14.00/day
3	$18.00/day
4	$24.00/day

8. Write a program which will print a depreciation schedule for an asset with cost C, salvage value S, and a useful life of N years. The values of C, S, and N are read from a card in the following format:

cost (C)   cols. 1–7   xxxxx.xx
salvage value (S)   11–17   xxxxx.xx
life (N)   21–22

Use straight line depreciation and sum of years digit to print the depreciation schedule. The form of the output should be something like the following.

DEPRECIATION SCHEDULE

YEAR	STRAIGHT LINE	SUM YEARS DIGIT
1	$xx,xxx.xx	$xx,xxx.xx
.	.	.
.	.	.
.	.	
N		

The formula to calculate **A**, the amount of depreciation during any year, assuming straight line depreciation, is

$$A = \frac{(C - S)}{N}$$

To calculate the amount of depreciation **D** during any year using the sum of years digit method, the formula is

$$D = \frac{(C - S)\, I}{\dfrac{N(N + 1)}{2}}$$

where $I = N$ in the first year
$I = N - 1$ in the second year
$I = N - 2$ in the third year

.

.

.

$I = 1$ in the Nth year

9. Write a program which will print a depreciation schedule for an asset with cost C, a useful life of N years, and which depreciates a percentage P each year. The values C, N, and P are read from a card in the following format.

cost (C)   cols. 1–7   xxxxx.xx
life (N)   11–12
percentage (P)   15–16   .xx

The output should be the following

DEPRECIATION SCHEDULE

COST $xx,xxx.xx
PERCENTAGE .xx

YEAR	DEP. EXPENSE	ACCUMULATED DEP.
1	$xx,xxx.xx	$xx,xxx.xx
.	.	.
.	.	.
.	.	.

For the first year, depreciation expense D_1 = accumulated depreciation A_1.

$$D_1 = A_1 = \frac{C\,P}{N}$$

In year 2, $D_2 = \dfrac{(C - A_1)\,P}{N}$ $A_2 = A_1 + D_2$

In year 3, $D_3 = \dfrac{(C - A_2)\,P}{N}$ $A_3 = A_2 + D_3$

.

.

.

In year N, $D_N = \dfrac{(C - A_{N-1})\,P}{N}$ $A_N = A_{N-1} + D_N$

6.4 Other Forms of the IF Statement[1]

Compound Tests

At the left margin is a segment from the flowchart in section 6.2. The decisions represented in the segment could have been expressed in one IF statement in COBOL. Instead of having the two tests in two separate IF statements, we could combine them into one compound test and say

```
IF CAT IS EQUAL TO '1A' AND AGE IS LESS THAN 27
    MOVE C-NAME TO NL-NAME
    MOVE NAME-LINE TO PRTLINE
    WRITE PRTLINE AFTER ADVANCING 2 LINES.
GO TO RLOOP.
```

The tests CAT IS EQUAL TO '1A' and AGE IS LESS THAN 27 have been joined with the word AND. When this command is executed, the computer checks to see if the category is 1A and if the age is less than 27. Only if both these tests are true does the computer execute the two MOVEs and the WRITE statement.

Sometimes we may wish to see if one thing or the other is true. For example, the following statement is asking if the contents of ANIMAL is either the word CAT or the word DOG.

```
IF ANIMAL IS EQUAL TO 'CAT' OR ANIMAL IS EQUAL TO
    'DOG' GO TO PET.
```

Since we used the word OR to connect the two tests, the computer will go to paragraph PET if either of the tests is true. If both the tests are false, the computer would execute the next sentence after the IF.

The word AND used to connect tests to form a compound test means "both" and the word OR means "either or both." In other words, in a compound test which uses AND, both tests must be true before the compound test will be true. If the tests were connected by the word OR, then the compound test will be true if either test is true or if both tests are true.

Three or more tests may be combined with AND or OR to form a compound test. For example, a test could be

```
ZIP = 62221 AND STREET = 'VIRGINIA' OR STREET = 'ADAMS'[2]
```

Just how do we interpret this compound test? If we include parentheses as in the following, then the test is less confusing.

```
ZIP = 62221 AND (STREET = 'VIRGINIA' OR STREET = 'ADAMS')
```

The computer will evaluate the condition within parentheses first and will use the result to evaluate the entire test. Therefore, if STREET were either VIRGINIA or ADAMS, then that part of the test would be true. If the ZIP

---

[1] The reader may wish to omit this section; all the options discussed are part of high level COBOL.

[2] In high level COBOL the equal sign (=) in an IF statement means the same as the phrase IS EQUAL TO.

were also 62221, then the entire test would be true, because each test connected by the AND was true. Even though tests could be very elaborate and complex, it is better to keep everything simple. Programmers are less likely to make mistakes and the programs are easier to change if necessary.

Rules for Compound Tests

1. Any two tests may be connected with the word AND or the word OR.
2. A compound test may be enclosed in parentheses and may be connected to another test with either the word AND or OR. The part in the innermost parentheses is evaluated first.
3. If AND joins two tests, the compound test will be true only if both parts are true. If one part or the other or both parts are false, the entire test is false.
4. If OR joins two tests, the compound test will be true if one or both parts are true. The compound test will be false only if both parts are false.

Relational Test

The arithmetic expression as explained in section 5.4 may be used in a relational test. The form of the test is

$$\begin{Bmatrix} \text{data-name} \\ \text{literal} \\ \text{arithmetic-expression} \end{Bmatrix} \text{relation} \begin{Bmatrix} \text{data-name} \\ \text{literal} \\ \text{arithmetic-expression} \end{Bmatrix}$$

The relation in the test may be any one of the following.

IS [NOT] GREATER THAN
IS [NOT] >   (> means greater than)
IS [NOT] LESS THAN
IS [NOT] <   (< means less than)
IS [NOT] EQUAL TO
IS [NOT] =

High level COBOL compilers allow the use of symbols to represent the relations of greater than, less than, or equal to. The following IF statements contain examples of relational tests.

IF B ** 2 − 4 * A * C < 0 GO TO IMAG.
IF SEX NOT = 'M' ADD 1 TO NONM.
IF CREDITS − DEBITS NOT < ZERO GO TO XP.

Sign Test

This test may be used to determine whether the value of a data-name or an arithmetic expression (see section 5.4) is positive, negative, or zero. The general form of this test follows.

$$\begin{Bmatrix} \text{data-name} \\ \text{arithmetic-expression} \end{Bmatrix} \text{IS [NOT]} \begin{Bmatrix} \text{POSITIVE} \\ \text{NEGATIVE} \\ \text{ZERO} \end{Bmatrix}$$

A value is positive if it is greater than zero and negative if it is less than zero. If an arithmetic expression is used, the computer finds its value and then checks it. For example, we may say

IF BALANCE IS NOT POSITIVE GO TO OVERDRAWN.

or

IF BALANCE IS NEGATIVE GO TO OVERDRAWN.

Both statements are asking the same question. In the statement

IF BAL — AMT IS NEGATIVE GO TO OVD.

the computer will subtract the value of AMT from the value of BAL and see if the result is negative.

Condition-names

Using condition-names in the DATA DIVISION can shorten our IF statements and make them more readable. Let us study the following example before discussing the technical aspects of condition-names.

Suppose our data card contains a code of 1 for males and 2 for females. To test for a male, we would write IF SEX IS EQUAL TO 1.... Looking at just the IF statement, we cannot tell what a code of 1 means, but if we describe SEX in the following way:

```
03   SEX PICTURE 9.
     88    MALE VALUE 1.
     88    FEMALE VALUE 2.
```

then our IF statement would become

IF MALE . . .

This commands the computer to see if the value of SEX is a 1 and is certainly a more lucid statement than the one which said

IF SEX IS EQUAL TO 1 . . .

The condition-names in the example are MALE and FEMALE. They are programmer-supplied and have the level number 88. Condition-names state the different values or range of values which a data-name may have. To test for a particular value, we use only the condition-name associated with that value.

A level 88 entry defines a condition-name and has the following general form.

$$88 \text{ condition-name} \begin{Bmatrix} \underline{VALUE} \text{ IS} \\ \underline{VALUES} \text{ ARE} \end{Bmatrix} \text{literal-1 } [\underline{THRU} \text{ literal-2}]$$
$$[\text{literal-3 } [\underline{THRU} \text{ literal-4}] \ . \ . \ . \ ] \ .$$

The level 88 entry states possible values of the elementary or independent item immediately preceding it. If the THRU phrase is included, a range of values from literal-1 through literal-2 is tested, including the values of literal-1 and literal-2. The value of literal-1 must be less than the value of literal-2, literal-3 less than literal-4, and so on.

For example, to test salary for different categories of

```
     0–$ 4,000   (low)
$ 4,001–$10,000   (middle)
$10,001–$20,000   (high)
```

we could describe salary and use three level 88 entries.

```
03   SALARY PICTURE 9(5).
     88   LOW VALUES 0 THRU 4000.
     88   MID VALUES 4001 THRU 10000.
     88   HIGH VALUES 10001 THRU 20000.
```

Then a command of

```
IF LOW . . .
```

would tell the computer to see if the value of SALARY is between 0 and 4000 dollars. If the SALARY were exactly 4000, the test would be true. For any salary above 4000, the test would be false.

Negated Test

Any test may be preceded by the word NOT. The test itself may not contain the word NOT. Following are examples of IF statements containing negated tests.

```
IF NOT SALARY LESS THAN 3000 GO TO WPASS.
IF HEIGHT GREATER THAN 72 AND NOT WEIGHT GREATER
    THAN 200 GO TO AXCEPT.
IF NOT SOLD GO TO XAMIN. (SOLD would be a condition-name)
```

Exercises

1. What will the computer do when it executes the following statement? Assume AGE = 24 and WGT = 120.

   IF AGE IS LESS THAN 25 AND WGT LESS THAN 115 GO TO OK.

2. What if AGE = 20 and WGT = 110 and the computer executes the command in exercise 1?

3. What will the computer do when it executes the following statement? Assume HT = 62 and WGT = 130.

   IF HT LESS THAN 65 OR WGT GREATER THAN 150 GO TO RFS.

4. What will happen if HT = 65 and WGT = 130 when the computer executes the command in exercise 3?

5. Write one IF statement to correspond to the following flowchart segment.

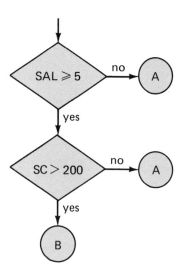

6. Write an IF statement using a sign test to express the following flowchart segment.

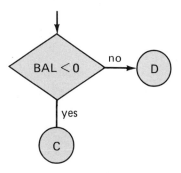

7. What does the following statement do?

  IF CBS — AMT POSITIVE NEXT SENTENCE ELSE GO TO OVD.

8. Describe KODE (a one-digit number) so that it may be tested for each of the values 1, 3, or 5.

9. Describe PASS (a 3-digit number) so that it may be tested for the values of 300 through 500.

10. Describe KXD (a 3-digit number) so that it may be tested for the values of 000 through 100 and 900 through 999. (Use one level 88.)

Programs

See the program assignments following section 6.3.

Chapter 7

Finding and Correcting Errors

7.1 Debugging Programs

When a program does not work, we say that it contains a "bug." Finding and correcting the errors (or debugging the program) requires some experience and perseverance. In this chapter we will discuss a general method to follow for debugging programs. Section 7.2 discusses pre-run errors: those which can and should be detected before submitting the program to the computer. Section 7.3 concerns post-run errors: those which the computer reports. While it is not possible to list all the sources of error, we will discuss and show how to correct errors most commonly made by the beginning programmer.

If we can detect mistakes before running the program on the computer, then we can save our time and machine time. Punctuation errors, misspelling, omission of necessary headings in the program are all things which may be corrected if the programmer takes time to proofread his program cards. Some errors will not show up until the program has been run on the computer and does not produce the desired results. Then the programmer must go over the statements carefully using some of the data and try to discover what is wrong.

The flowchart in Figure 7.1 illustrates a general method to follow when trying to find errors in a program. Boxes 1–9 illustrate the pre-run stage of finding errors; boxes 10–20 the post-run stage.

7.2 Pre-run Errors

Trace the Flowchart

After drawing a flowchart, the programmer should select some data and do a trace of the flowchart. The data should tell all possible decisions and paths in the flowchart. If there is something wrong, it can be corrected before the program is written.

We cannot overemphasize the importance of a flowchart. A flowchart is more than just an outline of a program—it shows the step-by-step instructions which the computer must follow to solve a problem. Time spent in designing a correct flowchart will more than compensate for the time lost in having to debug a program which was not written from a flowchart.

Proofread the Program

Compare the written program with the skeleton outline in Table 3.1 or Appendix B. Are all the words spelled correctly? Are there periods and hyphens where there should be? Are all the statements in the correct order? Amazingly enough, a mis-placed period can create havoc in a program.

Proofread the Punched Cards

The easiest way to proofread the punched cards is to obtain a printed listing of the cards. Most installations have their own computer program or

Figure 7.1

General Method for
Finding Program Errors

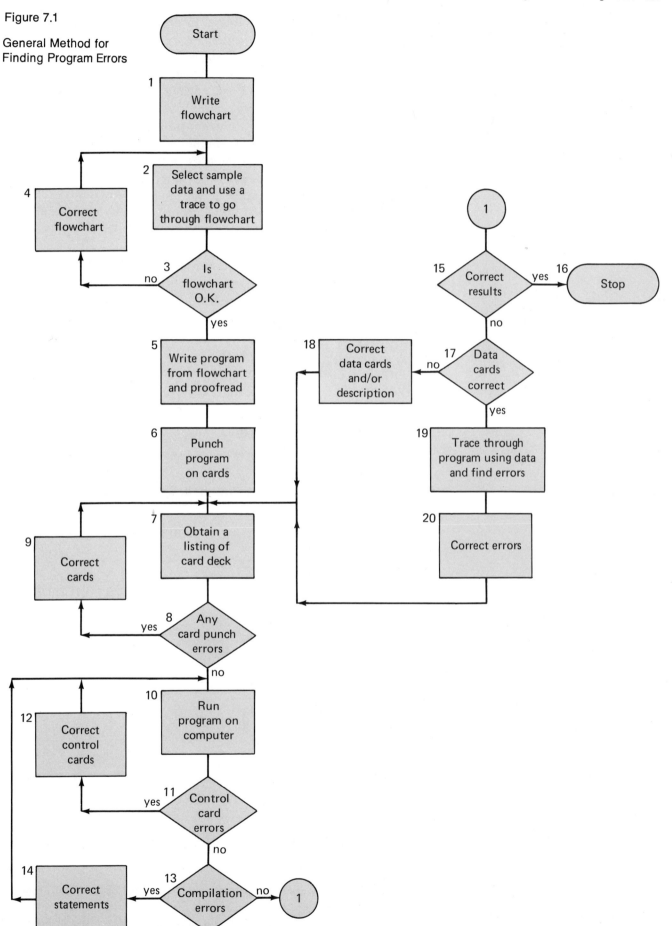

a machine which will produce the listing. If not, you may wish to use Program 3.1.

One of the important things to watch for in proofreading is the spacing of the statements on the cards. COBOL statements begin either in column 8 or column 12 and may not extend past column 72. If you see that a word may cause a line to go past column 72, place that word in column 12 of a new card. The computer will realize that the line goes from one card to the next because there will be no period at the end of the first card.

Remove mispunched cards from the deck. Be sure that all the zeros and O's are punched correctly. Check for misspelling; the names CHECK-SUM and CHECKSUM are *not* the same to the compiler. Are any of the programmer-supplied names reserved COBOL words? (Check with Appendix A.)

Exercise

The following program contains numerous card punching and COBOL grammatical errors. Identify as many as you can. A complete listing of the errors is given at the end of this chapter.

```
IDEMTIFICATION DIVISION.
PROGRAM ID. ERROR-PROG.
REMARKS. THIS PROGRAM CONTAINS MANY INTENTIONAL
    ERRORS. FIND AS MANY AS YOU CAN.
ENVIRONMENT DIVISION.
CONFIGURATION SECTION.
SOURCE-COMPUTER.   IBM-360.
OBJECT-COMPUTER.   IBM-360.
IMPUT-OUTPUT SECTION.
INPUT-OUTPUT SECTION.
FILE-CONTROL
     SELECT A ASSIGN TO SYS005-UR-2540R-S.
     SELECT B ASSIGN TO SYS006-UR-1403-S.
FILE SECTION.
FD    AFILE DATA RECORD AREC LABEL RECORDS OMITTED.
01    A-REC.
      03   NUM      PICTURE 999.
      03   FILLER   PICTURE X(77).
FD    B    DATARECORD BLINE LABEL RECORDS OMITTED.
01    BLINE
      03   FILLER   PICTURE X(20).
      03   SUM      PICTURE 9(5).
      03   FILLER   X(107).
PROCEDURE SECTION.
START. OPEN INPUT A. OPEN OUTPUT B.
       MOVE SPACE TO BLINE.
       MOVE ZERO TO SUM.
ADD-EM. READ AFILE AT END GO TO FINISH.
       ADD NUM TO SUM.
       GO TO ADD EM.
F.     WRITE BLINE AFTER NEWPAGE.
       CLOSE A B. STOP RUN.
```

7.3 Post-run Errors

Control Card Errors

Control cards are important because they instruct the computer what to do with your card deck. The control cards may tell the computer to compile your program, execute it, list it, etc. A slight punctuation error in a control card may mean that your program doesn't get processed by the computer. Check with your instructor for the appropriate control cards to use at your computer center.

Compilation Errors

The compiler checks the program to see if all the statements obey the correct form. One way to avoid compilation errors is to compare the program with the skeleton outline in Table 3.1 and with the forms of the commands given in sections 4.6, 5.3, 6.3, Appendix B, and throughout the book. Whenever the compiler detects an error, it prints a message and a line number. The line number points to the line in the program which contained the error; the message tells what caused the error. Some compilers list the program and then place all error messages on a separate page. Other compilers print errors as they occur in the listing of the program. Not all compilers give the same messages. Therefore, in the following example we will give a general idea of the type of error messages one might encounter and an explanation of them.

Example

Line No.	Statement
001	IDENTIFICATION DIVISION.
002	PROGRAM ID. COMP-ERRORS.
003	ENVIRONMENT DIVISION.
004	SOURCE-COMPUTER. IBM-360.
005	OBJECT-COMPUTER. IBM-360.
006	INPUT-OUTPUT SECTION.
007	FILE-CONTROL.
008	SELECT IFILE ASSIGN TO SYS005-UR-2540R-S.
009	SELECT PFILE ASSIGN TO SYS006-UR-1403-S.
010	DATA DIVISION.
011	FD I-FILE DATA RECORD CARD LABEL RECORDS OMITTED.
012	01 CARD.
014	I UNRECOGNIZABLE DESCRIPTION
023	I NO PARAGRAPH NAME
024	I NAME NOT DESCRIBED
025	I INCORRECT SYNTAX IN READ
025	I INCORRECT SYNTAX IN GO TO
026	I INCORRECT SYNTAX IN MOVE
027	I LITERAL MUST BE NUMERIC
029	D NO SELECT FOR FILE
029	I INCORRECT DATA NAME

Diagnostics

The word *diagnostic* means error message. In some cases we may be able to read the message and know immediately what the problem is. At other times the message may give only a clue to the problem. Being able to interpret diagnostics improves with practice.

Errors are classified into three or four categories depending upon the compiler. They are trivial (sometimes called minor or warning), intermediate (also called conditional), and major (catastrophic, disastrous). In this example W stands for trivial or warning errors, I for intermediate, and D for disastrous, or major, errors. Trivial errors are warnings to the programmer of possible trouble. For example, a statement which moves data from one area to a smaller area would receive a W error meaning that characters will be lost during the move. However, this may be what the programmer intended. W errors do not keep the program from executing. Intermediate errors cause one of two things to happen: either the statement in error is dropped from the program or it is compiled (possibly erroneously). If, for example, the DATA DIVISION contains two items with exactly the same name, then any statement using that name will receive an intermediate error. The compiler will not know which item the programmer meant to use so it will pick one (perhaps the wrong one). Catastrophic or disastrous errors are so serious that they keep the program from executing. Omitting a SELECT statement for a file will cause a D error.

Often one error may cause others. In the above example, spelling IFILE as I-FILE in the file description (FD) caused the errors in lines 26 and 29. I-FILE had no SELECT statement and therefore any time part of I-FILE was used an error was recorded. Correcting the spelling would erase the errors in lines 26 and 29. We will now explain the diagnostics in the above program and explain how to correct the mistakes.

002—Program Name Missing. There is a program name on line 2 and it is a valid name obeying the rules for programmer supplied names. The mistake is actually in the heading PROGRAM ID; there should be a hyphen between the two words. The compiler cannot always tell exactly what the error is, as in this case. Therefore, a programmer should use diagnostics as an aid to pointing out problems.

004—Missing Section Header. At first glance we may not be able to tell what is missing until we refer to the skeleton outline in Table 3.1 and see that CONFIGURATION SECTION should come before SOURCE-COMPUTER.

011—No SELECT for File. Misspelling caused this error. The FD should read IFILE and *not* I-FILE. The compiler sees these as two different words.

014—Unrecognizable Description. If we look at the description X(50), we may think that nothing is wrong. However, we have omitted the word PIC-TURE before the description.

023—No Paragraph Name. This diagnostic tells us exactly what is wrong. Every sentence in the PROCEDURE DIVISION must be in some paragraph and we have not included one here. We may correct this error by choosing a name according to the rules in Section 3.2.

024—Name Not Described. Referring to the DATA DIVISION we see that we have words named PFILE and CNT; SPACE and ZERO are special COBOL words which the compiler recognizes. What could be the problem? We should use the name PLINE instead of PFILE because that is the name of the memory area in which we wish to put blanks.

025—Incorrect Syntax in READ. If we compare the READ statement to its outline form, we will find that we should say READ file-name . . . . In this program IFILE is the file-name, not CARD.

025—Incorrect Syntax in GO TO. Comparing the GO TO statement to its general form, we find that we should say GO TO paragraph-name. Since STOP is the name of a paragraph, we should check to see if it is a valid name. The word STOP is a COBOL reserved word, so we must change the name of the paragraph and the GO TO statement. We could use something like STOP-PROG in both places.

026—Incorrect Syntax in MOVE. This error is caused by line 11. Spelling the file-name I-FILE instead of IFILE means that the compiler does not recognize the name INFO. Correcting line 11 will remove this error.

027—Literal Must Be Numeric. In any computation we must use numeric literals—ones without literal marks. To correct this we should write ADD 1 TO CNT.

029—No SELECT for File. Again, this is a case of misspelling. We should consistently use the word IFILE or I-FILE, but *not* both.

029—Incorrect Data-Name. COBOL reserved words may *not* be used for paragraph names. However, we could use the name STOP-PROG instead of STOP.

Data Card or Data Description Errors

The description of the data tells the computer exactly how the input cards are punched and how the output should be spaced. Any discrepancy between the description and the punched cards can make a great deal of difference in the output of the program. If, for example, the program says that a number is in columns 8–10 on the card and the number is actually in columns 9–11, the computer will not read the number correctly. Either the cards or the program would have to be changed. See example 1 below.

Another source of error is describing the location of the decimal point incorrectly. If a number such as 763 is to be read as 7.63, then its PICTURE must be 9V99 and *not* 999.

If the value of a number may be negative, then its PICTURE must contain an S. If a negative number is to be edited, the PICTURE should have a + — CR or DB.

Any value used in computation must have a numeric PICTURE, but the result computed may have an edited PICTURE. See example 2 below.

Numbers on the data cards must *not* contain an actual decimal point; the V in the PICTURE shows the location of the decimal point. Signed numbers must have the sign multi-punched in the same column as the right-most digit. Numbers not large enough to fill an entire field on a card should have zeros occupying the empty columns. See example 3 below.

Example 1

The following description does not match the format of the data card. Omitting the FILLER PICTURE X after SS says that NAME is in columns 10–29 and AMT is in columns 30–34, when NAME is actually in columns 11–30 and AMT is in columns 31–35.

```
social security number    cols.  1–9
name                            11–30
amount                          31–35
01 DCARD.
   03 SS       PICTURE 9(9).
←———————————————— 03 FILLER PICTURE X.    missing
   03 NAME   PICTURE A(20).
   03 AMT     PICTURE 9(5).
   03 FILLER  PICTURE X(46). ← should be X(45).
```

Example 2

Suppose the program has computed GROSSPAY and DEDUCT. It needs to subtract DEDUCT from GROSSPAY to compute NETPAY. The values of GROSSPAY, DEDUCT, and NETPAY are to be printed.

Since DEDUCT and GROSSPAY are used to compute a value, their PICTUREs must be numeric. Therefore, DEDUCT and GROSSPAY should be described in WORKING-STORAGE. To output them we will describe in the output area the items O-DEDUCT and O-GROSSPAY which will have edited pictures. NETPAY may be described in the output area if its value is not used to compute anything else.

```
FD    P-FILE . . .
01    O-LINE.
      .
      .
      .
      03    O-GROSSPAY    PICTURE    $ZZ,ZZZ.99.
      03    FILLER        PICTURE    X(10).
      03    O-DEDUCT      PICTURE    $ZZ,ZZZ.99.
      03    FILLER        PICTURE    X(10).
      03    NETPAY        PICTURE    $ZZ,ZZZ.99.
WORKING-STORAGE SECTION.
77    GROSSPAY      PICTURE    9(5)V99.
77    DEDUCT        PICTURE    9(5)V99.
      .
      .
      .
```

The commands in the PROCEDURE DIVISION to do the computing and editing would be

```
SUBTRACT DEDUCT FROM GROSSPAY GIVING NETPAY.
MOVE DEDUCT TO O-DEDUCT.
MOVE GROSSPAY TO O-GROSSPAY.
```

Example 3

If the card shown in this example is described in the following way

```
01    DCARD.
      03    AMT       PICTURE    999V99.
      03    FILLER    PICTURE    X(5).
      03    NUM       PICTURE    S999.
      03    FILLER    PICTURE    X(67).
```

then the value of AMT is 23.8 and NUM is -867. The first value illustrates that:

1. the decimal point is not on the card, but the computer reads the value correctly because of the V in the PICTURE.
2. the number does not occupy five columns, so two zeros are added to fill up the area.

The seven and the sign are multi-punched in column 13 to tell the computer that NUM is negative.

Forgetting to Put Spaces in the Output Area

When a program begins execution, the computer's memory is not blank. Most likely it contains the remains of another person's program. If we forget to put blanks where necessary in an output line, then several things may happen. The printed line may contain leftovers from a previous program. Or, the computer may not print the line because of garbage in the output line. Whenever the output is not exactly as planned, we should make sure the output line was blank initially.

If a line is not erased by the program after it is written, the line may reappear later when other things are printed. For example, suppose our output record is the following.

```
01   OUTREC.
     03   FILLER   PICTURE   X(26).
     03   C1       PICTURE   X(30).
     03   C2       PICTURE   X(20).
     03   C3       PICTURE   X(30).
     03   C4       PICTURE   X(26).
```

The commands

```
MOVE SPACE TO OUTREC.
MOVE 'CENSUS REPORT' TO C2.
WRITE OUTREC AFTER 2 LINES.
MOVE 'COUNTY' TO C1.
MOVE 'TOTALS' TO C4.
WRITE OUTREC AFTER 1 LINES.
```

will write the following.

	CENSUS REPORT	
COUNTY	CENSUS REPORT	TOTALS

The title "CENSUS REPORT" will reappear on every printed line unless it is erased by moving something into that area. To correct this we should include a MOVE SPACE TO OUTREC command after the first WRITE statement.

Forgetting to Initialize Data-Names

Initializing means giving a data-name its first value. If a program adds numbers, it should zero the area where the sum goes. If a program uses a data-name whose value does not change, it should use the VALUE phrase or a MOVE statement to give the data-name a value.

Example

The following WORKING-STORAGE SECTION will make SS-DEDUCT equal to .0585, ONE equal to 1, and TITLE equal to the phrase PLANT INVENTORY. The data-name TOTAL does not have an initial value. If we want it to be zero, we would need to include in the PROCEDURE DIVISION the command MOVE ZERO TO TOTAL.

```
WORKING-STORAGE SECTION.
77   SS-DEDUCT   PICTURE V9999    VALUE .0585.
77   ONE         PICTURE 9        VALUE 1.
77   TITLE       PICTURE A(15)    VALUE 'PLANT INVENTORY'.
77   TOTAL       PICTURE 9(5).
```

Editing Problems

Three things are important when describing numbers:

1. the PICTURE for input data should contain only the 9 V and S.
2. any values used in computation should have a numeric PICTURE (with 9 V S).
3. any values to be printed should be edited. Their PICTURE should contain some of the editing characters: $ 9 . , Z * B CR DB + or − but *no* V. The description of these values should be part of either the output area in the FILE SECTION or a line in WORKING-STORAGE which will be transferred to the output area for printing.

If PR = 26.75 and is described in the output record by PICTURE 99V99, then our printed output will contain the number 2675, which is not the correct value of PR. The description should be PICTURE 99.99 so that an actual decimal point will print.

Truncation (Not Saving Enough Room in Memory)

Truncation can occur during a MOVE or as the result of an arithmetic operation. It means that characters are dropped because the area where they are to be placed is not large enough for all the characters. Sometimes this is intentional. If a card contains information only in the first 30 columns and we say "move the entire card into an area 30 places long," the last 50 columns of the card would not be moved. However, if we are computing values, we want to make sure that the areas are large enough for the results. We may use the SIZE ERROR option to warn us if truncation has occurred and then we may increase the size of the area in the program. In practice we should describe our areas allowing plenty of room for a computed value. Even if we are positive a number will never be more than five digits, why not describe it with a PICTURE 9(6)? It certainly doesn't hurt, and may save time and effort later.

Time Limit

Most computers allot a certain amount of time to each program. If the program hasn't finished execution in that length of time, we say that it has exceeded its time limit. A large program may require more time, but frequently a never-ending loop is the cause of a time limit. Therefore, a programmer should check the program's logic very carefully to make certain that every loop has a way to stop.

Example

The following program segment contains a never-ending loop. Since VAL starts with a value of 1 and 2 is added to it each time through the loop, it will *never* be exactly equal to 10. Therefore, there is no way for the computer to get out of paragraph NEL. How could we correct this?

Program 7.1   Example of a Never-ending Loop

```
PROCEDURE DIVISION.
    .
    .
    .
INIT. MOVE 1 TO VAL.
NEL. IF VAL IS EQUAL TO 10 GO TO NEXTP.
    MULTIPLY 2 BY C.
    ADD C TO PRIN.
    WRITE OLINE.
    ADD 2 TO VAL.
    GO TO NEL.
NEXTP.  . . .
```

Errors in Converting the Flowchart to COBOL

Frequently programmers will write a flowchart, make certain it's correct by doing a trace, but will make a slight mistake when converting the flowchart into COBOL instructions. We may be able to spot a mistake such as this by comparing the flowchart and the program. Sometimes we are so familiar with our own program that when rereading it we may gloss over the mistake. In this case we may need to "play computer." *Playing computer* means going through each statement of the PROCEDURE DIVISION with the data and following all the instructions just as the computer would.

Example

The following flowchart was *incorrectly* converted to COBOL commands. What should we do to correct the instructions?

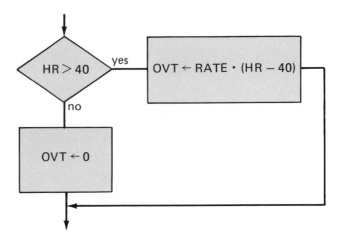

IF HR GREATER THAN 40 SUBTRACT 40 FROM HR GIVING OHR
 MULTIPLY OHR BY RATE GIVING OVT.
MOVE ZERO TO OVT.

Inserting DISPLAY Statements

In a long program or in one involving many computations, it may not be practical to play computer. To save our time we should have values printed as the program is executing. Looking at the values printed we may be able to find which part of the program caused the mistake. For example, if we had inserted the following statement

DISPLAY 'VAL = ' VAL.

in paragraph NEL of Program 7.1, we would have discovered that VAL was never equal to 10 and would have found the cause of the time limit. However, we would have gotten a lot of output from just the one DISPLAY statement.

See Chapter 10 for a discussion of the rules of the DISPLAY command, which provides an easy way of printing values. In the example above, the computer would have printed the phrase VAL = and followed it with the current value of the data-name VAL. In a program containing more than one DISPLAY statement, we should have the computer label the values printed to make it easier to decipher the output.

Adding DISPLAY statements liberally throughout the program could result in many pages of output. Therefore, we should use them only when necessary or we should run the program with just a few pieces of data.

Playing Computer

When none of the above suggestions have located the error, we should play computer with the program. This process may be slow, but it certainly is effective. Going through each statement and doing exactly what the computer does, we should be able to spot mistakes which we had glossed over previously.

Often a programmer is tempted to say, "This paragraph averages the scores; and this paragraph writes the values." If he had looked closer, he would realize he had forgotten to zero the area in which he was totaling scores or he had forgotten to move something to the output area. Minor errors which keep a program from working can usually be detected by playing computer.

Exercises

1. What are the control cards which should be used to run a program at your computer installation?

2. What is wrong with each of the following statements?

```
IMPUT-OUTPUT SECTION.
DATA SECTION.
77   FD          PICTURE 999.
77   AMT         999V99.
77   WH-SALE     PICTURE $ZZZ.99
     MOVE NUM TO 999.
     SUBTRACT '2.00' FROM BAL.
     MULTIPLY SAL BY 5.4% GIVING SS.
     STOP PROGRAM.
```

3. What is the largest value which may be placed in each of the following areas? What is the smallest?

```
77   A   PICTURE   9(5)V99.
77   B   PICTURE   $ZZZ.99.
77   C   PICTURE   $$$.99.
77   D   PICTURE   S9999.
```

4. How do you describe a three-digit number with no decimal places which may be negative? If this number were supposed to be −12, how would you punch it on the data card?

5. Describe an item named XMN and give it a value of 2.75.

Errors in Exercise on Page 120.

1. IDEMTIFICATION is misspelled
2. hyphen missing from PROGRAM ID.
3. IMPUT-OUTPUT SECTION. should be removed
4. FILE-CONTROL should end in a period
5. DATA DIVISION header is missing
6. AFILE should be named A as in the SELECT statement
7. AREC in the FD and A-REC in the line below should be spelled the same
8. DATARECORD should be two words
9. 01 BLINE should end in a period
10. PROCEDURE SECTION should be PROCEDURE DIVISION
11. READ A not AFILE
12. no paragraph named FINISH
13. GO TO ADD EM has a hyphen missing
14. space between NEWPAGE and period
15. SUMis a COBOL reserved word

Special Terms

1. *debugging*
2. *bug*
3. *pre-run errors*
4. *post-run errors*
5. *truncation*
6. *never-ending loop*
7. *time limit*
8. *playing computer*
9. *initialize*
10. *diagnostic*

Chapter 8

Subscripted Data-Names

8.1 Introduction

In this chapter we discuss ways to describe and use an entire group of information such as a group of estimates of which we wish to find the average or a group of weights from which we wish to find the largest. Section 8.2 introduces, through an example, a new way of working with a collection of items. In section 8.3 we study the rules involved. Section 8.4 discusses the concept of a table—a group of values which we normally refer to when looking for a particular piece of information. For example, a tax table would tell us how much income tax to pay; a time table would tell us when a particular flight leaves or arrives. Section 8.5 discusses one way to put values into a table and how to use the REDEFINES clause.

8.2 Beginning to Use Subscripted Names

Let us suppose that we have ten estimates punched on one card and we want to compute the average cost per estimate. How would we go about doing this? First of all we would need to name the estimates. Therefore, let us write the following description.

Figure 8.1A Describing Ten Estimates Without Subscripts

```
01   INFO.
     03   E1        PICTURE    99V99.
     03   E2        PICTURE    99V99.
     03   E3        PICTURE    99V99.
     03   E4        PICTURE    99V99.
                      .
                      .
                      .
     03   E10       PICTURE    99V99.
     03   FILLER    PICTURE    X(40).
```

Of course our actual description in the program would need to include all ten entries for the E's. The compiler would not be able to understand the ellipses in Figure 8.1A. To compute the average estimate we could say

```
ADD E1 E2 E3 E4 E5 E6 E7 E8 E9 E10 GIVING EST-TOTAL.
DIVIDE 10 INTO EST-TOTAL GIVING AVG-EST.
```

This method of giving each estimate a separate name certainly would work, even if it is lengthy. A shorter way is to give one name to the entire group of estimates and then distinguish one estimate from another by using what is called a subscript. For example, we could call the first estimate E (1), the second one E (2), and so on. The group name is E and the subscript is the number in parentheses. We would describe these in the following way.

Figure 8.1B Describing Ten Estimates With Subscripts

```
01   INFO.
     03   E OCCURS 10 TIMES    PICTURE    99V99.
     03   FILLER               PICTURE    X(40).
```

The phrase OCCURS 10 TIMES is saying that E is subscripted: that there are ten items in the group named E, and that their names are E (1), E (2), E (3), . . . and so on. The last one is named E (10).

How would we go about adding these numbers together? We could do it in a manner similar to the one above, or we could write the following.

```
ADD E (1)   TO EST-TOTAL.
ADD E (2)   TO EST-TOTAL.
ADD E (3)   TO EST-TOTAL.
              .
              .
              .
ADD E (10) TO EST-TOTAL.
```

Of course, we have assumed that EST-TOTAL has been made zero before E (1) was to be added to it. Also, in an actual program we would need to write all ten ADD statements. It would not be good enough to put . . . into the program; the compiler would not have any idea what we meant. By now, the reader may be wondering why we introduced subscripts, because they certainly have not made the procedure shorter.

Let us examine the preceding ADD statements and see if we notice any similarities. They all seem to be about the same—the only difference is the subscript. It keeps changing from 1 to 2 to 3 on up to the last value of 10. If we could use a data-name instead of a number for the subscript, then we could change the value of the data-name and thereby change the value of the subscript. For example, if we wrote

```
MOVE 1 TO I.
ADD E (I) TO EST-TOTAL.
```

I would be 1 and E (I) would be interpreted as E (1). Then we could change the value of I and form a loop by returning to the ADD statement as in the following.

```
ST. MOVE 1 TO I.
ADD-UP. ADD E (I) TO EST-TOTAL.
        ADD 1 TO I.
        GO TO ADD-UP.
```

First of all, I would be 1 and we would add E (1) to EST-TOTAL. Then I would increase to 2 and we would add E (2) to EST-TOTAL. Then I would be 3 and we would add E (3) to the total, and so on. What would stop this loop after we have added E (10)? So far, there is nothing. This is a good example of a never-ending loop and we must find a way to make it stop. Perhaps we should look at the flowchart which corresponds to these COBOL statements (see Figure 8.2) and decide how to fix it.

If the value of I is greater than 10 when we leave flowchart box 3, then we do not want to continue the loop. Therefore, let us insert a test to see if I is greater than 10 and leave the loop if it is.

Now we should correct our COBOL statements to correspond to the flowchart in Figure 8.3.

Figure 8.2

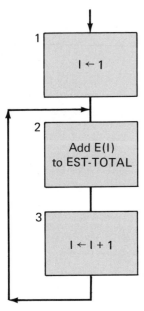

Figure 8.3 Flowchart to Add
Ten Subscripted
Data-Names

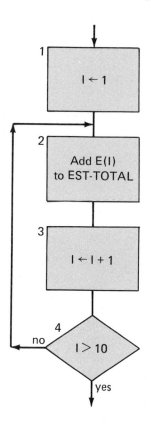

ST. MOVE 1 TO I.
ADD-UP. ADD E (I) TO EST-TOTAL.
    ADD 1 TO I.
    IF I NOT GREATER THAN 10 GO TO ADD-UP.

This new method of using subscripts has greatly shortened our description of the estimates and it has illustrated a basic way of adding subscripted data-names. What would we need to change in the flowchart in Figure 8.3 if we wanted to add 20 estimates instead of 10? Our only alteration would be in box 4, as shown in the margin at the left.

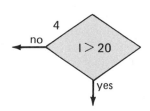

Our description of the estimates in Figure 8.1B says that E (1) is in columns 1–4, E (2) is in columns 5–8, E (3) is in columns 9–12, etc. This means that the numbers are punched next to each other with no spaces in between. What if the estimates had been punched in the following format?

E (1)   cols.   1–4
E (2)   6–9
E (3)   11–14
    .   .
    .   .
    .   .

In other words, there is one space between each number. This means our description would need to allow for the space.

01 INFO.
    03   ESTIMATES OCCURS 10 TIMES.
          05   E   PICTURE   99V99.
          05   FILLER   PICTURE   X.
    03   FILLER   PICTURE   X(30).

Here we are saying that a group (ESTIMATES) occurs 10 times. This means that ESTIMATES is subscripted. There are two parts in ESTIMATES (1)— E (1) and a FILLER. The two parts of ESTIMATES (2) are E (2) and a FILLER. In order to refer to the estimate (the value to be added) we still use E (1), E (2), and so on.

8.3 The OCCURS Clause

Any time we wish to use subscripts with a data-name, the data-name must be described with an OCCURS clause. Using subscripts means that we have a set of related data items which we are going to call by one name. To point to specific members in the group we use a number which is called a subscript. To reference the first item in the group, we use a subscript of 1; to reference the second we use a 2, and so on. The subscript, which may be a number or a data-name, is always enclosed in parentheses and is written following the name of the group. There must be a space between the name and the left parenthesis.

For example, the description

```
03    ANS OCCURS 50 TIMES    PICTURE 9.
```

says that there are 50 one-digit numbers all in the group named ANS. The first one is ANS (1), the second is ANS (2), the third is ANS (3), and so on. The last one is ANS (50).

The general form of the OCCURS clause is the following

<u>OCCURS</u> integer TIMES

Rules for the OCCURS Clause

1. The OCCURS clause may not be used on any item with the level number 01 or 77.

2. The OCCURS clause may appear in either the FILE or WORKING-STORAGE SECTION.

    For example, if we wanted to set up an area in WORKING-STORAGE where we could compute 30 different totals: TOT (1), TOT (2), . . . ,TOT (30), then our description would be

```
01    TOTALS.
      03    TOT OCCURS 30 TIMES    PICTURE 9(5).
```

3. If the OCCURS clause is used on a group item, then every elementary item in the group, as well as the group name, is subscripted.

    For example, in the description

```
03    NAME OCCURS 50 TIMES.
      05    FNAME    PICTURE    X(10).
      05    LNAME    PICTURE    X(10).
```

we have said that NAME is subscripted. But since FNAME and LNAME are part of the group NAME, they are also subscripted. We may picture this as the following.

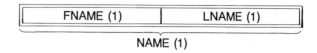

The double-outlined area is NAME (1). The PROCEDURE DIVISION may reference either NAME or FNAME or LNAME as long as each word is followed by a subscript whose value is between 1 and 50.

4. Any data-name described with an OCCURS clause must be subscripted.

5. The VALUE phrase may *not* be used on any subscripted data-name. (See the description in section 8.5 of the REDEFINES clause.)

6. Any subscripted name must be described with an OCCURS clause.

Rules for Subscripts

1. The subscript may be an integer or an elementary data-name which is not subscripted.
2. The value of the subscript must be positive and may not exceed the number in the OCCURS clause.
3. The subscript must be enclosed in parentheses. There must be at least one space between the data-name and the left parenthesis, but no spaces between the left parenthesis and the subscript and the right parenthesis.

8.4 Using a Table

Suppose we were asked to write a program to do the payroll for the Cogswell Manufacturing Company. Their salesmen receive salaries based upon a certain classification scale:

class 1	$2.00 an hour
class 2	$2.70 an hour
class 3	$3.25 an hour
class 4	$4.00 an hour

There is one card punched in the following format for each salesman.

social security number	cols. 1–9
name	10–30
number of hours worked	31–32
class	33

The program should produce a listing of salesmen's names and salaries.

We might be tempted to flowchart the problem in the manner shown in Figure 8.4 on the following page.

There is nothing wrong with the flowchart, but we should ask ourselves:

Figure 8.4 Flowchart of an
Operation to Compute
Salaries Based on a
Fixed Pay Class

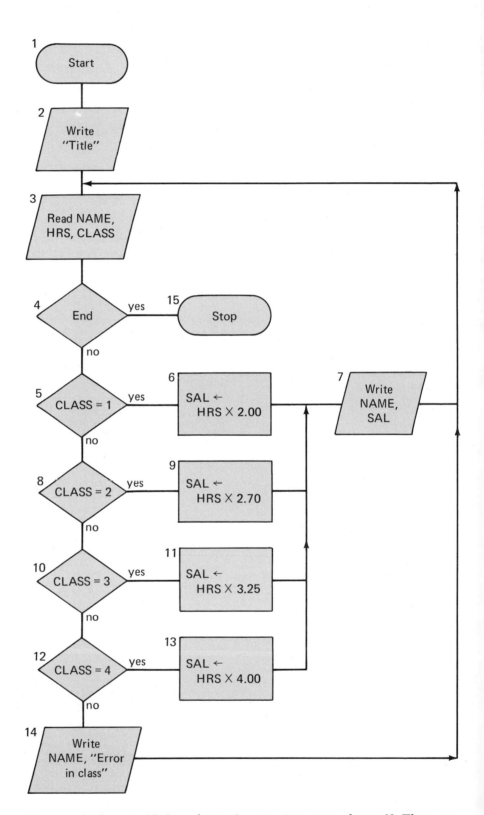

What would happen if the salesmen's pay rates were changed? Then our
flowchart and program no longer would be any good. We would need to
change the places in the program (corresponding to boxes 6, 9, 11, and 13 in
the flowchart) where the salary was computed. The reader might think that

it would be an easy matter to alter a few lines in the program, but it would be better if the program did not need to be altered at all. If this program is to be used by the payroll department, probably no one in the department would be able to change the program. Therefore, it would be necessary to hire a programmer to make the necessary modifications.

A better idea, to make the program more general, would be to punch cards containing the different rates for each class. The program could read the rates and save them in the form of a table in WORKING-STORAGE. Then, if the rates ever changed, we would need new data cards for the rates, but nothing would need to be done to the program. To calculate the salary the program would need to find out which rate to use. It could do this by referring to the table of rates.

Another possibility to consider is a modification to the number of pay classes. Instead of always being 4, they might be increased to 5 or decreased to 3. Our program should allow for a maximum number of classes, say 10. Then if the company wishes to change pay scales, it may do so without creating havoc to the program.

Our data deck will begin with the rate cards followed by the salesmen's payroll cards. Since our program is going to be general, we cannot tell it to read four rate cards just because there happen to be four rates at the time we are writing the program. Instead we must fix our data deck so that it tells the program how many rate cards there are. One way would be to begin the deck with a special card containing the number of rate cards which follow. After the last rate card would be the first salesman's card. This method is all right as long as the first card contains the correct amount; in this case it would be four.

Another method is to include an extra rate card following the last one. If this card contains a number which could never be an actual pay rate, then we can have our program check for this "dummy" rate card. We call it a "dummy" card because it is not part of the actual data but is used to signal the end of the rate cards. The following diagram shows a picture of the deck setup using a $0.00 rate card to separate the four rates from the salesmen's cards.

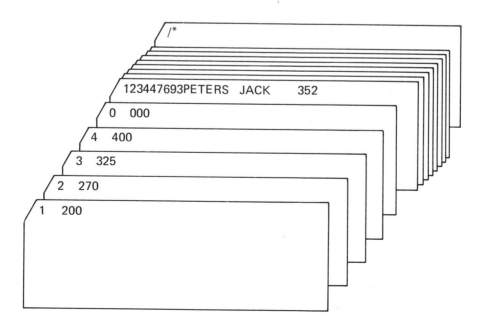

Our program can count the number of rate classes as it is reading the rates into the table in WORKING-STORAGE. When the $0.00 rate card is encountered, the program will know how many rates have been read. This number is stored in the data-name NUM. The flowchart in Figure 8.5 shows the rate card reading and data storage operation.

Figure 8.5 Flowchart of the
Operation to Store Any
Number of Pay Rates
and Classes in a Table

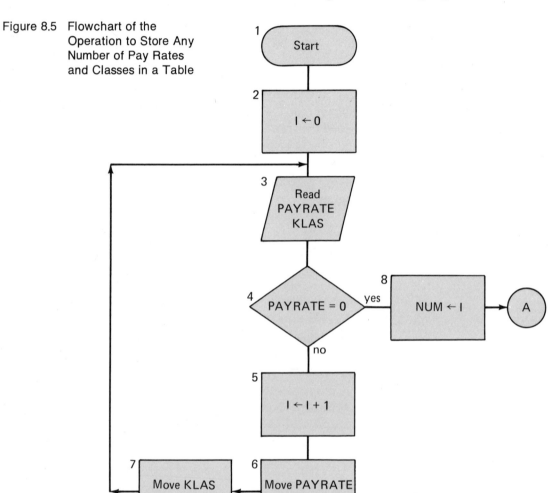

The names RATE and CLAS are subscripted and will be described in the following way in WORKING-STORAGE.

```
01   PAY-RATE-CLASSES.
     03   CLAS OCCURS 10 TIMES PICTURE 99.
     03   RATE OCCURS 10 TIMES PICTURE 9V99.
```

We may picture memory in the following way.

CLAS (1) ☐☐   RATE (1) ☐☐☐

CLAS (2) ☐☐   RATE (2) ☐☐☐

CLAS (3) ☐☐   RATE (3) ☐☐☐
                              ↑

CLAS (4) ☐☐   RATE (4) ☐☐☐
                              ↑

CLAS (5) ☐☐   RATE (5) ☐☐☐
                              ↑

CLAS (6) ☐☐   RATE (6) ☐☐☐
                              ↑

CLAS (7) ☐☐   RATE (7) ☐☐☐
                              ↑

CLAS (8) ☐☐   RATE (8) ☐☐☐
                              ↑

CLAS (9) ☐☐   RATE (9) ☐☐☐
                              ↑

CLAS (10) ☐☐   RATE (10) ☐☐☐
                              ↑

If there are only four classes, then we will not be using all of the memory spaces we saved. This is all right because our program will be able to handle anywhere from one to a maximum of ten classes.

After the rates and classes have been read, our next task is to process the salesmen's cards and to calculate salaries. We begin by reading NAME, HRS, and CLASSS from a card, as shown in the flowchart segment below. If it is the end card, we stop. Otherwise, we shall proceed to compute the salary.

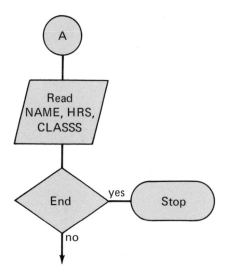

Before we can compute the salary, we will need to know the salesman's hourly rate of pay. We may determine his rate by referring to our PAY-RATE-CLASSES table in WORKING-STORAGE. If his CLASSS is the same as CLAS (1), then his rate is the value of RATE (1). If his CLASSS is equal to the value of CLAS (2), then his rate is the value of RATE (2), and so on. This procedure is shown in the following flowchart.

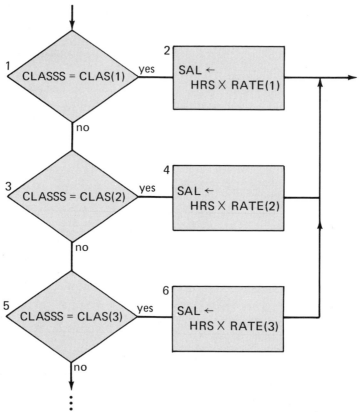

Our flowchart could become very lengthy, so let us see if we can't shorten it in some way. Is there anything similar between boxes 1 and 2 and boxes 3 and 4? Perhaps we could form some sort of loop if we find something which repeats. The only difference between box 1 and box 3 and box 5 is that the subscript of CLAS is different. The subscript begins at 1 and is increasing by 1. Therefore, if we use a data-name instead of a specific number, we will be able to form a loop and shorten our flowchart. We will let the first value of the subscript be 1 and will increase it by 1 each time we go through the loop. Our flowchart for this operation is shown below.

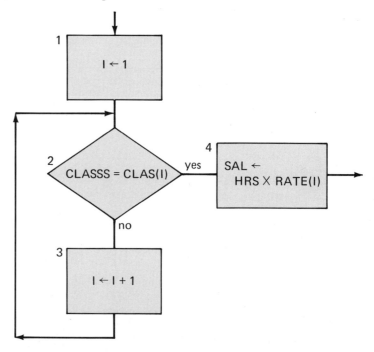

The only thing wrong with the loop that we have just formed is that it might never end. If someone punched a card wrong, we would have a never-ending loop. We should include a test somewhere so that we will have a way out of the loop if the value of I was ever larger than the value of NUM (the number of rate classes). If that happens, we should leave the loop and report that an error has occurred. The following flowchart contains the error reporting step.

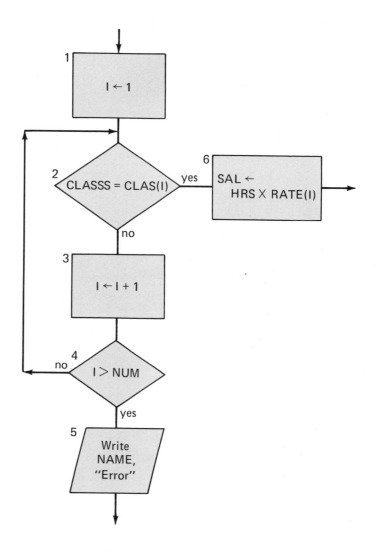

Now that we have computed the salary, we should tie that part of the flow-chart in with the beginning part which read in the class and rate cards (Figure 8.5) and form the complete flowchart shown in Figure 8.6 on page 142.

If the cards containing PAYRATE and KLAS are punched for the current problem in which there were four pay classes, then

Figure 8.6 Final Flowchart to
Compute Salaries from
a Rate and Class Table

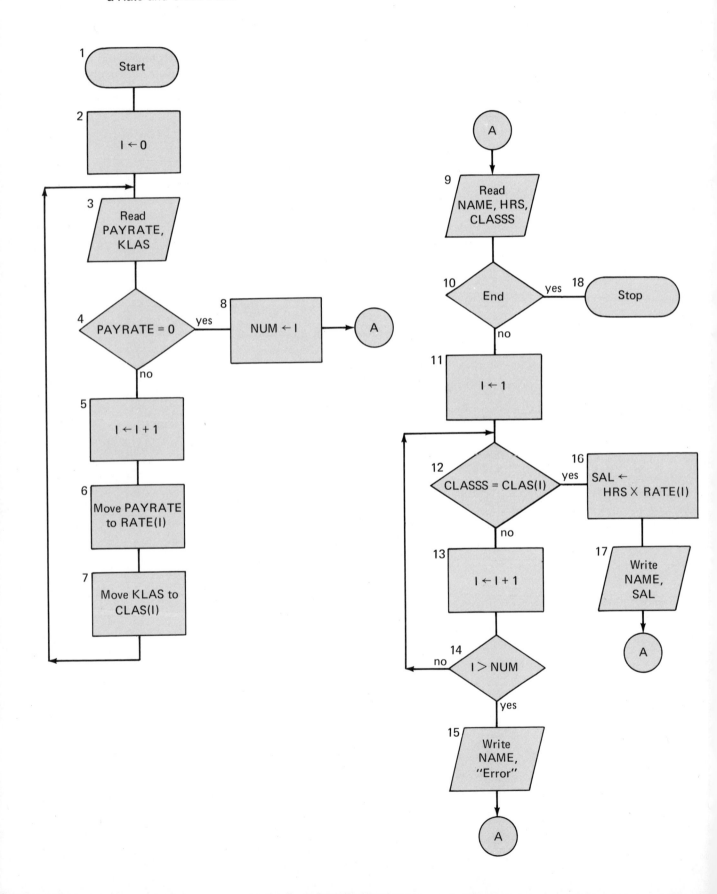

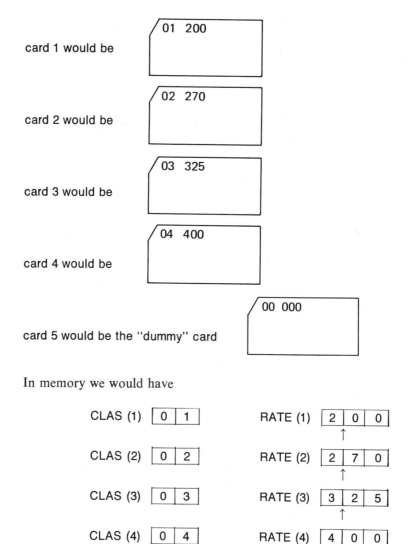

card 1 would be

01 200

card 2 would be

02 270

card 3 would be

03 325

card 4 would be

04 400

card 5 would be the "dummy" card

00 000

In memory we would have

CLAS (1) [0 | 1]   RATE (1) [2 | 0 | 0]

CLAS (2) [0 | 2]   RATE (2) [2 | 7 | 0]

CLAS (3) [0 | 3]   RATE (3) [3 | 2 | 5]

CLAS (4) [0 | 4]   RATE (4) [4 | 0 | 0]

We would have put nothing into CLAS (5) − CLAS (10) or into RATE (5) − RATE (10).

Looking closely at the value of each CLAS and the subscript of each, we realize that the subscript and the corresponding value is always the same. That is, CLAS (1) = 1, CLAS (2) = 2, CLAS (3) = 3, and CLAS (4) = 4. This means that in flowchart box 8 of Figure 8.6 when we read a value for CLASSS, it should be either 1, 2, 3, or 4. If CLASSS = 1, then the rate is RATE (1). If CLASSS = 2, then the rate is RATE (2). Whatever value CLASSS is, the corresponding rate will be RATE (CLASSS).

This fact could shorten our flowchart and program because we would not need to have CLAS in our table in WORKING-STORAGE, nor would we need the loop of boxes 11, 12, and 13. Instead, our flowchart could be the one in Figure 8.7.

Notice the differences between the flowchart in Figure 8.6 and the one in Figure 8.7. The latter one is good *only if* the class is the same number as the subscript of RATE. If our classes had been the letters A, B, C, and D, then we would have had to use the flowchart in Figure 8.6. Also notice box 10 in Figure 8.7. It was included as a safety measure to make sure that the value of CLASSS was between 1 and NUM. It should be read as: Is CLASSS less

Figure 8.7 Flowchart to Compute
Salaries Using Only a
Rate Table

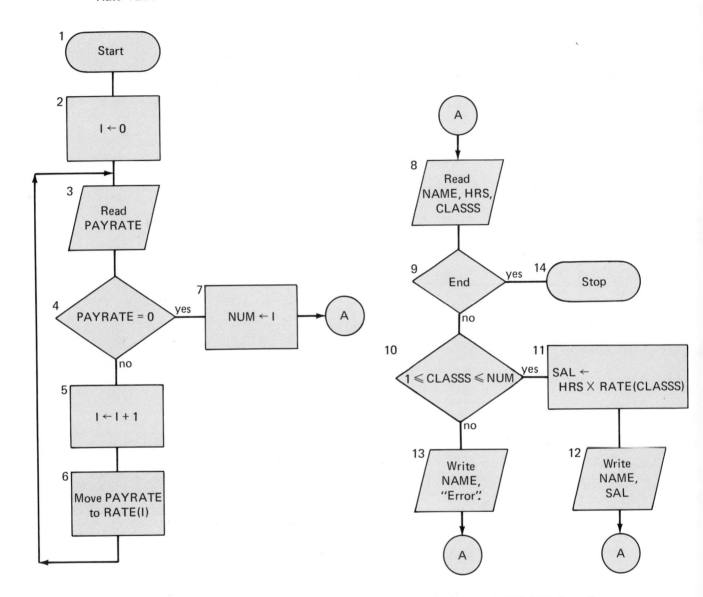

than or equal to NUM and is 1 less than or equal to CLASSS. This is saying
the same thing as is the value of CLASSS between 1 and the value of NUM;
CLASSS could be equal to 1 or NUM or any value in between.

We will now give programs which correspond to both flowcharts. Program
8.1 is a solution to the flowchart in Figure 8.6 and Program 8.2 a solution to
Figure 8.7. Notice that the EMPLOYEE file contains two records: RATE-
CARD and EMP. We include the two 01 record descriptions because there
are two different kinds of cards in the file. Remember that the entire deck of
cards is still *one* file even though it contains *two* types of cards. In paragraph
READ-PAY-CARDS the computer is reading the rate cards; in paragraph
A it is reading the salesmen's cards. We are aware of the difference because
we know how the data deck is set up. But to the computer, the command
READ EMPLOYEE . . . merely tells it to read a card into memory. It does
not know which kind of card to read; it merely takes the next available card

in the deck. Then, when our program mentions PAYRATE, the computer refers to the description of PAYRATE and determines that it is a number in columns 4–6 with an assumed decimal point between columns 4 and 5. On the other hand, if we refer to NAME, the computer looks at the information in columns 10–30 of the read area. Even though there are two 01 levels in the EMPLOYEE file, there is only one area reserved in memory for a record.

Notice other differences and similarities in each program. Which program is better? Which program is shorter? Why was PAYLINE made blank in paragraph A instead of in paragraph STARTOUT? (To shorten both programs in the text, neither prints a title.)

Program 8.1	Program 8.2

```
IDENTIFICATION DIVISION.
PROGRAM-ID.   VERSION-ONE.
ENVIRONMENT DIVISION.
CONFIGURATION SECTION.
SOURCE-COMPUTER.   IBM-360.
OBJECT-COMPUTER.   IBM-360.
INPUT-OUTPUT SECTION.
FILE-CONTROL.
     SELECT EMPLOYEE ASSIGN TO
        SYS005-UR-2540R-S.
     SELECT PAYROLL ASSIGN TO
        SYS006-UR-1403-S.
DATA DIVISION.
FILE SECTION.
FD   EMPLOYEE DATA RECORDS RATECARD
     EMP LABEL RECORDS OMITTED.
01   RATECARD.
     03   KLAS       PICTURE 99.
     03   FILLER     PICTURE X.
     03   PAYRATE    PICTURE 9V99.
     03   FILLER     PICTURE X(74).
01   EMP.
     03   FILLER     PICTURE X(9).
     03   E-NAME     PICTURE A(21).
     03   HRS        PICTURE 99.
     03   CLASSS     PICTURE 9.
     03   FILLER     PICTURE X(47).
FD   PAYROLL DATA RECORD PAYLINE
     LABEL RECORDS OMITTED.
01   PAYLINE.
     03   FILLER     PICTURE X(20).
     03   P-NAME     PICTURE A(21).
     03   FILLER     PICTURE X(10).
     03   SAL        PICTURE $***.99.
     03   MSG        PICTURE X(74).
WORKING-STORAGE SECTION.
77   I              PICTURE 99.
77   NUM            PICTURE 99.
01   PAY-RATE-CLASSES.
     03   CLAS OCCURS 10 TIMES
          PICTURE 99.
     03   RATE OCCURS 10 TIMES
          PICTURE 9V99.
PROCEDURE DIVISION.
STARTOUT.   OPEN INPUT EMPLOYEE.
     OPEN OUTPUT PAYROLL.
     MOVE 0 TO I.
READ-PAY-CARDS.
     READ EMPLOYEE AT END GO TO STOPIT.
```

```
IDENTIFICATION DIVISION.
PROGRAM-ID.   VERSION-TWO.
ENVIRONMENT DIVISION.
CONFIGURATION SECTION.
SOURCE-COMPUTER.   IBM-360.
OBJECT-COMPUTER.   IBM-360.
INPUT-OUTPUT SECTION.
FILE-CONTROL.
     SELECT EMPLOYEE ASSIGN TO
        SYS005-UR-2540R-S.
     SELECT PAYROLL ASSIGN TO
        SYS006-UR-1403-S.
DATA DIVISION.
FILE SECTION.
FD   EMPLOYEE DATA RECORDS RATECARD
     EMP LABEL RECORDS OMITTED.
01   RATECARD.
     03   FILLER     PICTURE XXX.
     03   PAYRATE    PICTURE 9V99.
     03   FILLER     PICTURE X(74).

01   EMP.
     03   FILLER     PICTURE X(9).
     03   E-NAME     PICTURE A(21).
     03   HRS        PICTURE 99.
     03   CLASSS     PICTURE 9.
     03   FILLER     PICTURE X(47).
FD   PAYROLL DATA RECORD PAYLINE
     LABEL RECORDS OMITTED.
01   PAYLINE.
     03   FILLER     PICTURE X(20).
     03   P-NAME     PICTURE A(21).
     03   FILLER     PICTURE X(10).
     03   SAL        PICTURE $***.99.
     03   MSG        PICTURE X(74).
WORKING-STORAGE SECTION.
77   I              PICTURE 99.
77   NUM            PICTURE 99.
01   PAY-RATE-CLASSES.
     03   RATE OCCURS 10 TIMES
          PICTURE 9V99.


PROCEDURE DIVISION.
STARTOUT.   OPEN INPUT EMPLOYEE.
     OPEN OUTPUT PAYROLL.
     MOVE 0 TO I.
READ-PAY-CARDS.
     READ EMPLOYEE AT END GO TO STOPIT.
```

Program 8.1	Program 8.2
``` IF PAYRATE IS EQUAL TO ZERO MOVE I TO NUM GO TO A. ADD 1 TO I. MOVE PAYRATE TO RATE (I). MOVE KLAS TO CLAS (I). GO TO READ-PAY-CARDS. A. READ EMPLOYEE AT END GO TO STOPIT. MOVE SPACE TO PAYLINE. MOVE E-NAME TO P-NAME. MOVE 1 TO I. CHECK-ANOTHER. IF CLASSS IS EQUAL TO CLAS (I) MULTIPLY HRS BY RATE (I) GIVING SAL WRITE PAYLINE AFTER ADVANCING 2 LINES GO TO A. ADD 1 TO I. IF I NOT GREATER THAN NUM GO TO CHECK-ANOTHER. MOVE ZERO TO SAL. MOVE 'ERROR IN CLASS' TO MSG. WRITE PAYLINE AFTER ADVANCING 2 LINES. GO TO A. STOPIT. CLOSE EMPLOYEE PAYROLL. STOP RUN. ```	``` IF PAYRATE IS EQUAL TO ZERO MOVE I TO NUM GO TO A. ADD 1 TO I. MOVE PAYRATE TO RATE (I). GO TO READ-PAY-CARDS. A. READ EMPLOYEE AT END GO TO STOPIT. MOVE SPACE TO PAYLINE. MOVE E-NAME TO P-NAME. IF CLASSS NOT LESS THAN 1 AND CLASSS NOT GREATER THAN NUM MULTIPLY HRS BY RATE (CLASSS) GIVING SAL WRITE PAYLINE AFTER ADVANCING 2 LINES GO TO A. MOVE ZERO TO SAL. MOVE 'ERROR IN CLASS' TO MSG. WRITE PAYLINE AFTER ADVANCING 2 LINES. GO TO A. STOPIT. CLOSE EMPLOYEE PAYROLL. STOP RUN. ```

Summary

Tables such as the one containing the pay rates are often used in programs where it is helpful to store information in memory. In our example, we formed a table of rates from data cards and used that table to calculate an employee's salary. The first solution to the problem searched the pay classes until it had found the correct one. This searching through a group of numbers to find a particular one is called a *table look-up*. The group of related numbers which are saved in memory is called a *table*. Often the elements in a table are subscripted for easy reference.

In the second solution to the problem (Program 8.2) we did not search the rates for the correct one. Instead, we used CLASSS, which was read in, to tell us immediately which RATE to use. In both programs though, PAY-RATE-CLASSES would be considered a table.

Tables are useful in many different types of programs. For example, a program which computes income tax might use a tax table to determine an individual's tax. Programs which keep track of a store's inventory stock could use a table to store such information as the amount on hand, current price, and item number of each item in the store. If a program needs a group of related items which must remain in memory throughout the program's execution, we could make the group into a table and use subscripts to shorten our work.

Exercises

1. Write a description for 100 items named COST (1), COST (2), COST (3), and so on. The last one is named COST (100). Each item is a 5-digit integer.

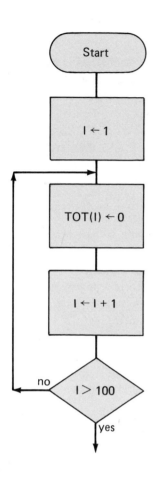

2. Convert the flowchart segment at the left into COBOL. Use paragraph names only where necessary.

3. If A (1) = 30, A (2) = 60, A (3) = 10, A (4) = 100, A (5) = 200, what will be computed as the final value of SUMA?

STARTOUT. MOVE 0 TO SUMA. MOVE 1 TO J.
ADDUP. ADD A (J) TO SUMA.
IF J LESS THAN 5 ADD 1 TO J GO TO ADDUP.

4. Give one reason why one would use subscripted names in a program.

5. Write a description for 50 people's names—NAME (1) through NAME (50). Each name should be divided according to a last name of 15 characters and a first name of 10 characters.

6. Draw a picture which represents the following description and the way the variables would be stored in memory.

```
01   PARTS-TABLE.
     03   ITEM OCCURS 75 TIMES.
          05   PART-NO   PICTURE   9(5).
          05   DESC      PICTURE   A(20).
          05   PRICE     PICTURE   99V99.
```

Programs

1. All the employees at Big H Industries have just taken a personal preference test to see how well they have adapted to working for the company. Currently all the results are on cards; therefore, the management wishes a report printed. The report should contain the following information:

last name
first name
score on preference test

The cards are in the following format:

first name	cols. 1–10
last name	cols. 11–20
score on part 1	21
score on part 2	22
score on part 3	23
.	.
.	.
.	.
score on part 20	40

Write a program which will total the scores on the 20 parts of the test and will write the desired report.

2. At Sunshine State University whenever a student government election is held, a card is punched for each student voting in the election. This card contains the student's name in the following columns

last name   cols. 1–10
first name   11–20

As votes are tabulated, it is necessary to determine the names of any students who voted more than once in the election. This would be an almost impossible task to do by hand, since there may be more than 5000 persons voting. Therefore, it is your assignment to write a program which will read in the students' names (and store them in WORKING-STOR-AGE in an area which has been subscripted), and then will write the names of any people who voted more than once. Start the output on a new page and label it appropriately.

3. As Secret Agent in charge of Data Processing, it is your assignment to write a program which will convert the nation's coded messages into a readable form.

The master deck will consist of 44 cards—each one with a letter, number, or other character (such as $. , / ') punched in column one. The first card will contain the character which corresponds to a code of 01. Card two will contain the character corresponding to a code 02. Card 44 will contain the character corresponding to code 44.

The message cards will contain numbers in columns 1–80. In columns 1–2 there will be a code number; 3–4 another code number, etc. Your program should change these codes into a readable message. There are two types of input:

> 44 cards containing the characters
> any number of cards to be decoded

The output should be a double-spaced printout of the decoded messages.

4. Revise program 6 of section 6.3 so that it checks to see if the same card appears twice in the payroll deck. If it does, print the card.

5. A company is investigating the salaries of its employees to see if there is any discrimination among the salaries for men and women. They want a program which will give the total number of males and the total number of females in each of the following salary brackets.

> 0–$ 3,000/year
> $ 3,001–$ 5,000
> $ 5,001–$ 7,000
> $ 7,001–$10,000
> $10,001–$15,000
> $15,001–$25,000

Also, compute the average male salary and the average female salary.

Input for the program comes from payroll cards. For each employee there is one card in the following format:

name   cols. 1–20
sex   21   (M-male; F-female)
salary   26–30 xxxxx

Output should include the salary bracket totals and the two average salaries.

6. The Payroll Department of the Machine Manufacturing Company needs a program which will process the weekly payroll, computing for each employee:

gross salary
income tax deduction
social security deduction (5.85% of gross salary)
net salary

Input consists of cards. The data deck is organized into two parts—income tax information and employee records. The income tax table is in the following form.

	Income Bracket	1 dependent	2 dep.	3 or more
1	100	.19	.16	.13
2	200	.20	.18	.15
3	250	.21	.19	.16
4	300	.23	.22	.20
.	.	.	.	.
.	.	.	.	.
.	.	.	.	.

The tax table gives the percentage of gross salary which is to be the income tax deduction. For example, an employee is in the first income bracket (line 1) if his weekly salary is less than or equal to the first amount (100). An employee is in the second income bracket if he is not in the first bracket and his salary is less than or equal to the second amount (200). An employee earning 276 per week would be in the 4th income bracket according to the sample tax table illustrated. If he has two dependents, his gross salary should be multiplied by .22 to compute his income tax deduction.

Each line of the income tax table is punched on cards in the following format:

income tax bracket   cols. 1–3   xxx
multiplier for 1 dep.   9–10   .xx
multiplier for 2 dep.   14–15   .xx
multiplier for 3 or more   19–20   .xx

A dummy data card has been placed at the end of the tax table cards; it has an income bracket of 000.

The format of the employee payroll cards is as follows.

name   cols. 1–20
weekly salary   21–25   xxx.xx
number of dependents   31

For output, place an appropriate title at the top of a new page. List below it for each employee: name, gross salary, number of dependents, income tax deduction, social security deduction, and net salary. It would be a good idea to print the income tax table to make sure the program read it correctly.

8.5 The REDEFINES Clause

One way to give values to a table in WORKING-STORAGE is to read the values and move them into the table. Another way is to use VALUE and REDEFINES. For example, suppose we want to set up a table of the months of the year so that MONTH (1) = JANUARY, MONTH (2) = FEBRUARY, and so on. This table might be used by a program which was to convert a numerical month code into the month name. In memory each table entry must be the same size. Since the longest month name (September) is 9 letters, each entry must be 9 characters long. We define the table in two sections: first we define the values and then we tell the compiler that we want the months subscripted. (Each b in the following description denotes a blank space.)

```
01    MONTH-VALUES.
      03    FILLER    PICTURE A(9)    VALUE 'JANUARYbb'.
      03    FILLER    PICTURE A(9)    VALUE 'FEBRUARYb'.
      03    FILLER    PICTURE A(9)    VALUE 'MARCHbbbb'.
      03    FILLER    PICTURE A(9)    VALUE 'APRILbbbb'.
      03    FILLER    PICTURE A(9)    VALUE 'MAYbbbbbb'.
      03    FILLER    PICTURE A(9)    VALUE 'JUNEbbbbb'.
      03    FILLER    PICTURE A(9)    VALUE 'JULYbbbbb'.
      03    FILLER    PICTURE A(9)    VALUE 'AUGUSTbbb'.
      03    FILLER    PICTURE A(9)    VALUE 'SEPTEMBER'.
      03    FILLER    PICTURE A(9)    VALUE 'OCTOBERbb'.
      03    FILLER    PICTURE A(9)    VALUE 'NOVEMBERb'.
      03    FILLER    PICTURE A(9)    VALUE 'DECEMBERb'.
01    MONTH-TABLE REDEFINES MONTH-VALUES.
      03    MONTH OCCURS 12 TIMES PICTURE A(9).
```

The REDEFINES clause tells the compiler that MONTH-TABLE and MONTH-VALUES are two names for the same memory area. Even though both are 01 level entries, no extra memory is set aside for MONTH-TABLE. Because the MONTH-VALUES group does not contain an OCCURS clause, we may use the VALUE phrase to define the twelve months of the year. We did not name the elementary items in MONTH-VALUES because they are named MONTH (1), MONTH (2), and so on by the MONTH-TABLE group.

Using the REDEFINES clause is a good way to set up a table in a program if the table values will never change or if the table is short. Just think how many lines we would need in a program to define a table of the 50 state names. If the table is long, it might be easier to have the program read values and store them in the table.

The general form of the REDEFINES clause is

level number data-name-1 <u>REDEFINES</u> data-name-2

Rules for REDEFINES

1. The level number of data-name-1 and data-name-2 must be the same.
2. This clause may not be used with 01 entries of the FILE SECTION.
3. The storage area defined by data-name-1 and data-name-2 must be the same size.

4. The entries redefining a storage area must immediately follow the entries defining the storage area.

   For example, the 01 MONTH-TABLE above immediately follows the end of the 01 MONTH-VALUES description.

5. The same storage area may be redefined several times. The description defining the storage area must be immediately followed by the descriptions containing the REDEFINES clauses. Each REDEFINES clause must use the name which defined the area.

   For example, the print line OLINE may print in one column either a social security number (SS-NUM), an error message (ERROR-CODE), or an employee number (EMPLOY-NUM). The following description shows how the area originally named SS-NUM may be used for ERROR-CODE or EMPLOY-NUM. Since ENUM is only six digits long, we added a FILLER so that EMPLOY-NUM is the same size as SS-NUM.

```
01    OLINE.
      03    FILLER    PICTURE X(10).
      03    SS-NUM    PICTURE 999B99B9999.
      03    ERROR-CODE    REDEFINES SS-NUM    PICTURE X(11).
      03    EMPLOY-NUM    REDEFINES SS-NUM.
            05    ENUM PICTURE 9(6).
            05    FILLER PICTURE X(5).
            .
            .
            .
```

6. The description of data-name-2 may *not* contain a REDEFINES or an OCCURS clause. Neither may data-name-2 be an elementary item or a subgroup of a group item containing a REDEFINES or an OCCURS clause.

7. The entries in the REDEFINES clause may not contain a VALUE phrase, but the entries defining the area may. For example, the following is allowed.

```
WORKING-STORAGE SECTION.
01    TITLELINE    PICTURE X(132) VALUE SPACES.
01    HEADS REDEFINES TITLELINE.
      03    HEADA    PICTURE X(30).
      03    HEADB    PICTURE X(72).
      03    HEADC    PICTURE X(30).
```

Neither HEADA, HEADB, nor HEADC may contain a VALUE phrase.

Programmers frequently use the REDEFINES clause to set up a table or to use the same area in memory for two different purposes. For example, suppose our print line will contain the following:

name   address   item-ordered   quantity   price   total-price

If an item is out of stock, then the program should not print the total-price, but it should print the message "OUT OF STOCK." We want to use the same column on the line to print a number or to print a phrase. Therefore, we describe this area in the following way.

```
01     PRINT-LINE.
       .
       .
       .
       03    MESSAGE              PICTURE X(12).
       03    TP    REDEFINES MESSAGE.
             05    TOTAL-PRICE    PICTURE $Z,ZZZ.99.
             05    TFILL          PICTURE XXX.
```

Since the size of TOTAL-PRICE is smaller than MESSAGE, we needed to add TFILL and make TOTAL-PRICE part of the group TP. In the PROCEDURE DIVISION we would have the command

```
MOVE 'OUT OF STOCK' TO MESSAGE.
```

if the item ordered was not on hand, and the commands

```
MOVE SPACE TO TFILL.
MULTIPLY QTY BY PRICE GIVING TOTAL-PRICE.
```

if the item was on hand.

Exercises

1. Write a description to set up a table in WORKING-STORAGE. Elements in the table should be named NUM (1), NUM (2), . . . , NUM (9) and should have values ONE, TWO, . . . , NINE respectively.

2. If the following entries appear in a program, draw a picture of the contents of memory after each of the following MOVEs is executed.

```
03    AMT    PICTURE $Z.99.
03    NC REDEFINES AMT    PICTURE X(5).
      . . .
MOVE 1.50 TO AMT.
MOVE 'FREE' TO NC.
```

3. Tell what is wrong with each of the following REDEFINES.

```
FD    CFILE . . .
01    INFO.
      03    ENAME    PICTURE A(20).
      03    ENUM REDEFINES ENAME PICTURE 9(6).
      03    FILLER    PICTURE X(10).
      03    KODE REDEFINES NUM PICTURE X.
      03    NUM       PICTURE 9.
      03    FILLER    PICTURE X(59).
01    STAT REDEFINES INFO.
      .
      .
      .
```

4. Correct the following REDEFINES clause.

```
03    SAL PICTURE $ZZZ.99.
04    MSG REDEFINES SAL PICTURE X(7).
```

Programs

1. The Durable Gas and Electric Company uses punched cards for its bills. When a bill is paid, the date is punched on the card. Write a program which will convert a numerical date such as 040874 into APRIL 8, 1974. The input cards contain

name	cols.	1–20	
amount paid		21–25	xxx.xx
account number		31–37	
date paid		51–56	
(month in 51–52)			
(day in 53–54)			
(year in 55–56)			

   The program should list on one line for each customer: name, amount paid, and date paid. The output should start on a new page with an appropriate title.

2. The U.S. Weather Bureau punches rainfall amounts on cards. Whenever there is no rainfall, they record zeros in columns 1–3. If there is a trace, they punch a T in column 1. Otherwise, they record the amount of rain in columns 1–3 in the form x.xx.

   Write a program which will compute and print the number of days reported, the total rainfall, and the average rainfall. What should your program do if a trace of rain is recorded? Label each value printed.

3. Use the data in program 2 and write a program to find the largest amount of rainfall recorded.

Chapter 9

Techniques for Handling Loops

9.1 Introduction

A program containing subscripted data-names frequently has a loop in which a process is executed repeatedly. In section 9.2 we discuss the PERFORM statement which effectively controls a loop. In section 9.3 we discuss other kinds of loops in which the EXIT statement is needed. Section 9.4 explains nested loops: a situation in which one loop is completely contained within another. For now, let us study a simple loop and see how we can control it with the PERFORM statement.

```
ST. MOVE 1 TO I.
ADD-UP. ADD E (I) TO EST-TOTAL.
    ADD 1 TO I.
    IF I NOT GREATER THAN 10 GO TO ADD-UP.
```

We may use the PERFORM instruction to tell the computer to execute paragraph ADD-UP ten times and thus eliminate the need for the IF statement.

```
ST. MOVE 1 TO I.
    PERFORM ADD-UP 10 TIMES.
      .
      .
      .
ADD-UP. ADD E (I) TO EST-TOTAL.
    ADD 1 TO I.
```

The program segments above accomplish the same purpose. The PERFORM statement instructs the computer to execute paragraph ADD-UP ten times. When it is finished, it goes to the next statement after the PERFORM. If paragraph ADD-UP immediately follows the PERFORM statement, the computer will execute it an eleventh time. If we replaced the ellipses with a GO TO statement, the computer would skip over the ADD-UP paragraph.

Another version of the PERFORM statement[1] can eliminate the need for the MOVE and ADD statements above. For example, we could write

```
ST. PERFORM ADD-UP VARYING I FROM 1 BY 1
    UNTIL I GREATER THAN 10.
      .
      .
      .
ADD-UP. ADD E (I) TO EST-TOTAL.
```

The action of the PERFORM statement is the following:

1. the value of I is set to 1.
2. a test is made: Is I greater than 10? If so, the PERFORM is finished. If not, go on to step 3.
3. paragraph ADD-UP is executed.
4. the value of I is increased by 1.
5. return to step 2.

[1]Not available on low level COBOL.

This program segment, like the other two, is telling the computer to add E (1) to EST-TOTAL, add E (2) to EST-TOTAL, add E (3), and so on. E (10) is the last item added to EST-TOTAL.

Although the PERFORM statement is frequently used in a program containing subscripted data-names, it can also be used to control loops or to simplify a large problem. This is illustrated in examples 4 and 5 of section 9.2 and example 6 in section 9.3.

9.2 The PERFORM Command

The PERFORM statement has several forms.

Form 1: <u>PERFORM</u> procedure-name [<u>THRU</u> procedure-name].

Form 2: <u>PERFORM</u> procedure-name [<u>THRU</u> procedure-name]
$$\begin{Bmatrix} \text{data-name} \\ \text{integer} \end{Bmatrix} \underline{\text{TIMES}}.$$

Form 3:[2] <u>PERFORM</u> procedure-name [<u>THRU</u> procedure-name]
$$\underline{\text{VARYING}} \text{ data-name } \underline{\text{FROM}} \begin{Bmatrix} \text{literal-1} \\ \text{data-name-1} \end{Bmatrix}$$
$$\underline{\text{BY}} \begin{Bmatrix} \text{literal-2} \\ \text{data-name-2} \end{Bmatrix} \underline{\text{UNTIL}} \text{ condition}.$$

The procedure-name is a paragraph name or a section name. The data-name must be an elementary numeric item with no decimal digits. The literal must be a numeric literal with no decimal digits. The condition is any test which could be used in an IF statement.

Rules for the PERFORM Statement

1. The PERFORM statement instructs the computer to begin executing the first statement in the procedure named. After executing the last statement in the procedure, the computer will return to execute the statement following the PERFORM command. If the procedure contains an IF or a GO TO statement which causes the computer to leave the instructions being PERFORMed, the computer will not return to the statement following the PERFORM. For example,

```
PA. PERFORM AB.
    ADD 1 TO OVER.
       .
       .
       .
AB. READ CARD AT END GO TO EC.
    IF AGE LESS THAN 21 GO TO UNDER.
```

When the computer comes to paragraph PA, it finds the instruction PERFORM AB. From there it goes to paragraph AB where it reads a card and checks the age. If the end card is not read and if AGE is 21 or greater, the computer will return to the ADD statement. However, if the

---

[2] This form is not available in low level COBOL.

end card is read or if AGE is less than 21, the computer will go to paragraph EC or UNDER respectively and will not return to the ADD statement.

2. The THRU procedure-name option will cause the computer to execute several paragraphs or several sections. It begins with the first statement of the first procedure and finishes with the last statement in the second procedure named. For example,

PB. PERFORM TST THRU COM.

.
.
.

TST. . . .
CK. . . .
COM. . . .

The computer will execute paragraphs TST, CK, and COM, unless a statement causes the computer to leave one of those paragraphs and not return.

3. Form 1 is the basic PERFORM statement. The statements in the procedure mentioned are executed one time. Then the computer returns to the statement following the PERFORM.

4. In Form 2, the procedure is performed the number of times specified. If an integer is used, it must be positive. If a data-name is used which has a negative or zero value, the computer ignores the PERFORM command and goes to the statement following the PERFORM. While the PERFORM is being executed, the value of the data-name may *not* be changed.

For example,

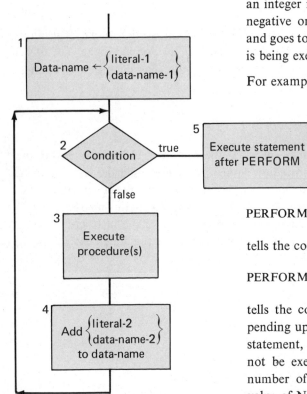

PERFORM ADD-EM 10 TIMES.

tells the computer to execute ADD-EM a total of ten times.

PERFORM READCD N TIMES.

tells the computer to execute READCD a certain number of times depending upon the value of N. When the computer reaches the PERFORM statement, N must have a value. If N is zero or negative, READCD will not be executed. If N is positive, the procedure will be performed the number of times specified. No statement in READCD may change the value of N.

5. In Form 3, the PERFORM statement works as shown in the flowchart at the left.

If the condition is true at the beginning of the PERFORM, the procedures are not executed; the computer goes on to execute the statement after the PERFORM.

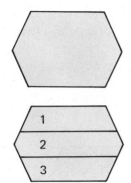

Another way of flowcharting this form of the PERFORM statement is to use the preparation symbol, shown at the left, and divide it into three parts, also shown in the left-hand margin. In part 1 we initialize the data-name; in part 2 we test the condition. If the condition is true, we exit from the PER-FORM loop; if not, we execute the procedure(s) and return to part 3 of the PERFORM to increase our data-name. From part 3 we return to part 2 and test again to see whether or not we continue the PERFORM. Diagrammatically this is shown below.

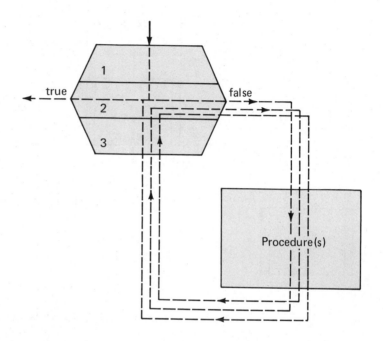

The following flowchart illustrates the way in which form 3 of the PERFORM statement works. In this diagram we have separated the tasks of the PER-FORM statement (box 1) from the procedure(s) executed (box 2).

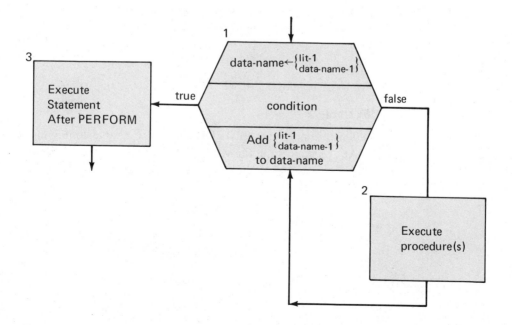

Example 1

Using the PERFORM statement, make each item of a group of subscripted data-names zero.

We may flowchart the procedure in one of two ways.

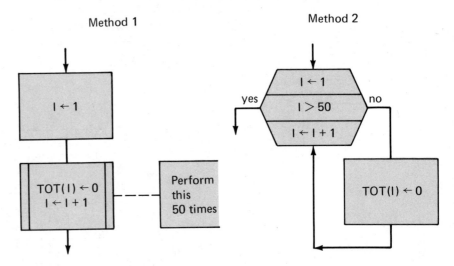

Method 1   Method 2

The flowchart in Method 1 uses the predefined process symbol, shown at left, to show everything which is to be performed 50 times. If just a few instructions are to be executed, we may write them inside the flowchart box. If the procedure is long, we may place them in a separate flowchart. See example 3.

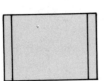

We may convert the above flowcharts into COBOL in the following ways.

```
Method 1: RPT. MOVE 1 TO I.
               PERFORM ZRO 50 TIMES.
               .
               .
               .
          ZRO. MOVE ZERO TO TOT (I).
               ADD 1 TO I.


Method 2: RPT. PERFORM ZRO VARYING I FROM 1 BY 1 UNTIL
               I GREATER THAN 50.
               .
               .
               .
          ZRO. MOVE ZERO TO TOT (I).
```

Example 2

This example uses PERFORM to write a table containing N entries.

At execution time the value of N tells how many entries of the subscripted data-name SCALE there are. Our output should look like the following diagram.

```
SCALE (1) = 37.5
SCALE (2) = 46.1
SCALE (3) = 49.2
     .          .
     .          .
     .          .
```

Two flowcharts for writing the table follow.

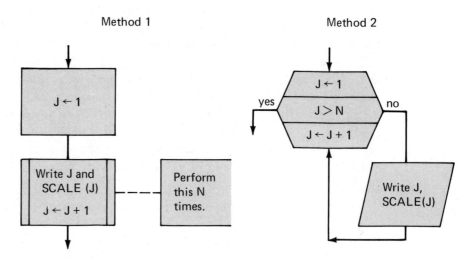

Method 1   Method 2

Let us describe the output line by the following.

```
01   TLINE.
     03   FILLER    PICTURE X(57).
     03   MSA       PICTURE X(7).
     03   JNUM      PICTURE Z9.
     03   MSB       PICTURE X(4).
     03   SVAL      PICTURE ZZZ.9.
     03   FILLER    PICTURE X(57).
```

The flowcharts may be written in COBOL in two ways.

```
Method 1: WRIT. MOVE SPACE TO TLINE.
                MOVE 'SCALEb(' TO MSA.
                MOVE ')b=b' TO MSB.
                MOVE 1 TO J.
                PERFORM WS N TIMES.
                    .
                    .
                    .
          WS. MOVE J TO JNUM.
                MOVE SCALE (J) TO SVAL.
                WRITE TLINE.
                ADD 1 TO J.
```

```
Method 2: WRIT. MOVE SPACE TO TLINE.
                MOVE 'SCALEb(' TO MSA.
                MOVE ')b=b' TO MSB.
                PERFORM WS VARYING J FROM 1 BY 1
                UNTIL J GREATER THAN N.
                    .
                    .
                    .
          WS. MOVE J TO JNUM.
                MOVE SCALE (J) TO SVAL.
                WRITE TLINE.
```

Example 3

This example uses PERFORM to find the largest value in a group of subscripted data-names.

We have 100 numbers named SAL (1), SAL (2), through SAL (100) and want to find the largest. LARG will contain the value of the largest. Our procedure will be to set LARG to the value of SAL (1). Then we compare LARG and SAL (2). If SAL (2) is bigger than LARG, we move SAL (2) into LARG. Then we proceed to compare LARG to SAL (3), SAL (4), and so on. Whenever we find a value which is bigger than our current value of LARG, we move that value into LARG. The following flowcharts illustrate our procedure. Since FIND cannot easily be written as just one flowchart box, we have made a separate flowchart of it. The exit box shows the end of the FIND procedure. There is no loop in FIND because the PERFORM causes FIND to be executed repeatedly 99 times.

Two ways to convert the flowcharts into COBOL follow.

Method 1: INIT. MOVE SAL (1) TO LARG.
           MOVE 2 TO I.
           PERFORM FIND 99 TIMES.
           .
           .
           .

        FIND. IF SAL (I) GREATER THAN LARG MOVE SAL (I) TO LARG.
           ADD 1 TO I.

Method 1

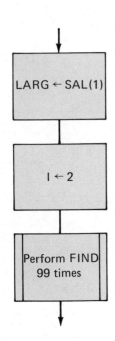

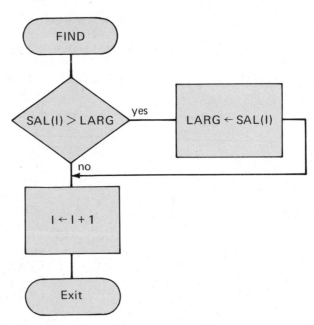

Method 2: INIT. MOVE SAL (1) TO LARG.
           PERFORM FIND VARYING I FROM 2 BY 1 UNTIL I GREATER THAN 100.
           .
           .
           .

        FIND. IF SAL (I) GREATER THAN LARG MOVE SAL (I) TO LARG.

Method 2

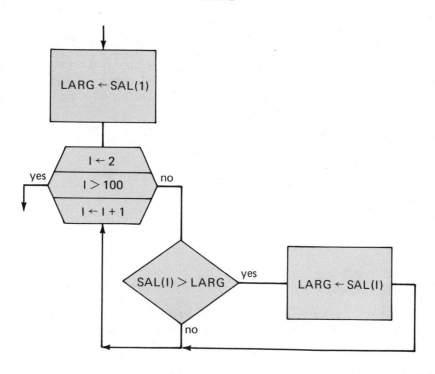

Example 4

Here we use PERFORM to write only 50 lines per page and title every page. The flowchart of our procedure follows.

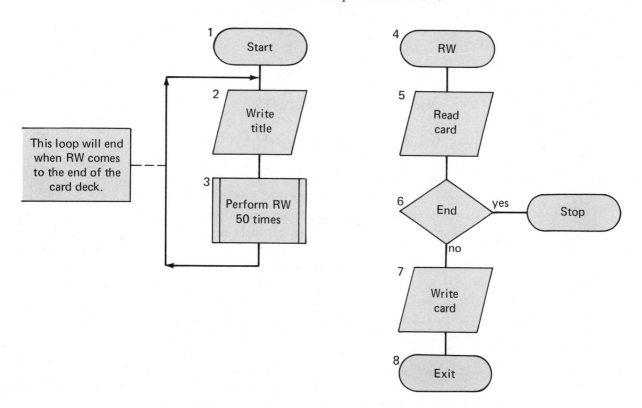

Notice several things about the RW flowchart:

Figure 9.1 Rough Flowchart for a
Payroll Problem

1. instead of a start box, the beginning symbol contains the name RW.
2. the flowchart has a stop and an exit. The stop means stop execution. The exit shows the end of the RW procedure. In this example if we said PERFORM RW one time, the computer would read a card, check for the end, and write the card. There is no loop to make the computer read more than one card. Telling the computer to PERFORM RW 50 TIMES means read and write 50 cards. The loop in the main flowchart will keep the computer executing the PERFORM and hence keep reading cards until it comes to the end.

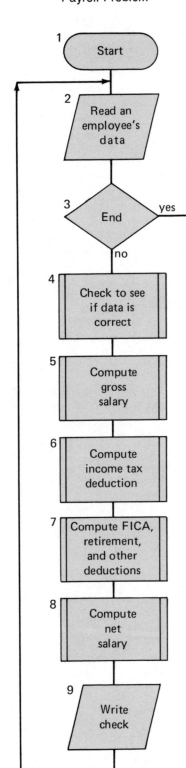

We will write only the PROCEDURE DIVISION for the flowchart.

```
PROCEDURE DIVISION.
INIT. OPEN INPUT CARD-FILE. OPEN OUTPUT PRINTER-FILE.
MAIN. MOVE TITLE TO PLINE.
      WRITE PLINE AFTER NEW-PAGE.
      MOVE SPACE TO PLINE.
      PERFORM RW 50 TIMES.
      GO TO MAIN.
RW. READ CARD-FILE AT END GO TO FNSH.
      MOVE INFO TO CTR.
      WRITE PLINE AFTER ADVANCING 1 LINES.
FNSH. CLOSE CARD-FILE PRINTER-FILE.
      STOP RUN.
```

Each time the computer performs paragraph RW it reads, moves, and writes. When it has executed RW 50 times, the computer returns to the statement immediately following the PERFORM (the GO TO statement). This causes it to write a title on a new page and then perform RW again. Only when the end card is read will the computer go to paragraph FNSH.

Example 5

Here we use the PERFORM to divide a large program into smaller parts to organize it and make it easier to debug. For example, if we were doing a complete payroll program, we might begin our work with a rough flowchart.

We could keep the flowchart in Figure 9.1 as our basic flowchart and make separate flowcharts for each of the procedures in boxes 4–8. This way we are dividing our work into smaller tasks. When we write the program, boxes 4–8 will become PERFORM statements. To test the program we need to check each procedure to see if it is computing the correct results. If procedure 5 does not compute the gross salary correctly, none of the following procedures will get the right answer because their work depends upon the gross salary. To test each procedure we could include DISPLAY statements after each of the PERFORM statements. If we get incorrect values at one point, then we will know which procedure to examine.

9.3 The EXIT Statement

Example 6

In this example we will flowchart the procedure of box 5 in Figure 9.1. To compute gross salary, we assume that we know RATE and HOURS and will pay time and a half for any hours worked over 40. The flowchart for the GS procedure follows.

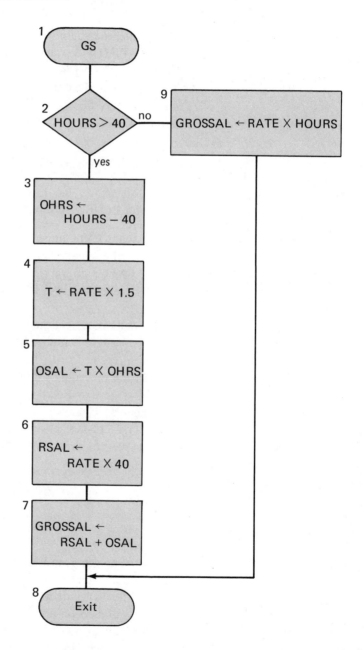

When we convert the procedure into COBOL, we use the EXIT statement to tell the computer that it has reached the end of the GS procedure. Notice that the EXIT is in a separate paragraph.

```
GS. IF HOURS GREATER THAN 40 NEXT SENTENCE
      ELSE GO TO NO-OVER.
```

```
          SUBTRACT 40 FROM HOURS GIVING OHRS.
          MULTIPLY RATE BY 1.5 GIVING T.
          MULTIPLY T BY OHRS GIVING OSAL.
          MULTIPLY RATE BY 40 GIVING RSAL.
          ADD RSAL OSAL GIVING GROSSAL.
          GO TO EXIT-GS.
      NO-OVER. MULTIPLY RATE BY HOURS GIVING GROSSAL.
      EXIT-GS. EXIT.
```

When we finish computing the salary plus overtime in paragraph GS, we want to tell the computer that the procedure is finished. We do this by saying GO TO EXIT-GS, our EXIT paragraph. This also gives us a way to skip over the NO-OVER paragraph which computes salary without overtime. The PERFORM statement to execute this procedure is the following. We must use the THRU option since our procedure includes more than one paragraph.

```
      PERFORM GS THRU EXIT-GS.
```

Rules for the EXIT Statement

1. The word EXIT must appear in a sentence by itself.
2. The EXIT sentence must be the only sentence in a paragraph.
3. The EXIT paragraph may be used to denote the last paragraph in a procedure executed by a PERFORM statement.

Normally the EXIT statement is used to emphasize the end of a procedure. If the procedure contains decisions (IF statements), then an EXIT paragraph may be necessary so that the different paths to follow will all have the same end. In the preceding example EXIT-GS was the end of the procedure. The computer gets to EXIT-GS either from paragraph NO-OVER or from the statement which says GO TO EXIT-GS. There is no need to use the word EXIT in EXIT-GS, but it does point out that this is the end of the GS procedure. We could just as well have named it END-GS or any other valid paragraph-name.

9.4 Nested Loops

Study the flowchart in Figure 9.2. HR (1), HR (2), HR (3), HR (4), and HR (5) are the number of hours worked by an employee on Monday, Tuesday, and so on. The flowchart will find the total number of hours worked on Monday, Tuesday, and so on and will place the answers in T (1), T (2), T (3), T (4), and T (5), respectively.

The flowchart in Figure 9.2 contains three loops: one loop is determined by the PERFORM on box 3, the second is boxes 4–8, and the third is box 7 which also is executed by a PERFORM. The third loop is completely contained inside the second loop. Whenever one loop is surrounded by another loop, the inner loop is said to be *nested*. Nested loops are most easily identified in a flowchart.

Figure 9.2 Flowchart Showing a
Nested Loop

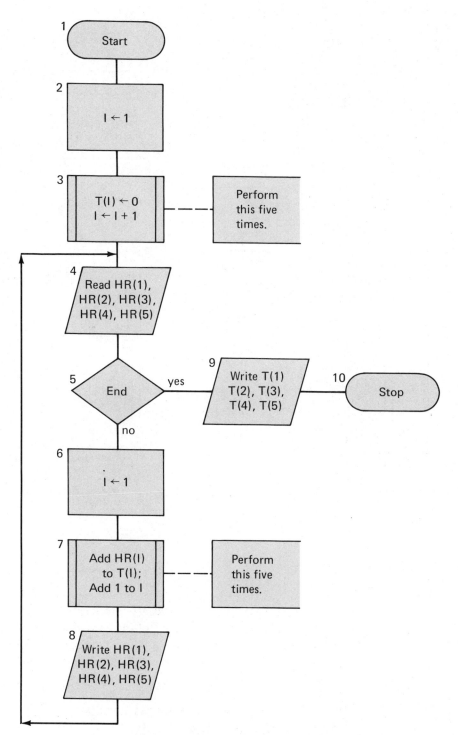

Figure 9.3 is a modification of Figure 9.2. Its only change is that it prints the employees' hours 50 lines to a page. It also titles every page.

Although it is not immediately evident, the flowchart in Figure 9.3 contains nested loops. We may think of box 5 as a loop which controls the TOTAL procedure. It says execute TOTAL repeatedly, and the repetition determines a loop.

Figure 9.3 Expanded Version of
Flowchart 9.2 to Write
50 Lines Per Page

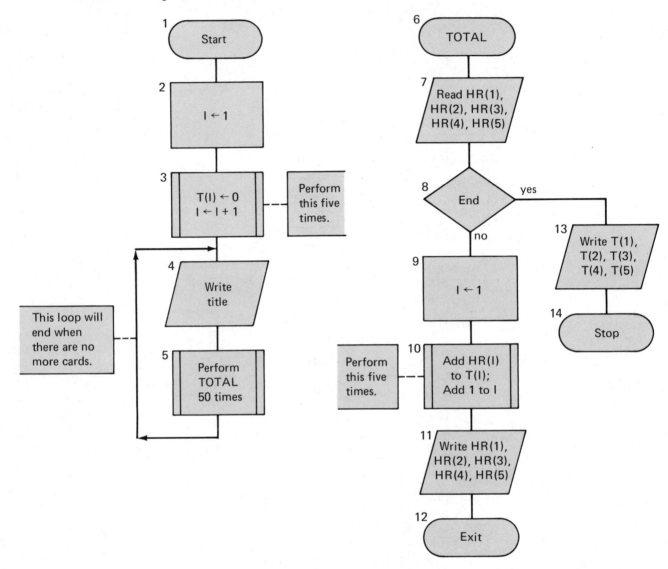

When we convert this flowchart into a COBOL program, we would use PERFORM statements to control the execution of box 3 and box 10. Study the following program segment which corresponds to flowchart boxes 4–14. Paragraph MOVE-EM will move the hours into the output area so they may be printed.

Program 9.1

```
NEW-PAGE. MOVE TITLE TO PRTLINE.
     WRITE PRTLINE AFTER NP.
     PERFORM TOTAL THRU T-EXIT 50 TIMES.
     GO TO NEW-PAGE.
TOTAL. READ EMPLOYEE-HOURS AT END GO TO SUMRY.
     MOVE 1 TO I.
     PERFORM ADD-UP 5 TIMES.
     MOVE 1 TO I.
     PERFORM MOVE-EM 5 TIMES.
     WRITE HOURS AFTER 1 LINES.
```

```
       GO TO T-EXIT.
ADD-UP. ADD HR (I) TO T (I).
       ADD 1 TO I.
MOVE-EM. MOVE HR (I) TO H (I).
       ADD 1 TO I.
T-EXIT. EXIT.
```

What happens when the computer comes to the PERFORM TOTAL THRU T-EXIT 50 TIMES command? It goes to paragraph TOTAL and begins executing the statements there. When it comes to the PERFORM ADD-UP command, it goes to paragraph ADD-UP, adds HR (1) to T (1), makes I = 2, and then continues executing ADD-UP four more times. When it finishes the PERFORM ADD-UP command, the computer returns to the second MOVE 1 TO I statement in paragraph TOTAL. Next the PERFORM MOVE-EM command makes the computer leave paragraph TOTAL, go to paragraph MOVE-EM, execute it five times, and then return to the WRITE statement. When it finally gets to T-EXIT, the procedures in TOTAL THRU T-EXIT have been executed one time. The computer realizes that it must execute the procedures a total of 50 times, so it returns to paragraph TOTAL to begin again. The fiftieth time the computer reaches the EXIT paragraph, it returns to the GO TO NEW-PAGE command because it has completed performing TOTAL THRU T-EXIT 50 times.

At each step along the way, the computer remembers whether or not it is performing a procedure and knows where to return when it finishes. In this example, we have seen how a PERFORM within a PERFORM works. The commands PERFORM ADD-UP and PERFORM MOVE-EM are nested within the PERFORM TOTAL THRU T-EXIT command. Each time the computer executes TOTAL, it performs paragraphs ADD-UP and MOVE-EM and returns to TOTAL. Only when the computer reaches paragraph T-EXIT has it completed one full execution of the TOTAL through T-EXIT procedure.

Rules for Nested PERFORM Commands

1. If a sequence of statements referred to by a PERFORM statement includes another PERFORM statement, the procedures associated with the nested PERFORM must be totally included in or totally excluded from the logical sequence referred to by the first PERFORM.

   For example, in Program 9.1 PERFORM ADD-UP is included within the statements referred to by the PERFORM TOTAL THRU T-EXIT command. Paragraph ADD-UP is totally included in the procedure TOTAL through T-EXIT. Program 9.1 could have been written in the following manner in which paragraphs ADD-UP and MOVE-EM are totally excluded from the procedure TOTAL through T-EXIT. Notice that the GO TO T-EXIT has been omitted.

Program 9.2

```
                  .
                  .
                  .
TOTAL. READ EMPLOYEE-HOURS AT END GO TO SUMRY.
       MOVE 1 TO I.
       PERFORM ADD-UP 5 TIMES.
       MOVE 1 TO I.
```

```
        PERFORM MOVE-EM 5 TIMES.
        WRITE HOURS AFTER 1 LINES.
T-EXIT. EXIT.
ADD-UP. ADD HR (I) TO T (I).
        ADD 1 TO I.
MOVE-EM. MOVE HR (I) TO H (I).
        ADD 1 TO I.
```

An example in which the procedures associated with the nested PER-FORM would *not* be totally included or excluded in the sequence referred to by the first PERFORM is the following.

```
XXX. PERFORM A THRU A-EXIT 5 TIMES.
     GO TO XY.
A.   PERFORM B THRU B-EXIT.
     .
     .
     .

B.   MOVE ZERO TO TOT.
     .
     .
     .

A-EXIT. EXIT.
B-EXIT. EXIT.
```

The procedure **B THRU B-EXIT** should be either inside *or* outside the procedure **A THRU A-EXIT**. In this case the two procedures overlap. We may picture this as

Following are diagrams of the correct inclusion or exclusion of procedures as was done in Programs 9.1 and 9.2 respectively.

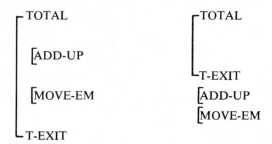

2. A nested PERFORM statement may not have the same exit as the outer PERFORM. For example, the following is *not* allowed.

A.   PERFORM RA THRU RE.

.

.

.

RA. PERFORM RM THRU RE.   *not allowed*

.

.

.

RM.

.

.

.

RE.

Exercises

1. What would be the values computed if the computer executes the following commands?

       MOVE 1 TO I.
       PERFORM INIT 100 TIMES.

       .

       .

       .

  INIT. MOVE I TO NUM (I).
       ADD 1 TO I.

2. Write instructions which will make all elements in the S table (S (1), S (2), . . . , S (50)) have the value zero.

3. Write instructions which will make N (1), N (3), N (5), . . . , N (9) zero and will make N (2), N (4), . . . , N (10) equal to one.

4. If C (1) = 50, C (2) = 10, C (3) = 100, C (4) = 20, and BAL = 500 what will be the final value of BAL? Which paragraph will the computer begin to execute at the conclusion of the following statements?

  A.   MOVE 1 TO I.
       PERFORM SUB 4 TIMES.
  B.   . . .
  SUB. SUBTRACT C (I) FROM BAL.
       IF BAL LESS THAN ZERO GO TO ZB.
       ADD 1 TO I.

5. Use the following values with exercise 4. BAL = 200, C (1) = 50, C (2) = 120, C (3) = 60, C (4) = 10

6. How many paragraphs will be executed if we say PERFORM C1 THRU C3.

```
C1. READ CFILE AT END GO TO C2.
    .
    .
    .
C2. . . .
C3. EXIT.
```

7. How many times will paragraph COMP be executed by each of the following PERFORM statements?

```
PERFORM COMP VARYING N FROM 1 BY 1 UNTIL N IS
   GREATER THAN 20.
PERFORM COMP VARYING N FROM 1 BY 1 UNTIL N IS
   EQUAL TO 20.
PERFORM COMP VARYING N FROM 2 BY 1 UNTIL N IS
   EQUAL TO 20.
```

8. Rewrite the following using a PERFORM statement.

```
ZERO-NUM. MOVE 1 TO NUM.
REP.    MULTIPLY AMT (NUM) BY QTY (NUM) GIVING PRICE.
        ADD PRICE TO TOTAL-PRICE.
        ADD 1 TO NUM.
        IF NUM GREATER THAN 10 GO TO REPORT-IT ELSE
           GO TO REP.
```

9. What is the value of SUMM at the end of each of the following paragraphs?

   a. BEGIN   b. MULT   c. DO-TWO   d. CHNGE

```
WORKING-STORAGE SECTION.
77  SUMM   PICTURE 9999   VALUE ZERO.
77  ONE    PICTURE 9      VALUE 1.
PROCEDURE DIVISION.
BEGIN. PERFORM ADNO.
MULT. PERFORM ADNO 200 TIMES.
DO-TWO. PERFORM ADNO THRU SUBSOME.
CHNGE. PERFORM ADNO VARYING NOTIMES FROM 1 BY 1
   UNTIL NOTIMES IS EQUAL TO 3.
   STOP RUN.
ADNO. ADD ONE TO SUMM.
SUBSOME. SUBTRACT 100 FROM SUMM.
```

10. How many cards will be read by the following statements?

```
START-OUT. OPEN INPUT CARD-FILE.
   PERFORM R 25 TIMES.
R. READ CARD-FILE AT END GO TO C.
NEXTP. . . .
```

Programs

1. Revise one of your previous programs so that it writes only 40 lines on every page and titles every page.

2. Write a program which will allow you to check a data deck by printing every tenth card. Use any cards for input and any format for output.

3. Do any of the program assignments in Chapter 8.

Chapter 10

Advanced Topics

10.1 Introduction

This chapter discusses a variety of topics not normally needed in elementary programs. Section 10.2 discusses how to input and output small amounts of data without having to set up files. Section 10.3 concerns documenting a program. Section 10.4 explains the EXAMINE command which is frequently used in correcting invalid data. Section 10.5 discusses the ALTER statement and the GO TO DEPENDING statement, both of which are ways to alter the path of a program. Section 10.6 lists all the figurative constants available. Section 10.7 describes the use of data-names with two or three subscripts. Section 10.8 discusses qualification and the CORRESPONDING option of the ADD, MOVE, and SUBTRACT statements.

The reader should study these topics whenever needed. All sections are independent and do not have to be covered in any order.

10.2 Input and Output of Small Amounts of Data

Reading and writing data is usually time-consuming for a programmer because he is forced to describe files and get them ready before he can do any input or output. A program with magnetic tape as its primary means of input and output would have tape files. If this program reads one card containing the current date, it would define a card file. Printing one message telling the number of records processed would require a printer file. However, if the program uses the ACCEPT command to read the date card and the DISPLAY command to print the message, it does not need to establish a card file or a printer file. These commands make reading and writing easier, but they should be used sparingly because they are much slower than the READ and WRITE instructions.

The ACCEPT Statement

This command may be used to transfer a small volume of data from an input device into the computer's memory. Frequently the input device is either the card reader or the computer's console. The console has a keyboard similar to a typewriter which a computer operator uses to enter information or instructions into the computer. The two forms of the ACCEPT command are as follows.

Form 1: <u>ACCEPT</u> data-name.

Form 2:[1] <u>ACCEPT</u> data-name [<u>FROM</u> mnemonic-name].

The data-name may be an independent, elementary, or group item described anywhere in the DATA DIVISION. Most compilers put restrictions on the number of characters which may be read into memory at one time.

[1] High level COBOL.

Since there is no standard maximum, we suggest you refer to your manufacturer's reference manual.

Form 1 of the ACCEPT will read data from the computer's standard input device. For most machines this means the card reader. (Check with your installation to be sure.)

The FROM option of form 2 reads data from an input device other than the standard one. The mnemonic-name is a programmer-supplied name given to the device in the SPECIAL-NAMES paragraph of the ENVIRONMENT DIVISION. For example, CONSOLE is the special COBOL word for the computer's console. Writing

SPECIAL-NAMES. CONSOLE IS KEYBOARD.

allows us to write the command

ACCEPT DATE FROM KEYBOARD.

This statement causes the computer to wait until someone enters the date at the console. Some computer centers do not allow operators to type in data for a program, because it wastes too much time. Reading a punched card containing the date would be faster. If a program uses the FROM option of the ACCEPT, it may not be able to READ from the same input device.[2]

Example

```
WORKING-STORAGE SECTION.
77    OPTION        PICTURE XXX.
01    DATE.
      03    MONTH    PICTURE 99.
      03    DAY      PICTURE 99.
      03    YEAR     PICTURE 99.
```

Assuming the computer's standard input device is the card reader, the following commands would read two cards. The contents of columns 1–3 of the first card would go into the memory area named OPTION and columns 1–6 of the second card would go into DATE. The value of MONTH would come from columns 1–2, DAY from columns 3–4, and YEAR from 5–6.

```
ACCEPT OPTION.
ACCEPT DATE.
```

The DISPLAY Statement

This command may be used to write a small amount of data onto an output device. Usually a computer's standard output device is the printer, so a DISPLAY statement will print a line. Another common device is the console which may have a typewriter or a cathode ray tube screen for outputting messages to the operator. A program which accepts data from the console should display instructions before asking the operator to type any information.

The two forms of the DISPLAY statement follow.

Form 1: $\underline{\text{DISPLAY}}$ $\left\{ \begin{matrix} \text{data-name} \\ \text{literal} \end{matrix} \right\}$ $\left[\left\{ \begin{matrix} \text{data-name} \\ \text{literal} \end{matrix} \right\} \cdots \right]$.

[2] Check your computer's reference manual.

$$\text{Form 2:}^3 \ \underline{\text{DISPLAY}} \ \begin{Bmatrix} \text{data-name} \\ \text{literal} \end{Bmatrix} \begin{bmatrix} \begin{Bmatrix} \text{data-name} \\ \text{literal} \end{Bmatrix} \cdots \end{bmatrix}$$

[<u>UPON</u> mnemonic-name].

The data-name may be a group, elementary, or independent item. It may be subscripted. The literal may be numeric or non-numeric. Refer to the manufacturer's reference manual to find out the maximum number of characters which may be displayed in one statement.

Form 1 will print the data on the computer's standard output device, which for most machines is the printer.

The UPON option of form 2 prints information on the output device defined in the SPECIAL-NAMES paragraph of the ENVIRONMENT DIVISION. For example,

SPECIAL-NAMES. CONSOLE IS SCREEN.

gives the programmer-supplied mnemonic-name SCREEN to the computer's console. A command such as the following would write a message to the operator.

DISPLAY 'TURN ON SWITCH 1' UPON SCREEN.

Some compilers will not allow a program to use WRITE and DISPLAY on the same device. Refer to your installation's reference manual for details.

Examples

DISPLAY NUM-RECORDS 'RECORDS PROCESSED'.

will print the value of NUM-RECORDS followed by the words RECORDS PROCESSED.

DISPLAY A.
DISPLAY B.

will print two lines with the value of A on the first and the value of B on the second.

DISPLAY A B.

will print the values of A and B on the same line with *no* spaces in between.

DISPLAY A SPACE B.

will include one space between the value of A and the value of B.

Exercises

1. Describe a card so that the date may be read from it with an ACCEPT command. The numeric date is punched in columns 51–56. What would the ACCEPT command be?

2. How many values may be read with an ACCEPT statement?

³ High level COBOL.

3. Write a DISPLAY statement which will print COUNT = followed by the value of the data-name COUNT.

4. If MAX = 500 and CASE = 50, what will be printed by the following DISPLAY statement?

DISPLAY MAX ' ' CASE.

10.3 Documenting a Program

Program documentation in its simplest form means putting comments in a program to explain what the program does, what it uses for input, and what it outputs. The comments within a program should be general, brief, and concise. Several sentences in the REMARKS paragraph of the IDENTIFICATION DIVISION can explain the purpose of the program. NOTE paragraphs used liberally in the PROCEDURE DIVISION can summarize the purpose of groups of instructions. More formal documentation often required by a company of its programmers includes detailed descriptions and instructions for the running of the program.

The NOTE Sentence

The NOTE sentence allows a programmer to put comments in the PROCEDURE DIVISION. The sentence is printed in the program's listing, but is not compiled.

Form: <u>NOTE</u> sentence. [sentence] . . .

If a NOTE sentence begins a paragraph, the entire paragraph is considered a comment and is ignored by the compiler. If the NOTE sentence is not the first one in a paragraph, the comment ends when the compiler sees the first period after the word NOTE. Therefore, we may include one or more sentences as comments anywhere in the PROCEDURE DIVISION.

Examples

```
PROCEDURE DIVISION.
NOTE-1. NOTE THIS PROGRAM ASSUMES THE DATA IS CODED
     1, 2, 3 OR 4. IF ANY OTHER CODE APPEARS, A MESSAGE
     OF 'INCORRECT CODE' IS PRINTED AND THAT PIECE
     OF DATA IS IGNORED.
INIT. OPEN INPUT DATA-FILE.
          .
          .
          .

COMPUTE-AVG. IF COUNT IS EQUAL TO ZERO GO TO ER-1.
     NOTE THE PROGRAM STOPS THE COMPUTER FROM
          DIVIDING BY ZERO.
     DIVIDE TOTAL BY COUNT GIVING AVERAGE.
```

All the sentences in paragraph NOTE-1 are printed on the program listing but are ignored by the compiler during the compilation process. The computer begins its execution with the OPEN statement in paragraph INIT. In paragraph COMPUTE-AVG the computer executes the IF statement and if it does not go to ER-1, it will continue to divide TOTAL by COUNT. It does nothing to the NOTE sentence.

Suppose, for example, a program contains the following paragraph.

```
COMPUTE-OVERTIME. SUBTRACT 40 FROM HOURS GIVING
    HRS-OVER-40.
    MULTIPLY RATE BY 1.5 GIVING TIME-N-HALF.
    MULTIPLY TIME-N-HALF BY HRS-OVER-40 GIVING
        OVERTIME-PAY.
    MULTIPLY RATE BY 40 GIVING REG-PAY.
    ADD REG-PAY OVERTIME-PAY GIVING GROSS-PAY.
```

Since the programmer used meaningful names, anyone familiar with COBOL should be able to read through the paragraph and figure out that it computes gross salary, paying time and a half for any hours worked over 40. However, it would save time if we inserted the following comment before the COM-PUTE-OVERTIME paragraph.

```
NOTE-3. NOTE THAT AN EMPLOYEE RECEIVES TIME AND A
    HALF FOR ANY HOURS WORKED OVER 40.
```

Formal documentation is often compiled in the form of a manual because it includes so much information about the program. All of the following should be part of this manual.

1. program title
2. programmer's name
3. date of program's completion and date of last revision
4. instructions telling how to run the program, how to set up the data
5. list of control cards
6. sample input data and the output resulting from running the program with the data
7. general flowchart
8. semi-detailed flowcharts of special procedures
9. file descriptions on layout forms
10. instructions to the operator telling which tapes to use (if any), procedures to follow in case of error, average run time, where to deliver output, etc.
11. program listing including a 2 or 3 paragraph description of the program
12. suggestions for future changes and warning about possible trouble areas

After a program is completed, tested, and documented, it may need revision from time to time. There may be errors in the program which do not turn up until a certain set of data is run. New tax laws may require different calculation methods. Management may request new reports printed. Running a program may show that certain features need to be added and others are no longer necessary. Revising programs is such an important task that many companies have full-time employees who do nothing but update programs.

To write programs which will be easy to work with and with less chance for error follow these suggestions:

1. Write one statement per line.
2. Do not split clauses between lines.
3. Indent level numbers in the DATA DIVISION so that the same level numbers are in a column.
4. Align the PICTURE and VALUE clauses so that they are in columns.
5. Do not use special options which only work for a particular computer.

6. Use meaningful names.
7. Begin all data-names belonging to the same file with the same two letters. For example, PY-HOUR and PY-DATE could name items in the PAYROLL file and SY-HOUR and SY-DATE names in the SALARY file.
8. Begin each paragraph name with a number. Use names like 10-START, 20-WRITE-HEADINGS, 30-READ-DATA. If the paragraphs are numbered with ascending numbers, finding a particular paragraph is easier. Also, using numbers like 10, 20, and 30 instead of 1, 2, and 3 leaves room to insert a paragraph between 10 and 20 and keep the numbers in order.
9. Define data-names with a value in the WORKING-STORAGE SECTION and use them in place of numeric literals in the PROCEDURE DIVISION. For example, instead of writing the current interest rate or a salary deduction amount, make these items constants in WORKING-STORAGE. Then if the interest rate changes, we do not need to search the PROCEDURE DIVISION and correct every line which used the interest rate. Our only change would be in the line defining the value of the interest rate.
10. If a code could be A, B, C, or D, check for all four possibilities. Do not test for just A, B, and C, and assume that the code must be a D if it is not one of the first three.
11. Don't do unnecessary computations. For example, to calculate the formulas $A = P(1 + R)$ and $X = M/(1 + R)$, compute $1 + R$ and use that value in both formulas. Don't compute $1 + R$ twice.
12. Use the ROUNDED and SIZE ERROR options only where necessary to save computer time.
13. In a series of IF statements, test for the most likely condition first. For example, in looking for people over 6 feet tall who weigh less than 200 pounds, the first test should see if the person is over 6 feet. If a person is not that tall, it would be unnecessary to check his weight.
14. To avoid termination of the program, test all numeric fields for valid data before doing arithmetic. If the computer finds invalid data, it will stop executing the program unless instructed otherwise.
15. If the input data is supposed to be in a certain order, the program should check for it.

Documentation is an important part of programming. People who will use the program need precise instructions in addition to a working program. Those who must modify a program will find their job easier if the program is well documented.

10.4 The EXAMINE Command

The EXAMINE command has many variations. It can look at the contents of a data item and count the number of occurrences of a particular character or it can change the contents of a data item by replacing one character with another. For example, a numeric area cannot contain blanks. If our data contained blanks instead of zeros in a numeric field, we could use the EXAMINE command to replace the blanks with zeros. The general form of the EXAMINE statement follows.

Form: EXAMINE data-name

$$
\left\{
\begin{array}{l}
\text{TALLYING} \left\{ \begin{array}{l} \text{UNTIL FIRST} \\ \text{ALL} \\ \text{LEADING} \end{array} \right\} \text{literal-1 [REPLACING BY literal-2]} \\
\\
\text{REPLACING} \left\{ \begin{array}{l} \text{ALL} \\ \text{LEADING} \\ \text{[UNTIL] FIRST} \end{array} \right\} \text{literal-3 BY literal-4}
\end{array}
\right\}.
$$

Each literal must be a single character; its class must be consistent with the class of the data-name. The EXAMINE begins with the leftmost character of the data-name and moves from left to right. It ignores the sign of a numeric area.

The TALLYING option counts characters in the item examined and places the total in a special data-name called TALLY. The program does not need to describe TALLY since the compiler takes care of defining it. Each time the EXAMINE command uses the TALLYING option, TALLY is initialized at zero. Therefore, a program should reference TALLY before its value is lost. The three variations of TALLYING work in the following way:

1. UNTIL FIRST counts the number of characters to the left of the first appearance of literal-1.
2. ALL counts the number of times literal-1 appears.
3. LEADING counts the times literal-1 appears in the leftmost portion of the area. Counting stops when a character other than literal-1 is encountered.

The TALLYING option may be used to count certain characters and to replace them with literal-2 if the REPLACING BY is included.

The REPLACING option will change the contents of the data-name examined. Its variations work in the following way:

1. ALL says that each occurrence of literal-3 will be changed to literal-4.
2. LEADING changes only those occurrences of literal-3 which are in the leftmost portion of the data-name. The replacement stops with the first character not equal to literal-3.
3. UNTIL FIRST replaces all characters with literal-4 until literal-3 or the end of the data is encountered.
4. FIRST replaces the first appearance of literal-3 with literal-4.

Examples

EXAMINE WORD TALLYING UNTIL FIRST SPACE.

H	E		I	S	

WORD

TALLY = 2

EXAMINE WORD TALLYING ALL 'E'.

H	E		I	S	

WORD

TALLY = 1

EXAMINE BAL TALLYING LEADING 0.

0	2	5	0	

BAL

TALLY = 1

EXAMINE BAL TALLYING LEADING 0 REPLACING BY '*'.

0	2	5	0

BAL(before)

*	2	5	0

BAL(after)

TALLY = 1

EXAMINE NUM REPLACING ALL SPACE BY 0.

	2	3	

NUM(before)

0	2	3	0

NUM(after)

EXAMINE NUM REPLACING LEADING SPACE BY 0.

	2	3	

NUM(before)

0	2	3	

NUM(after)

EXAMINE MSG REPLACING FIRST SPACE BY '*'.

T	E	N	T	

MSG(before)

T	E	N	T	*

MSG(after)

EXAMINE TXT REPLACING UNTIL FIRST '*' BY SPACE.

H	E	R	E	*

TXT(before)

				*

TXT(after)

EXAMINE can be used to put hyphens in a social security number or to put slashes in a date. For example, suppose SOC-SEC is read as a 9-digit number and DATE is a 6-digit number.

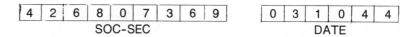

To print the social security number as 426-80-7369 and the date as 03/10/44 we need to move each number into a larger area which will leave room for the hyphens or slashes. Therefore, we define (probably as part of the output line) SOC-SEC-ED with a PICTURE 999B99B9999 and DATE-ED with PICTURE 99B99B99. The commands

```
MOVE SOC-SEC TO SOC-SEC-ED.
EXAMINE SOC-SEC-ED REPLACING ALL SPACE BY '-'.
```

will put hyphens in the social security number, and the commands

```
MOVE DATE TO DATE-ED.
EXAMINE DATE-ED REPLACING ALL SPACE BY '/'.
```

will put slashes in the date.

Exercises

1. Write a statement which will count the number of occurrences of 1's in the contents of the data-name TEST-SCORE.

2. Write statements which will count the number of occurrences of A's and E's in the area named PREFERENCE.

3. Write a statement which will change every comma (,) in MONEY to a decimal point (.).

4. Write a statement which will replace leading blanks in SAL with asterisks (*).

5. Write a statement which will count the number of characters preceding the first period in TEXT.

10.5 Altering the Path of a Program

Normally the computer executes the statements in a program in the order in which they are listed. It proceeds from one sentence to the next and from one paragraph to the next unless a GO TO statement tells it to proceed to another portion of the program. If this happens, we say that the GO TO alters the path of the program. In this section we will study two additional ways to change the sequence in which instructions are executed. The GO TO DE-PENDING command can be thought of as a many branch IF. Its application is somewhat limited, but often it can replace a series of IF statements. The

ALTER command can change a GO TO statement while the program is executing so that it tells the computer to proceed to a different paragraph. Let us study examples to see how we might use each of these statements.

Example Using GO TO DEPENDING

Suppose a program tests for a class of 1, 2, 3, 4, or 5 and goes to paragraphs C-1, C-2, C-3, C-4, or C-5 respectively. The flowchart segment might look like the following.

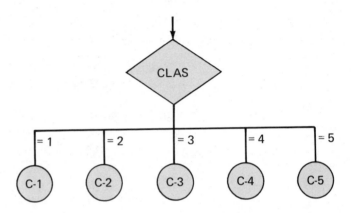

The program could contain either five IF statements testing for each value of CLAS or the following GO TO DEPENDING statement.

GO TO C-1 C-2 C-3 C-4 C-5 DEPENDING ON CLAS.

If the value of CLAS is 1, the computer goes to the first paragraph, C-1. If CLAS is 2, the computer goes to the second paragraph, C-2, and so on. If CLAS is 5, the computer goes to C-5. If CLAS is something other than 1, 2, 3, 4, or 5, the computer proceeds to the statement immediately following the GO TO and the GO TO has no effect.

The GO TO DEPENDING Statement

The general form of the GO TO DEPENDING statement is the following.

Form: GO TO procedure-name-1 [procedure-name-2] . . .
procedure-name-n DEPENDING ON data-name.

The procedure-names are paragraph names or section names. The data-name is an elementary numeric item with no decimal digits. If the value of the data-name is 1, the computer goes to procedure-name-1. If the value of the data-name is 2, the computer goes to procedure-name-2, and so on. If the data-name is not 1, 2, 3, . . . , or n, the GO TO has no effect.

Example Using ALTER

The following program is written for tape input but can be adapted for card input. The first data card contains a code (KODE) which is a T if the input is on tape. If the code is not T, input is assumed to be on cards and the program changes itself so that it will read cards instead of tape.

Initially the program is set up so that at paragraph EVAL-BRANCH it returns to paragraph GET-TAPE to read more tape. If the data is on cards, we want to change the program so that EVAL-BRANCH says GO TO GET-CARD, so it will read cards instead of tape. The ALTER statement in paragraph INIT does just that. Even though the listing of the program reads

    EVAL-BRANCH. GO TO GET-TAPE.

the ALTER statement changes the machine language version of the program and EVAL-BRANCH becomes the GO TO GET-CARD command. If the data is on tape, the computer never executes the ALTER statement and EVAL-BRANCH does not change.

```
PROCEDURE DIVISION.
INIT. OPEN INPUT CARD-FILE. OPEN OUTPUT RPT.
    READ CARD-FILE AT END GO TO NO-DATA.
    IF KODE = 'T' OPEN INPUT TAPE-FILE GO TO GET-TAPE.
    ALTER EVAL-BRANCH TO GET-CARD.
    GO TO GET-CARD.
GET-TAPE. READ TAPE-FILE AT END GO TO END-TAPE.
    MOVE TAPE-REC TO WORK-AREA.
    .
    .
    .
EVAL.
    .
    .
    .
EVAL-BRANCH. GO TO GET-TAPE.
    .
    .
    .
GET-CARD. READ CARD-FILE AT END GO TO END-CARD.
    MOVE CARD-REC TO WORK-AREA.
    GO TO EVAL.
    .
    .
    .
NO-DATA.
    .
    .
    .
```

The ALTER Statement

Form: <u>ALTER</u> procedure-name-1 <u>TO</u> [<u>PROCEED TO</u>] procedure-name-2.

Procedure-name-1 must be the name of a paragraph containing only a GO TO statement without the DEPENDING option. Procedure-name-2 may be the name of a paragraph or a section.

The ALTER statement changes the command in the paragraph named procedure-name-1 so that it becomes GO TO procedure-name-2. Since the change is made during execution, the program listing is the same as it was written. Only the machine language version of the program is different.

Exercises

1. Write statements so that the statement GO TO READ-DATA may be altered to GO TO END-OF-JOB.

2. Write a statement which will go to paragraph UNDER-GRAD if CLAS is equal to 1, 2, 3, or 4, to paragraph GRAD if CLAS is 5, and to SPECIAL-STU if CLAS is 6.

3. Write a statement which will go to paragraph SNGL if DEP is 1 and FSM if DEP is 3, 4, or 5.

4. Write statements which will use the GO TO DEPENDING to go to paragraph A-1 if AGE is between 10 and 19, to A-2 if AGE is between 20 and 29, to A-3 if AGE is between 30 and 39, A-4 if AGE is between 40 and 49, A-5 if AGE is between 50 and 59, and A-6 if AGE is between 60 and 69.

10.6 Figurative Constants

In section 4.6, we discussed two figurative constants SPACE and ZERO. The COBOL compiler recognizes other figurative constants which are listed below. High level COBOL may use any of the spellings of the constants; low level COBOL may use only those in the first column.

Low level	Alternate Spellings (high level)	Meaning
ZERO	ZEROS, ZEROES	The value 0 or the character zero depending upon the PICTURE of the item involved.
SPACE	SPACES	One or more blanks.
HIGH-VALUE	HIGH-VALUES	One or more occurrences of the character which has the highest value on the computer.
LOW-VALUE	LOW-VALUES	One or more occurrences of the character which has the lowest value on the computer.
QUOTE	QUOTES	One or more occurrences of the literal mark (quote mark). The word QUOTE may not be used in place of the literal marks enclosing a non-numeric literal.
not-available	ALL literal	One or more occurrences of the programmer-supplied literal, which may be a non-numeric literal or one of the figurative constants above.

All the characters available on a computer are ordered in what is termed the collating sequence. This sequence is often used in sorting. For example, the collating sequence of one computer is   blank > .) ; + $ * − / , (= ≠ < A B C D E F G H I J K L M N O P Q R] S T U V W X Y Z 0 1 2 3 4 5 6 7 8 9 where 9 has the highest value and blank the lowest value. In this case HIGH-VALUE would be 9 and LOW-VALUE would be the blank. Consult your computer's manual for its particular collating sequence.

Rules for Figurative Constants

1. When a figurative constant is moved into a memory area, the entire area is filled with the constant's character.
2. When a figurative constant is compared to a data-name, the constant is repeated character by character until it is the same size as the data-name.
3. When a figurative constant is used in a DISPLAY or an EXAMINE statement, the constant is one character long. The constant ALL literal may not be used with a DISPLAY or an EXAMINE command.

Examples

In the following let PLACE be described by PICTURE X(7). The b denotes a blank; HIGH-VALUE is 9 and LOW-VALUE is a blank.

Command	Result
MOVE ZERO TO PLACE.	`0 0 0 0 0 0 0` PLACE
MOVE SPACE TO PLACE.	`b b b b b b b` PLACE
MOVE HIGH-VALUE TO PLACE.	`9 9 9 9 9 9 9` PLACE
MOVE LOW-VALUE TO PLACE.	`b b b b b b b` PLACE
MOVE ALL '*-' TO PLACE.	`* - * - * - *` PLACE
DISPLAY 'HE SAID, ' QUOTE 'I AM GOING.' QUOTE.	HE SAID, 'I AM GOING.'

10.7 Data-names with Two and Three Subscripts[4]

In Chapter 8 we saw how useful subscripted data-names are. In some applications we may need to use two or three subscripts on a data-name. If our data is in the form of a rectangular table with rows and columns, we could use two subscripts to refer to each item—one for the row number and another for the column. For example, following is a table showing the percentage of tax to deduct based on the payroll class and the number of dependents claimed.

Number of Dependents

		1	2	3	4	5	6 or more
Payroll Class	1	.18	.16	.15	.14	.13	.12
	2	.20	.19	.18	.16	.15	.14
	3	.23	.22	.21	.19	.17	.16
	4	.28	.26	.24	.22	.21	.19

[4] Available only on high level COBOL.

Knowing the payroll class and number of dependents tells us how much of the salary should be deducted for tax. A person in class 3 with 4 dependents would have 19% of his salary deducted for tax.

In a COBOL program this table would be described in WORKING-STORAGE in the following way:

```
01   TAX-TABLE-1.
     03   PAYROLL-CLASS OCCURS 4 TIMES.
          05   PCT-TAX OCCURS 6 TIMES   PICTURE V99.
```

This description says that there are four payroll classes. In other words, PAYROLL-CLASS is subscripted and the maximum subscript is four. Within each PAYROLL-CLASS there are six items called PCT-TAX. Altogether there are twenty-four (four times six) elements called PCT-TAX and to refer to any one of them we use two subscripts. The first subscript tells the number of the PAYROLL-CLASS and the second subscript tells the number of dependents. Thus, PCT-TAX (2, 3) = .18 according to the table above and PCT-TAX (3, 2) = .22. The maximum value of the second subscript is 6. Therefore, a person in class 4 with 8 dependents would have a percentage rate of PCT-TAX (4, 6).

If we wish to use VALUE to define the tax table in memory and the RE-DEFINES clause to give the table subscripts, we would do it in the following way. We would need to list all 24 values in a program, but have not done so here because of space limitations.

```
01   TAX-TABLE-VALUES.
     03   FILLER   PICTURE V99   VALUE .18.
     03   FILLER   PICTURE V99   VALUE .16.
     03   FILLER   PICTURE V99   VALUE .15.
     03   FILLER   PICTURE V99   VALUE .14.
     03   FILLER   PICTURE V99   VALUE .13.
     03   FILLER   PICTURE V99   VALUE .12.
     03   FILLER   PICTURE V99   VALUE .20.
     03   FILLER   PICTURE V99   VALUE .19.
     03   FILLER   PICTURE V99   VALUE .18.
                      .
                      .
                      .
01   TAX-TABLE-1 REDEFINES TAX-TABLE-VALUES.
     03   PAYROLL-CLASS OCCURS 4 TIMES.
          05   PCT-TAX OCCURS 6 TIMES   PICTURE V99.
```

Three subscripts on a data-name would be useful if we could picture the data as several pages of rectangular tables. For example, if we had a tax table for full-time employees and another table for part-time employees, then we could use three subscripts on PCT-TAX. One subscript would tell the payroll class, another the number of dependents, and the third would designate part-time or full-time employee. We could use a 1 for full-time and a 2 for part-time. For example, PCT-TAX (1, 3, 2) could represent the percentage of salary to deduct from a full-time person in class 3 with 2 dependents. The order in which we write the subscripts is not important, just as long as we are consistent. In this case the meaning of each subscript is the following.

PCT-TAX (part or full-time, payroll-class, dependents)

The description of this table would be

```
01   TAX-TABLE-2.
     03   PART-OR-FULL OCCURS 2 TIMES.
          04   PAYROLL-CLASS OCCURS 4 TIMES.
               05   PCT-TAX OCCURS 6 TIMES   PICTURE V99.
```

Altogether there are forty-eight (2 times 4 times 6) elements named PCT-TAX.

Rules for Data-names with Two or Three Subscripts

1. To describe a name which will have two subscripts use an OCCURS clause on an item which is part of a group containing an OCCURS clause. In the description of TAX-TABLE-1, PCT-TAX contained an OCCURS clause and was part of a group (PAYROLL-CLASS) containing an OCCURS clause.

2. If a data-name which has two subscripts is a group item, then every element in the group has two subscripts. For example,

```
01   A-TABLE.
     03   A-LINE OCCURS 5 TIMES.
          05   PARTS OCCURS 10 TIMES.
               06   PART-NO     PIC 9999.
               06   PART-COST   PIC 99V99.
```

Both PART-NO and PART-COST as well as PARTS have two subscripts.

3. To describe a name which will have three subscripts use an OCCURS clause on an item which is part of a group referenced with two subscripts, as shown in the following example.

```
01   RESERVATIONS.
     03   FLOOR OCCURS 3 TIMES.
          05   AISLE OCCURS 25 TIMES.
               07   SEAT OCCURS 20 TIMES   PIC X.
```

The data-name FLOOR has one subscript, AISLE has two, and SEAT has three.

4. The subscripts are enclosed in parentheses and separated by commas. There must be at least one space between the data-name and the left parenthesis and at least one space after each comma. For example, PART-NO (3, 8) and PCT-TAX (2, 1, 4).

5. The rules for subscripts are the same as those discussed in section 8.3.

Exercises

1. Refer to the description below to tell if there is an item named HRS (8, 1), one named HRS (1, 8). How many items are there named HRS?

```
01    EMPLOYEE-DATA.
   03    INFO OCCURS 1000 TIMES.
      05    NAME    PICTURE A(20).
      05    HRS       OCCURS 7 TIMES    PICTURE 99.
```

2. If

W (1, 1) = 7	W (2, 1) = 5	W (3, 1) = 10
W (1, 2) = 6	W (2, 2) = 6	W (3, 2) = 8
W (1, 3) = 7	W (2, 3) = 8	W (3, 3) = 7
W (1, 4) = 8	W (2, 4) = 7	W (3, 4) = 0
W (1, 5) = 9	W (2, 5) = 7	W (3, 5) = 5

Using the above data in the following program, what will be the values computed for DAY (1), DAY (2), and DAY (3)?

```
BEGIN. MOVE 1 TO J.
NEW-DAY. MOVE 1 TO I.
    MOVE ZERO TO DAY (J).
SUMUP. ADD W (J, I) TO DAY (J).
    ADD 1 TO I.
    IF I NOT GREATER THAN 5 GO TO SUMUP.
    ADD 1 TO J.
    IF J NOT GREATER THAN 3 GO TO NEW-DAY.
```

3. Describe an item named COST so that it will have 2 subscripts. The first subscript has a maximum value of 25; the second a maximum value of 12.

4. An auditorium is divided into 3 levels. Each level contains 25 rows and each row contains 20 seats. Describe the seats in the auditorium using 3 subscripts with the data-name SEAT so that the meaning of the subscript is

SEAT (level, row, seat #)

Programs

1. Write a program which will process reservation requests for the auditorium described in exercise 4 above. Originally no seat is reserved, so the entire SEAT area should be zero or blank (or whatever desired). Each input card contains a level number (col. 1), a row number (cols. 3–4), a seat number (cols. 6–7), and a person's name (cols. 11–30). As a seat is reserved the correct entry in the SEAT table should be changed from 0 to 1. If someone requests a seat which is already reserved, the program should print a message saying that the seat is taken. The output should include the number of seats reserved and a printout of the auditorium by level so that we can see which seats were reserved.

2. Write a program which will use a tax table similar to the one discussed in the text to calculate income tax deduction based on pay class and number of dependents. Input should be in the following form:

name	cols. 1–20	
social security number	21–29	
number of dependents	31	
pay class	33	
salary	36–40	xxx.xx

Output should include name, number of dependents, pay class, gross salary, income tax deduction, and net salary.

3. Write a program which will use a table with two subscripts to represent a piece of paper on which to draw a graph. The dimensions of the table should be something like 50 lines long and 100 characters wide. Each line would represent a line of the page. Initially the table should be blank. The program should place *'s or X's or some character in the appropriate areas of the table to draw a graph. After all points are plotted, print the entire table.

10.8 Qualification and the CORRESPONDING Option[5]

Normally every item in the DATA DIVISION has a unique name. If two or more items have identical names, we must qualify the name so there is no confusion about which memory area we are referencing. Qualification means using a unique group name which will identify the group to which the item belongs. For example, suppose C-REC is a record in the card file and P-REC is a record in our printer file.

```
01   C-REC.
     03   RATE      PICTURE 9V99.
     03   HRS       PICTURE 99.
          .
          .
          .

01   P-REC.
     03   FILLER    PICTURE X(10).
     03   RATE      PICTURE $9.99.
          .
          .
          .
```

In order to compute salary we must say

MULTIPLY RATE OF C-REC BY HRS GIVING SAL.

The phrase OF C-REC qualifies RATE and tells the compiler that we wish to multiply with the RATE which belongs to the card file.

Rules for Qualification

1. A data-name or a condition-name may be qualified in the following way.

$$\begin{Bmatrix} \text{data-name-1} \\ \text{condition-name} \end{Bmatrix} \begin{Bmatrix} \underline{OF} \\ \underline{IN} \end{Bmatrix} \text{data-name-2}$$

Data-name-2 must be a group to which data-name-1 or the condition-name belongs. Data-name-2 must be unique so there is no ambiguity about which item is referenced. The words OF and IN do not affect the qualification; either may be used.

[5] Available only on high level COBOL.

2. If two or more items have identical names, each name must be qualified every time it is referenced in the PROCEDURE DIVISION.

3. A name may be qualified even though it does not need to be.

The CORRESPONDING option, available on the MOVE, ADD, and SUBTRACT commands, makes it advantageous to use identical names on different data items. When properly utilized the CORRESPONDING option can reduce many statements into one.

For example, if we describe C-REC from the card file and P-REC from the printer file as the following:

```
01   C-REC.                              01   P-REC.
     03   NAME    PIC A(20).                  03   FILLER   PIC X(17).
     03   ADRES   PIC X(30).                  03   NAME     PIC A(20).
     03   FONE    PIC X(8).                   03   FILLER   PIC X(10).
     03   FILLER  PIC X(22).                  03   FONE     PIC X(8).
                                              03   FILLER   PIC X(10).
                                              03   ADRES    PIC X(30).
                                              03   FILLER   PIC X(10).
                                              03   DATE     PIC X(10).
                                              03   FILLER   PIC X(17).
```

To move NAME, ADRES, and FONE from C-REC to P-REC we say

    MOVE CORRESPONDING C-REC TO P-REC.

This one statement has the same effect as the following three.

```
MOVE NAME OF C-REC TO NAME OF P-REC.
MOVE ADRES OF C-REC TO ADRES OF P-REC.
MOVE FONE OF C-REC TO FONE OF P-REC.
```

The MOVE CORRESPONDING picks out all the names which appear in both C-REC and P-REC and moves those items from C-REC to P-REC. Since the name DATE does not appear in C-REC nothing is moved into the DATE area in P-REC.

The ADD CORRESPONDING statement will add each elementary item from one group to an elementary item of the same name in another group. The SUBTRACT CORRESPONDING works similarly, except that it subtracts elements of one group from elements of another group.

The general form of these statements is the following.

$$\underline{\text{MOVE}} \left\{ \begin{array}{l} \text{CORRESPONDING} \\ \text{CORR} \end{array} \right\} \text{data-name-1} \ \underline{\text{TO}} \ \text{data-name-2}.$$

$$\underline{\text{ADD}} \left\{ \begin{array}{l} \text{CORRESPONDING} \\ \text{CORR} \end{array} \right\} \text{data-name-1} \ \underline{\text{TO}} \ \text{data-name-2} \ [\underline{\text{ROUNDED}}] \\ [\text{ON} \ \underline{\text{SIZE ERROR}} \ \text{statement} \ . \ . \ . \ ] \ .$$

$$\underline{\text{SUBTRACT}} \left\{ \begin{array}{l} \text{CORRESPONDING} \\ \text{CORR} \end{array} \right\} \text{data-name-1} \ \underline{\text{FROM}} \ \text{data-name-2} \\ [\underline{\text{ROUNDED}}] \ [\text{ON} \ \underline{\text{SIZE ERROR}} \\ \text{statement} \ . \ . \ . \ ] \ .$$

Data-name-1 and data-name-2 must be group names; neither may have a level number 77 or 88. The elementary items which are moved, added, or subtracted are those which have the same name and belong to the same groups (except for data-name-1) as those in data-name-2. In an ADD or SUBTRACT statement all items referenced with the CORRESPONDING option must be numeric.

Example 1

MOVE CORR A TO B.

With the following descriptions of A and B, the items PNO and Y will be moved. PID is not moved since in A it belongs to the P group and in B it does not. X is not moved because there is nothing named X in B. The level numbers and order of the items have no effect on the MOVE.

01	A.				01	B.			
	03	X		PIC X(10).		04	Y		PIC A(30).
	03	P.				04	P.		
		05	PID	PIC XX.			06	PNO	PIC 999.
		05	PNO	PIC 999.			06	PCS	PIC $9.99.
	03	Y		PIC A(30).		04	PID		PIC XX.
	03	FILLER		PIC X(35).		04	FILLER		PIC X(43).

Example 2

ADD CORR C TO TOTS.

The value of NET in C will be added to the value of NET in TOTS; DED in C will be added to DED in TOTS; BONS in C will be added to BONS in TOTS. The results of the addition will be in the items in TOTS. Nothing will happen to NAME since NAME is not a part of TOTS.

01	C.			01	TOTS.	
	03	NET	PIC 9(5).		03	NET	PIC 9(8).
	03	DED	PIC 9(5).		03	DED	PIC 9(8).
	03	BONS	PIC 9(5).		03	BONS	PIC 9(8).
	03	NAME	PIC X(25).			
	03	FILLER	PIC X(40).			

Exercises

1. Tell which items in the following description would be moved by the command

   MOVE CORRESPONDING CENSUS-DATA TO REPORT-LINE.

01	CENSUS-DATA.		01	REPORT-LINE.	
	03	COUNTY	PIC X(15).		03	FILLER	PIC X(10).
	03	TOTALS.			03	COUNTY	PIC X(15).
		05	UNDER-65	PIC 9(5).		03	FILLER	PIC X(10).
		05	OVER-65	PIC 9(5).		03	OVER-65	PIC 9(5).
	03	FILLER	PIC X(55).		03	FILLER	PIC X(92).

2. Describe the PERSONNEL record and PER-TOTALS so we can say

ADD CORRESPONDING PERSONNEL TO PER-TOTALS.

and add the number of employees, number of departments and number of sections to their respective totals. The format of the PERSONNEL record follows.

plant name	cols.	1–10
city		11–25
number of employees		26–30
number of departments		36–37
number of sections		41–43

Chapter 11

Writing Reports

11.1 Introduction

This chapter explains basic concepts in writing reports. Section 11.2 discusses a many-paged report and writing titles on each page. Section 11.3 introduces the idea of a control: an item which determines when certain heading and summary lines are printed. The remaining sections introduce the Report Writer, a special feature of COBOL not available on every computer. However, these sections may be omitted without affecting the study of the remainder of the text. Section 11.4 introduces the Report Writer through a sample program; section 11.5 discusses rules of the Report Writer; and section 11.6 shows the use of controls with Report Writer.

11.2 Writing a Many-paged Report

Normally when we write a program, we title the output and start it on a new page. Then we begin printing line after line of output. Unless we include instructions to tell the computer to begin each page with a title, our output would look like the following diagram.

The printer writes one line after another even across the perforation in the paper. If the pages were separated, they could easily get out of order. **191**

Figure 11.1   Flowchart to Title
Every Page of Output

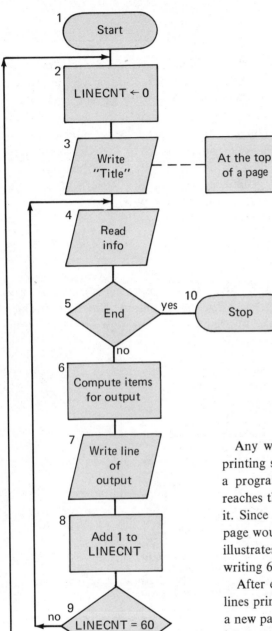

Any written report should have each page numbered and titled, and the printing should stop an inch or so from the bottom of the paper. To do this a program must count the lines as they are written. When the line count reaches the desired maximum, the program should start a new page and title it. Since printer paper contains approximately 66 lines, writing 60 lines per page would leave an inch margin at the bottom. The flowchart in Figure 11.1 illustrates the procedure of counting the lines and starting a new page after writing 60 lines.

After every line is written we add 1 to LINECNT to count the number of lines printed on a page. Whenever LINECNT is 60 we want to put a title on a new page and set the line count back to zero. To number the pages we could have another name such as PAGENUM to count the pages. Its value would be 1 initially and would be increased by 1 after a complete page is written. (See exercise 1.)

11.3 Controls in a Report

A *control* determines when a specific heading or summary line is printed. For example, if we were printing an employee roster listing employees by department, we would want to print the department name at the beginning of each department list. The control would be the department. Whenever it changes, we would print the new department name. In order to tell whether or not the department has changed, we need to save the department's name so that we may compare it to the new department name when it is read. In the flowchart in Figure 11.2 we store the department name and compare it to NEW-DEPT. Initially OLD-DEPT gets its value from the first data card. Whenever the department changes, we write the new name and change the value of OLD-DEPT to the new name.

Figure 11.2   Flowchart to Print Employee Roster by Department

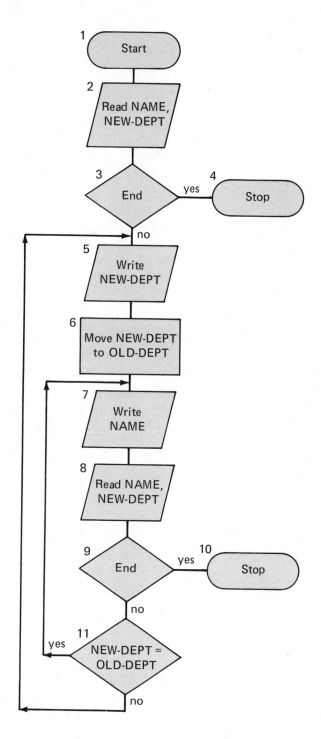

Instead of or in addition to writing headings our task might be to print a line at the end of each department list, telling the number of employees in the department. We would print this line when the department changed and before writing the new department title. Referring to Figure 11.2, we see that this would be included after the "no" branch on box 11. (See exercise 3.)

Figure 11.3 Flowchart to Print
Employee Roster by
Section and
Department

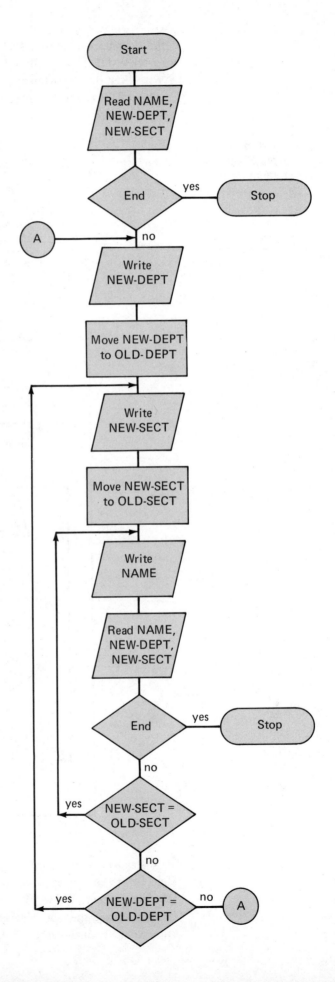

A report may have several controls—one more important than another one. For example, if our employee listing were by department and section with titles for both, the controls would be department and section. Since each department is divided into several sections, department is the *major control* (more important one) and section is the *minor control* (less important one). We would need to modify the flowchart in Figure 11.2 and check for a section change as well as a department change. These additions appear in Figure 11.3 in which OLD-SECT saves the section name.

Since section is the minor control, we must check for it first. If the section has changed we proceed to see if the department has changed. If it has, we print the new department and the new section names. If only the section is different, we print just the section heading.

Exercises

1. Draw a flowchart which will number the pages of a report and will write only 50 lines per page. Each page should be titled.

2. Write a flowchart which will print an inventory report of all the cars owned by Hurts Rent-A-Car Service. Each input card contains a car's make and model, the January 1 mileage, and current mileage. The report should be a listing of the input data followed by a summary page giving the number of cars owned and the total number of miles traveled.

3. Draw a flowchart which will count the number of employees in each department and will list the employees by department. Each total should be printed at the end of the department's list.

4. Design a flowchart which will take the data in exercise 2 and assume that it is organized by make and model. That is, all the cards for one make are grouped together and within that group the models are together. The flowchart should print a report listing the cars, the total number of each model, and the total number of each make.

11.4 Introduction to the Report Writer

An alternate way to do a report is to describe it in the REPORT SECTION and use the COBOL Report Writer. The Report Writer automatically takes care of printing titles, counting lines, numbering pages, moving data, and checking for controls. This feature is not available on all computers because it requires a machine with a large memory. Check with your computer installation to see if you may use the Report Writer. If not, the remainder of the chapter may be omitted since it is not referenced by other portions of the text.

Every report is divided into different parts—headings, footings, and details. A heading is something written at the beginning of a group of output. For example, a page heading goes at the top of every page. Footings are printed at the end of a group of information. If we were to number every page at the bottom, the page number would be in a page footing. Details are the body or main part of a report.

When we set up a report, we should decide what we want the output to look like and then decide whether to use headings, details, and/or footings. To illustrate how the Report Writer works, we will study a sample program which prints an employee roster. On each line we will write an employee's name and social security number. We will title the roster and number every page at the bottom. This means that our report will have a heading (the title), a detail (the line containing an employee's name and social security number), and a footing (the page number). Our data comes from cards in which the name is punched in columns 1–30 and the social security number in columns 31–39.

We begin our program with

```
IDENTIFICATION DIVISION.
PROGRAM-ID. ROSTER.
ENVIRONMENT DIVISION.
CONFIGURATION SECTION.
SOURCE-COMPUTER.    IBM-360.
OBJECT-COMPUTER.    IBM-360.
INPUT-OUTPUT SECTION.
FILE-CONTROL. SELECT EMPLOYEES ASSIGN TO
    SYS005-UR-2540R-S.
    SELECT EMP-ROSTER ASSIGN TO SYS006-UR-1403-S.
DATA DIVISION.
FILE SECTION.
FD    EMPLOYEES DATA RECORD EMP LABEL RECORDS
        OMITTED.
01    EMP.
    03    NAME     PICTURE A(30).
    03    SS       PICTURE 9(9).
    03    FILLER   PICTURE X(41).
FD    EMP-ROSTER LABEL RECORDS OMITTED REPORT LISTING.
```

We have named our report LISTING and have said that it will be written on the printer file named EMP-ROSTER. We have no 01 levels beneath the file description of EMP-ROSTER. All our output is described in the REPORT SECTION. We will discuss each part as it is written. The REPORT SECTION follows the end of the WORKING-STORAGE SECTION. Since there is no WORKING-STORAGE SECTION in this program, the REPORT SECTION follows the FILE SECTION.

```
REPORT SECTION.
RD    LISTING PAGE LIMIT 60 LINES LAST DETAIL 58.
```

The letters RD stand for the words Report Description and the phrase PAGE LIMIT 60 LINES means that nothing will be written after the 60th line on the page. The last detail line will be written on line 58. This leaves room for our page number after line 58.

```
01    TYPE PAGE HEADING NEXT GROUP PLUS 2.
    03    LINE 1.
        05    COLUMN 59 PICTURE X(15) VALUE
                'EMPLOYEE ROSTER'.
    03    LINE 4.
        05    COLUMN 41 PICTURE X(4) VALUE 'NAME'.
        05    COLUMN 75 PICTURE X(22)
                VALUE 'SOCIAL SECURITY NUMBER'.
```

The phrase 01 TYPE PAGE HEADING says that this group is the page heading which will be written at the top of every page. The phrase NEXT GROUP PLUS 2 tells the printer to space 2 lines down the page after writing the last line of the heading. This will leave some room between the column headings NAME and SOCIAL SECURITY NUMBER and the first employee listed. Our page heading consists of two parts: the 03 level groups. The first group is actually the title EMPLOYEE ROSTER and will be written on the first line of the page. The title will begin in column 59 and will be 15 characters long. The next group is composed of two parts and will be written on line 4, the fourth line of the page. This means that lines 2 and 3 will be blank. Line 4 contains the column heading NAME, which begins in column 41, and the column heading SOCIAL SECURITY NUMBER, which starts in column 75. Our page heading is actually two printed lines. (It could have been any number of lines.) We now proceed to describe our detail line containing an employee's name and social security number.

```
01    E-LINE TYPE DETAIL LINE PLUS 1.
03    COLUMN 41 PICTURE A(30) SOURCE NAME.
03    COLUMN 81 PICTURE 999B99B9999 SOURCE SS.
```

The name E-LINE is the name of our detail line. When we wish to print this line we will say GENERATE E-LINE. We do not need to name headings or footings because the Report Writer will print them automatically at the proper time. Since we write the phrase LINE PLUS 1 at the 01 level we are telling the computer that the entire detail will be written on a single line, one line down from the last printed line of the report. In other words, LINE PLUS 1 means single space. The detail has two parts, one beginning in column 41 and the other in column 81. When we tell the computer to print this line, it first must get the data to print. The phrase SOURCE NAME instructs the computer to move the contents of NAME (which is part of the file EMPLOYEES) into this area starting in column 41. Similarly, SOURCE SS tells the computer to get the social security number, edit it, and start it in column 81 of the line. Notice how blanks will be inserted into the social security number to make it more readable.

The third type of line which the report will print is a page footing. It is described by

```
01    TYPE PAGE FOOTING LINE PLUS 2.
03    COLUMN 63    PICTURE X(4)    VALUE 'PAGE'.
03    COLUMN 68    PICTURE ZZ    SOURCE PAGE-COUNTER.
```

The phrase LINE PLUS 2 says that the footing will be written two lines below the last detail line. Since we said in the RD that the last detail goes on line 58, the page footing will be on line 60. The word PAGE will be written along with the page number. Report Writer has a special area named PAGE-COUNTER in which it counts the pages as they are written. PAGE-COUNTER does not need to be described anywhere in the program; we merely need to use it. It is automatically set to one when the report begins and is increased by one at the end of every page. We have edited PAGE-COUNTER in this footing so that it will print without leading zeros.

Now we proceed to give the instructions to the computer. Our flowchart is basically the one in Figure 11.1. There is one difference however. We will not be giving instructions for the computer to use LINECNT to determine when to start a new page. The Report Writer will take care of this for us.

There are only three commands to use with the Report Writer: INITIATE, GENERATE, and TERMINATE. GENERATE tells the Report Writer to write a detail line. INITIATE gets the report ready and sets the PAGE-COUNTER to one. TERMINATE finishes the report and writes any final footings. Page headings and footings are written automatically at the top and bottom of every page. Let us examine the PROCEDURE DIVISION of our program and see how these commands are used.

```
PROCEDURE DIVISION.
INIT. OPEN INPUT EMPLOYEES. OPEN OUTPUT EMP-ROSTER.
    INITIATE LISTING.
READ-WRITE-LOOP. READ EMPLOYEES AT END GO TO
    FINISH-UP.
    GENERATE E-LINE.
    GO TO READ-WRITE-LOOP.
FINISH-UP. TERMINATE LISTING.
    CLOSE EMPLOYEES EMP-ROSTER.
    STOP RUN.
```

We have very few instructions in the program. First we open the files and then initiate the report by saying INITIATE LISTING. The first time the computer executes the GENERATE command it will write the title and column headings. Then it will move the contents of NAME and SS into the output area and write the line. We do not need to include any MOVEs in our program to get data printed. After E-LINE is written, the computer checks to see if it has reached line 58. If it has, then it will write the page footing, start a new page and title it. If not, it will write only the detail line. When we reach the end of the employee file we TERMINATE LISTING. This will write the page number at the bottom of the last page. Then we close our files and stop the computer. The complete program follows.

```
IDENTIFICATION DIVISION.
PROGRAM-ID. ROSTER.
ENVIRONMENT DIVISION.
CONFIGURATION SECTION.
SOURCE-COMPUTER.    IBM-360.
OBJECT-COMPUTER.    IBM-360.
INPUT-OUTPUT SECTION.
FILE-CONTROL. SELECT EMPLOYEES ASSIGN TO
    SYS005-UR-2540R-S.
    SELECT EMP-ROSTER ASSIGN TO SYS006-UR-1403-S.
DATA DIVISION.
FILE SECTION.
FD    EMPLOYEES DATA RECORD EMP LABEL RECORDS
        OMITTED.
01    EMP.
        03    NAME      PICTURE A(30).
        03    SS        PICTURE 9(9).
        03    FILLER    PICTURE X(41).
FD    EMP-ROSTER LABEL RECORDS OMITTED REPORT LISTING.
REPORT SECTION.
RD    LISTING PAGE LIMIT 60 LINES LAST DETAIL 58.
01    TYPE PAGE HEADING NEXT GROUP PLUS 2.
        03    LINE 1.
            05    COLUMN 59    PICTURE X(15)    VALUE
                'EMPLOYEE ROSTER'.
```

```
        03   LINE 4.
             05   COLUMN 41   PICTURE X(4)     VALUE 'NAME'.
             05   COLUMN 75   PICTURE X(22)
                       VALUE 'SOCIAL SECURITY NUMBER'.
01    E-LINE TYPE DETAIL LINE PLUS 1.
      03   COLUMN 41   PICTURE A(30)        SOURCE NAME.
      03   COLUMN 81   PICTURE 999B99B9999  SOURCE SS.
01    TYPE PAGE FOOTING LINE PLUS 2.
      03   COLUMN 63   PICTURE X(4)   VALUE 'PAGE'.
      03   COLUMN 68   PICTURE ZZ     SOURCE
                                       PAGE-COUNTER.
PROCEDURE DIVISION.
INIT. OPEN INPUT EMPLOYEES. OPEN OUTPUT EMP-ROSTER.
      INITIATE LISTING.
READ-WRITE-LOOP. READ EMPLOYEES AT END GO TO
      FINISH-UP.
      GENERATE E-LINE.
      GO TO READ-WRITE-LOOP.
FINISH-UP. TERMINATE LISTING.
      CLOSE EMPLOYEES EMP-ROSTER.
      STOP RUN.
```

11.5 Guidelines for Using the Report Writer

The Report Description

The first item in the REPORT SECTION is the report description (RD). It names the report and gives information about the layout of each page. The general form of the RD is the following.

$$\text{RD report-name} \left[\begin{Bmatrix} \text{CONTROL IS} \\ \text{CONTROLS ARE} \end{Bmatrix} \begin{Bmatrix} \text{FINAL} \\ \text{data-name} \ldots \\ \text{FINAL data-name} \ldots \end{Bmatrix} \right]$$

$$\left[\text{PAGE} \begin{Bmatrix} \text{LIMIT IS} \\ \text{LIMITS ARE} \end{Bmatrix} \text{integer} \begin{Bmatrix} \text{LINE} \\ \text{LINES} \end{Bmatrix} \right]$$

[HEADING integer] [FIRST DETAIL integer]

[LAST DETAIL integer] [FOOTING integer].

The CONTROL phrase is used if there are CONTROL HEADINGs or CONTROL FOOTINGs in the report. This phrase will be explained in section 11.6 since it is available only with high level COBOL.

The PAGE LIMIT phrase tells the number of the last line to be printed on a page. This phrase must be included if the report has headings or footings or uses the phrase LINE NUMBER or NEXT GROUP. Lines are numbered consecutively from the top of a page. Therefore, PAGE LIMIT 33 LINES means that the report would be written on the top half of each sheet of paper.

The HEADING phrase specifies the first line on which a heading can be printed. The number of the line must be greater than or equal to 1. If no HEADING is mentioned, the Report Writer assumes HEADING 1.

The FIRST DETAIL phrase tells the first line on which to write a detail. If this phrase is omitted, then the first detail may be written on or after the line number in the HEADING phrase.

The LAST DETAIL phrase tells the number of the last line on which details may be written. This phrase must be included if the report has any footings. If the phrase is omitted, the line number of the first detail is the same as the number specified in the FOOTING phrase.

The FOOTING phrase tells the number of the first line on which a page footing may be written and last line on which a control footing may be written. If omitted, the line number is the same as the number specified in the LAST DETAIL phrase. If both are omitted, the line number is the one specified in PAGE LIMITS.

Example

RD   A-REPORT PAGE LIMIT 60 LINES HEADING 6 FIRST
         DETAIL 10 LAST DETAIL 58 FOOTING 59.

The name of the report is A-REPORT and it will be written on lines 1–60 of each page. This **RD** determines the general layout of the report in the following way:

Report group	May be written on lines	Lines determined by
REPORT HEADING, REPORT FOOTING	6–60	HEADING—PAGE LIMIT
PAGE HEADING	6–10	HEADING—FIRST DETAIL
DETAIL, CONTROL HEADING	10–58	FIRST DETAIL—LAST DETAIL
CONTROL FOOTING	10–59	FIRST DETAIL—FOOTING
PAGE FOOTING	59–60	FOOTING—PAGE LIMIT

The 01 Level

Each part of a report—heading, footing, or detail—is described in a separate group using level numbers. The 01 level tells the type of the group: PAGE HEADING, PAGE FOOTING, DETAIL, and so on. Also, it may specify on what line the entire group will be written and any spacing desired after the group is written. A group may consist of several printed lines.

The general form of the 01 level is the following.

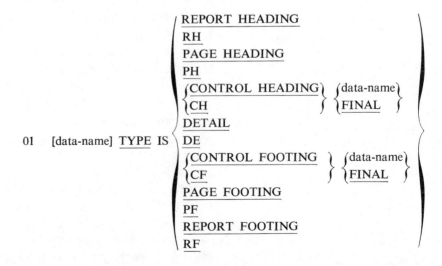

01   [data-name] TYPE IS
      REPORT HEADING
      RH
      PAGE HEADING
      PH
      {CONTROL HEADING / CH} {data-name / FINAL}
      DETAIL
      DE
      {CONTROL FOOTING / CF} {data-name / FINAL}
      PAGE FOOTING
      PF
      REPORT FOOTING
      RF

$$\left[\underline{\text{LINE}} \text{ NUMBER } \begin{Bmatrix} \text{integer} \\ \underline{\text{PLUS}} \text{ integer} \\ \underline{\text{NEXT PAGE}} \end{Bmatrix} \right]$$

$$\left[\underline{\text{NEXT GROUP}} \text{ IS } \begin{Bmatrix} \text{integer} \\ \underline{\text{PLUS}} \text{ integer} \\ \underline{\text{NEXT PAGE}} \end{Bmatrix} \right].$$

All integers used must be positive. The only required phrase at the 01 level is TYPE. We may use abbreviations such as RH instead of the words RE-PORT HEADING.

Only DETAIL lines need to have a data-name at the 01 level, because they are referred to by the GENERATE command. Headings and footings may have data-names, but it is not necessary because they will be printed automatically.

If LINE is used at the 01 level, then everything in the group must be written on the line specified. If the group contains several lines, then LINE must be used in the first level beneath the 01 level. Using an integer in the LINE phrase tells exactly on what line this part of the report will be written. This line must be in the range specified by PAGE LIMITS. The PLUS integer phrase tells the computer to write this group so many lines down from the last line written. The phrase NEXT PAGE says go to a new page; it may be used only at the 01 level.

The NEXT GROUP phrase tells the computer how many lines to space after writing this part of the report and before writing the next group. Frequently NEXT GROUP is used to leave several blank lines between a title and the first detail line. It may be used only at the 01 level.

If the 01 level is not subdivided, then it must contain the COLUMN phrase, a PICTURE phrase, and either the SOURCE or VALUE phrase. These are explained below. For example, the following description tells the Report Writer to center the title ABC MANUFACTURING COMPANY on every page.

```
01    TYPE PH LINE 3 COLUMN 53 PICTURE A(25) VALUE
      'ABC MANUFACTURING COMPANY'.
```

This title would be written on line 3 and would start in column 53. There is no need to use FILLER to center the title. Instead, we specify the column in which to start the title.

If we wanted to have a heading which writes a title and column headings (two lines in one page heading) we would need to enlarge the PH and sub-divide it into several subgroups containing elementary items. Refer to the section immediately following for an example of this.

Describing Items Which Are Part of a Group

The general form of any item which is part of a group is

nn   [data-name] [$\underline{\text{COLUMN}}$ NUMBER IS integer]

$$\left[\underline{\text{LINE}} \text{ NUMBER IS } \begin{Bmatrix} \text{integer} \\ \underline{\text{PLUS}} \text{ integer} \\ \underline{\text{NEXT PAGE}} \end{Bmatrix} \right]$$

$$\left[\left\{ \begin{array}{l} \underline{SOURCE} \ IS \left\{ \begin{array}{l} \text{data-name} \\ \underline{LINE\text{-}COUNTER} \\ \underline{PAGE\text{-}COUNTER} \end{array} \right\} \\ \underline{SUM} \ \text{data-name} \end{array} \right\} \right]$$

$$[\underline{VALUE} \ IS \ \text{literal}]$$

$$\left[\left\{ \begin{array}{l} \underline{PICTURE} \\ \underline{PIC} \end{array} \right\} \ IS \ \text{character-string} \right].$$

where

nn   is some level number from 02 through 10 (02 through 49 for high level
            COBOL). It is not necessary to name this item.

integer   is positive.

Items to be written on one line must be listed in the group in the order in which they are to be written. In other words, the column numbers of the items must be in ascending order. If COLUMN NUMBER is specified, then PICTURE and either SOURCE or VALUE must also be included. COLUMN NUMBER may be used only on elementary items.

The value of LINE-COUNTER is the number of the last line printed or the number of the last line skipped. The Report Writer uses LINE-COUNTER to determine when to write the PAGE HEADING and PAGE FOOTING. It is initially zero and is automatically incremented each time a line is written or skipped. It is reset to zero whenever the end of a page is reached.

PAGE-COUNTER is initialized at one and is increased by one at the end of every page (after printing a PAGE FOOTING but before printing a PAGE HEADING). If PAGE-COUNTER is referenced in more than one part of the report, the size of the item must be the same in every place. Also, the size must be large enough to accommodate the page number.

Example

```
01    TYPE PH NEXT GROUP PLUS 1.
    03    LINE 3.
        05    COLUMN 56    PICTURE A(25)
                    VALUE 'ABC MANUFACTURING COMPANY'.
    03    LINE 6.
        05    COLUMN 40    PICTURE XXXX    VALUE 'ITEM'.
        05    COLUMN 96    PICTURE X(5)    VALUE 'PRICE'.
```

This report group says that the PAGE HEADING is composed of two parts—a title to be written on line 3 and column headings to be written on line 6. The line of column headings has two parts (one heading for ITEM and one for PRICE) which are listed in ascending order. One line will be skipped after the column headings are printed because of the NEXT GROUP PLUS 1 command.

The INITIATE Command

The general form of the INITIATE command is

INITIATE report-name [report-name . . .] .

INITIATE gets a report ready to be printed. It sets the LINE-COUNTER to zero and the PAGE-COUNTER to one. Before a report is initiated, the file on which it is to be written must be OPEN. If we are printing several reports we may INITIATE all of them at once.

The TERMINATE Command

The general form of the TERMINATE command is

TERMINATE report-name [report-name . . .] .

TERMINATE finishes up the printing of groups which come at the end of a report—PAGE FOOTING, CONTROL FOOTING, REPORT FOOTING. TERMINATE should be used once at the end of a report.

The GENERATE Command

The general form of the GENERATE command is

GENERATE data-name.

The data-name must be the name of a DETAIL group. Besides printing DETAIL items, GENERATE increases the LINE-COUNTER, moves and edits any data needed in the DETAIL group, writes the line, and prints any headings or footings that are required.

Rules

1. In a report there may be only one PAGE HEADING, one PAGE FOOT-ING, one REPORT HEADING, and one REPORT FOOTING.

2. Each DETAIL must have a unique name.

3. In low level COBOL there may be only one report per file. High level COBOL allows multiple reports per file and control groups in a report (discussed in section 11.6).

4. Any report group may consist of several lines.

```
01    TYPE PH . . .
      03    LINE . . .
      03    LINE . . .
      03    LINE . . .
```

We may specify where these lines are to be written by telling the exact line number or by telling their relation to the preceding line written. For example,

```
01    TYPE PH . . .
      03    LINE 1 . . .
      03    LINE 3 . . .
      03    LINE 6 . . .
```

is telling exactly the lines on which we want the PAGE HEADING printed; whereas, the following example uses relative spacing.

```
01    TYPE PH . . .
      03    LINE PLUS 1 . . .
      03    LINE PLUS 2 . . .
      03    LINE PLUS 3 . . .
```

The first line will be one line down from anything which may precede it on the page (such as the REPORT HEADING). The second line will be written two lines below the first line; the third one will be written three lines below the second line. It is not a good idea to combine the two types of line numberings in one group. In fact, if we use relative spacing first, then we cannot use specific line numbers in the same report group.

5. The general form of the File Description for the file on which a report is written is the following.

FD   file-name LABEL RECORDS OMITTED
      { REPORT report-name   }
      { REPORTS report-name . . . } .

11.6 Using Controls in a Report

The Report Writer automatically checks for controls and prints headings and/or footings whenever the value of the control changes. It also can be used to sum numbers which are printed in a DETAIL line. Let us study the following example which utilizes control headings and footings.

The Greene County tax collector has a card for each taxpayer in the county. The card contains the following information:

last name	cols. 1–15	
first name	16–25	
street address	26–40	
city	41–55	
zip code	56–60	
property tax	61–67	xxxxx.xx
P (if tax has been paid)	70	

If no tax has been paid, column 70 will be blank. The tax collector wants the computer to take these cards and produce a listing for each town in the county. The listing should contain the taxpayers' names, their addresses, zip codes, and either the amount paid or the amount owed. At the end of the town's report, there should be a line showing the total amount paid and the total amount due. At the conclusion of the report there should be a summary line showing the total amount paid to the county and the amount owed. The report should look like the following diagram.

```
                          CITY A
JONES      BILL     110 ELM      21097      $300.00
MARTIN     J W      207 PARK     21097                      $400.00
   .          .          .                      .               .
   .          .          .                      .               .
   .          .          .                                      .
WATERS     MARK     321 ADAMS    21093                      $215.00
***TOTAL***                                 $367,389.00   $93,625.00
                          CITY B
ARNOLD     M T      102 SOUTH    21094      $560.00
   .          .          .                      .               .
   .          .          .                      .               .
```

The city will be a control to tell when to print the city heading and city total. To print the county totals we will use a FINAL control footing. This is a special control which is more important than any other control. A FINAL control heading prints once before any other control headings and a FINAL control footing prints at the end of the report after all other control footings.

In our report we will need two DETAIL lines—one to print if the person has paid his taxes and one to print if he owes money.

If we want the report to print the data by cities, then the cards will need to be arranged so that all of one city's data is grouped together in the card deck. We could arrange the cards by using a card sorter or a program which would do the task. For this problem we will assume that the cards are in the correct order. Let us begin our program by describing all the files we need.

```
IDENTIFICATION DIVISION.
PROGRAM-ID. TAX-REPORT.
ENVIRONMENT DIVISION.
CONFIGURATION SECTION.
SOURCE-COMPUTER.    IBM-360.
OBJECT-COMPUTER.    IBM-360.
INPUT-OUTPUT SECTION.
FILE-CONTROL. SELECT CARD-DECK ASSIGN TO
    SYS005-UR-2540R-S. SELECT PRINTOUT ASSIGN TO
    SYS006-UR-1403-S.
DATA DIVISION.
FILE SECTION.
FD     CARD-DECK DATA RECORD TAXPAYER LABEL RECORDS
           OMITTED.
01     TAXPAYER.
       03   NAME        PICTURE X(25).
       03   ADRES       PICTURE X(15).
       03   CITY        PICTURE X(15).
       03   ZIP         PICTURE 9(5).
       03   AMT         PICTURE 9(5)V99.
       03   FILLER      PICTURE XX.
       03   PAID        PICTURE A.
       03   FILLER      PICTURE X(10).
FD     PRINTOUT LABEL RECORDS OMITTED REPORT TAXES.
WORKING-STORAGE SECTION.
77     AMOUNT-PAID   PICTURE 9(5)V99.
77     AMOUNT-DUE    PICTURE 9(5)V99.
```

We have included AMOUNT-PAID and AMOUNT-DUE so that we can get the amount added to the correct sum. After a card is read, we will determine whether AMT is an amount paid or an amount due and will move it to the correct area in WORKING-STORAGE.

As we begin to describe our report we will need to tell the Report Writer the controls which we will use. These are CITY and FINAL. The CITY control will tell the Report Writer when to print the heading and when to print the city total line. The FINAL control will tell the Report Writer to print the county total line at the conclusion of the report. The controls are listed in their order of importance in the report description (RD); the FINAL control precedes all other controls. Following the RD we describe our headings and footings.

```
REPORT SECTION.
RD     TAXES CONTROLS FINAL CITY PAGE LIMIT 60 LINES
           FIRST DETAIL 5.
01     TYPE CH CITY LINE NEXT PAGE.
```

```
            03    COLUMN 59    PICTURE X(15) SOURCE CITY.
01    TYPE CF CITY LINE PLUS 2.
            03    COLUMN 84    PICTURE $$$$,$$$,$$$.99
                  SUM AMOUNT-PAID.
            03    COLUMN 104   PICTURE $$$$,$$$,$$$.99
                  SUM AMOUNT-DUE.
01    TYPE CF FINAL LINE PLUS 3.
            03    COLUMN 18    PICTURE X(11)
                  VALUE 'AMOUNT PAID'.
            03    COLUMN 31    PICTURE $$$$,$$$,$$$.99
                  SUM AMOUNT-PAID.
            03    COLUMN 68    PICTURE X(10)
                  VALUE 'AMOUNT DUE'.
            03    COLUMN 82    PICTURE $$$$,$$$,$$$.99
                  SUM AMOUNT-DUE.
```

Since we have used SUM in four places, the Report Writer will set up four separate areas where it can compute these totals. When the report is initiated, all four areas will be set to zero. When a DETAIL containing AMOUNT-PAID is printed, the value of AMOUNT-PAID will be added to the appropriate sum areas. When the CONTROL FOOTING on CITY is printed, its two sum areas will be set to zero so that the Report Writer can start computing the totals for the second city.

We will now describe our two DETAIL lines—one which will be used if we are printing an amount paid and one for printing an amount due. Notice that AMOUNT-DUE and AMOUNT-PAID will be in different columns on the output line.

```
01    TAXPAID TYPE DETAIL LINE PLUS 1.
            03    COLUMN 14    PICTURE X(25)      SOURCE NAME.
            03    COLUMN 49    PICTURE X(15)      SOURCE ADRES.
            03    COLUMN 74    PICTURE 9(5)       SOURCE ZIP.
            03    COLUMN 90    PICTURE $Z(5).99   SOURCE
                  AMOUNT-PAID.
01    TAXDUE TYPE DETAIL LINE PLUS 1.
            03    COLUMN 14    PICTURE X(25)      SOURCE NAME.
            03    COLUMN 49    PICTURE X(15)      SOURCE ADRES.
            03    COLUMN 74    PICTURE 9(5)       SOURCE ZIP.
            03    COLUMN 110   PICTURE $Z(5).99   SOURCE
                  AMOUNT-DUE.
```

Now that the report has been described we will write the PROCEDURE DIVISION. We begin by opening our files and initiating our report.

```
PROCEDURE DIVISION.
START. OPEN INPUT CARD-DECK. OPEN OUTPUT PRINTOUT.
   INITIATE TAXES.
```

As we read a card we must determine if AMT is an amount paid or one due. We will then move it to the appropriate area in WORKING-STORAGE so that when we generate our detail line, the amount will be added to the correct sum. If we had said SUM AMT, then the Report Writer would not be able to distinguish a paid amount from one which is due and all the amounts would be added together into one sum.

```
REPORT-TAXES. READ CARD-DECK AT END GO TO TERM.
   IF PAID = 'P' MOVE AMT TO AMOUNT-PAID GENERATE
```

```
        TAXPAID ELSE MOVE AMT TO AMOUNT-DUE GENERATE
        TAXDUE.
    GO TO REPORT-TAXES.
TERM. TERMINATE TAXES.
    CLOSE CARD-DECK PRINTOUT.
    STOP RUN.
```

The GENERATE command in this program does more than just move values and print lines. Since we have CONTROL HEADINGs and FOOT-INGs, the GENERATE checks to see if we are still in the same control group and prints the appropriate heading and/or footing. For example, when the first card is read, we tell the computer to GENERATE either TAXPAID or TAXDUE. The Report Writer realizes that we are at the beginning of a new city. Therefore, it prints the CH CITY and then prints the DETAIL line. As long as our data is from the first city no other CH or CF will be written. However, when the computer reads the first card of the second city and we give the command GENERATE, the computer will print the CF CITY for the first city, a CH CITY for the second city and then the DETAIL line. The TERMINATE command prints the CF CITY for the last city and the CF FINAL.

The complete program follows.

```
IDENTIFICATION DIVISION.
PROGRAM-ID. TAX-REPORT.
ENVIRONMENT DIVISION.
CONFIGURATION SECTION.
SOURCE-COMPUTER.    IBM-360.
OBJECT-COMPUTER.    IBM-360.
INPUT-OUTPUT SECTION.
FILE-CONTROL. SELECT CARD-DECK ASSIGN TO
    SYS005-UR-2540R-S. SELECT PRINTOUT ASSIGN TO
    SYS006-UR-1403-S.
DATA DIVISION.
FILE SECTION.
FD   CARD-DECK DATA RECORD TAXPAYER LABEL RECORDS
        OMITTED.
01   TAXPAYER.
        03   NAME           PICTURE X(25).
        03   ADRES          PICTURE X(15).
        03   CITY           PICTURE X(15).
        03   ZIP            PICTURE 9(5).
        03   AMT            PICTURE 9(5)V99.
        03   FILLER         PICTURE XX.
        03   PAID           PICTURE A.
        03   FILLER         PICTURE X(10).
FD   PRINTOUT LABEL RECORDS OMITTED REPORT TAXES.
WORKING-STORAGE SECTION.
77   AMOUNT-PAID        PICTURE 9(5)V99.
77   AMOUNT-DUE         PICTURE 9(5)V99.
REPORT SECTION.
RD   TAXES CONTROLS FINAL CITY PAGE LIMIT 60 LINES
        FIRST DETAIL 5.
01   TYPE CH CITY LINE NEXT PAGE.
        03   COLUMN 59    PICTURE X(15)            SOURCE CITY.
01   TYPE CF CITY LINE PLUS 2.
        03   COLUMN 84    PICTURE $$$$,$$$,$$$.99
                SUM AMOUNT-PAID.
```

```
                    03    COLUMN 104   PICTURE $$$$,$$$,$$$.99
                          SUM AMOUNT-DUE.
          01        TYPE CF FINAL LINE PLUS 3.
                    03    COLUMN 18    PICTURE X(11)
                          VALUE 'AMOUNT PAID'.
                    03    COLUMN 31    PICTURE $$$$,$$$,$$$.99
                          SUM AMOUNT-PAID.
                    03    COLUMN 68    PICTURE X(10)
                          VALUE 'AMOUNT DUE'.
                    03    COLUMN 82    PICTURE $$$$,$$$,$$$.99
                          SUM AMOUNT-DUE.
          01        TAXPAID TYPE DETAIL LINE PLUS 1.
                    03    COLUMN 14    PICTURE X(25)         SOURCE NAME.
                    03    COLUMN 49    PICTURE X(15)         SOURCE ADRES.
                    03    COLUMN 74    PICTURE 9(5)          SOURCE ZIP.
                    03    COLUMN 90    PICTURE $Z(5).99      SOURCE
                          AMOUNT-PAID.
          01        TAXDUE TYPE DETAIL LINE PLUS 1.
                    03    COLUMN 14    PICTURE X(25)         SOURCE NAME.
                    03    COLUMN 49    PICTURE X(15)         SOURCE ADRES.
                    03    COLUMN 74    PICTURE 9(5)          SOURCE ZIP.
                    03    COLUMN 110   PICTURE $Z(5).99      SOURCE
                          AMOUNT-DUE.
     PROCEDURE DIVISION.
     START. OPEN INPUT CARD-DECK. OPEN OUTPUT PRINTOUT.
          INITIATE TAXES.
     REPORT-TAXES. READ CARD-DECK AT END GO TO TERM.
          IF PAID IS EQUAL TO 'P' MOVE AMT TO AMOUNT-PAID
             GENERATE TAXPAID ELSE MOVE AMT TO
             AMOUNT-DUE GENERATE TAXDUE.
          GO TO REPORT-TAXES.
     TERM. TERMINATE TAXES.
          CLOSE CARD-DECK PRINTOUT.
          STOP RUN.
```

Rules for Using Controls

1. In the CONTROL phrase of the RD we must mention all items which will control the printing of control headings or footings. The controls must be listed in order of importance with the most important one coming first.
2. The SUM phrase may be used only in an elementary item of a CONTROL FOOTING. The value added must be printed in a DETAIL line. Each time the DETAIL line is printed the value will be added to a sum area set up by the Report Writer.
3. The word FINAL is a special COBOL word which refers to the most important control. A CONTROL HEADING FINAL will be printed once *before* any other control headings. A CONTROL FOOTING FINAL will be printed once *after* any other control footings.

Exercises

Refer to the following description to answer questions 1–5.

```
     RD     REPORT-FILE PAGE LIMIT 50 LINES HEADING 5 FIRST
            DETAIL 15 LAST DETAIL 50.
     01     TYPE PAGE HEADING LINE NEXT PAGE.
            03     COLUMN 25    PICTURE A(27)
                   VALUE 'REPORT SHOWING YTD EXPENSES'.
```

1. What is the name of the report?

2. What does PAGE LIMIT 50 LINES mean?

3. On what lines may the DETAILS be written?

4. On what line will the PAGE HEADING be written?

5. In what columns will the title be written?

6. If we want to number the pages of a report what name do we reference?

7. What does the phrase NEXT GROUP PLUS 2 mean?

8. What is the difference between saying LINE 2 and LINE PLUS 2?

9. How is the SOURCE phrase used?

10. What command is used to print DETAIL lines?

11. What does the INITIATE command do?

12. What does the TERMINATE command do?

13. In what types of report lines may the SUM phrase be used?

14. What is a control?

15. May a PAGE HEADING be written on several lines?

16. When is a REPORT HEADING written?

17. If we have a report in a program, may we use the WRITE command?

18. What does the SUM phrase do?

19. What does the phrase HEADING 5 mean?

20. RD is an abbreviation of _____ _____.

Programs

Any of the programs at the end of Chapters 4–6, 8–9, and 13 may have their output done with the Report Writer.

1. We are given a stack of cards on which is written the name of a stock, the number of shares which a company wants to sell, and the price per share at which to sell them. The format of each card is:

stock name	cols. 1–7	
number of shares to sell	11–13	
price at which to sell	15–20	xxx.xxx

Design a program which will compute the investment for each stock (multiply number of shares by price per share) and will add the investments to yield a total investment.

The printout should be titled "STOCK SUMMARY" with column headings "NAME" and "INVESTMENT." The appropriate values should be printed below the headings. At the end of the report print and label the total investment.

2. A company's payroll department has one card punched for each of its employees. The information on the cards is in the following format:

social security number	cols. 1–9	
last name	10–22	
first name	23–32	
middle initial	33	
rate of pay	60–62	x.xx
hours worked	64–65	

Write a program to make a listing of the following items:

employee's name
rate of pay
hours worked
weekly salary
social security deduction (5.85% of weekly salary)
net salary (weekly salary − deduction)

Start the listing on a new page and number each page. At the end of the listing write the following:

total salary paid
number of employees

Edit all numbers where necessary and title the listing.

Chapter 12

File Manipulation

12.1 Introduction

The basic structure of data in a COBOL program is the file. Files may be written on many kinds of devices—printer, card punch, tape drive, disk, drum—yet the way a COBOL program handles a file is basically the same, no matter what kind of file it is. The file and its records are described in the DATA DIVISION; the OPEN, CLOSE, READ, and WRITE commands process the file. In this chapter we will discuss the basic concepts of magnetic tape and disk files as well as details for handling files in COBOL. In section 12.2 we describe magnetic tape; in section 12.3, the disk. Section 12.4 discusses the ENVIRONMENT DIVISION; section 12.5, the DATA DIVISION; and section 12.6, the PROCEDURE DIVISION. These sections are intended to bridge the gap between an elementary text and the more technical reference manual.

As the programmer writes programs which handle a variety of file types, he should keep in mind that all files are basically the same. The record descriptions for a tape file are similar to those for a card file. Some of the few differences are in the ENVIRONMENT DIVISION where files are assigned to specific devices and their physical attributes described. From then on, the PROCEDURE DIVISION elements remain the same for any file type.

If it is ever necessary to convert a program from one computer to another, most of the changes should be in the ENVIRONMENT DIVISION. That is the portion of the program which contains all of the specifics for a particular machine.

Figure 12.1   Diagram of a Tape Drive

12.2 Magnetic Tape

Magnetic tape files are frequently used in applications involving a large volume of data. A tape is more economical, faster to input and output, and less cumbersome than cards. The standard tape is a 1/2″ wide strip of plastic which is coated with a magnetic substance and wound on a reel. Most tapes are 2400 feet long, although 1200, 600, and 250 foot lengths are available. Data is recorded on the tape by magnetizing certain areas (see Figure 1.10 for an example), and one 2400 foot tape may contain the equivalent of 22 boxes of cards (2000 cards per box).

The tape drive pictured in Figure 12.1 is a device which can read and write a tape. When the drive gets ready to write data on a tape, it must go from a stopped position to its average speed of 10 feet per second. As this acceleration takes place some tape passes by the read/write head and remains blank. After the data is written, the drive slows down and stops. Once again a portion of the tape has no data on it. This starting and stopping leaves a space between the records called an *inter-record gap* or *IRG*. Normally an

Figure 12.2   Diagram of a Tape Showing Inter-Record Gaps

Data	IRG	Data	IRG	Data	IRG

IRG is 3/4 or 3/5 of an inch long. See Figure 12.2. Several feet from the beginning of the tape is a metallic strip stuck to the plastic. This strip is the *load point* and denotes the beginning of the tape on which data may be recorded. The part of the tape preceding the load point is the *leader*. It contains no data because it is wound around another reel on the tape drive. Near the end of the tape is another silver strip, which is the *end of tape mark* (sometimes called end of reel mark). If a file does not fill a tape completely, an end of file mark shows its end. The *end of file mark*, sometimes called a tape mark, is a special character written on the tape by the tape drive. There may be several files on a single tape. In this case we have a *multi-file reel*. On the other hand, a file may be so voluminous that it occupies several reels of tape; this is a *multi-volume file*.

Many tapes contain labels at the beginning and end of the data to identify the reel. The header label at the beginning normally contains such information as the file name, date created, and date to destroy. The trailer label at the end is the same as the header label and includes a block count. If the file is a multi-volume file, a volume label may appear before the header label to identify the reel number. See Figure 12.3. Labels on a tape are a safety pre-

Figure 12.3   Diagram Representing Tape Labels (IRG not pictured)

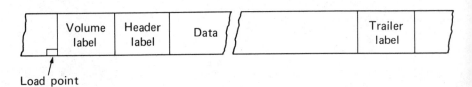

Load point

caution to keep a program from reading the wrong tape or writing on one which contains needed information. Once a tape's destroy date has past, we may write new data over the old. Checking standard labels on an input tape or writing labels on an output tape is taken care of by the OPEN statement in a COBOL program. A programmer has the option of using non-standard labels, but must provide his own label processing routines. Since most installations use either standard labels or no labels at all, we will limit our discussion to these types.

The tape drive can read and write information in a certain *density*, which is the number of characters per inch. Some common densities are 200, 556, 800, and 1600 bpi. *Bpi* is an abbreviation for bytes (characters) per inch. As technology improves, tape densities increase, making it possible to store more information on a single reel and process it at a faster pace. Most tape drives have controls to set the density of the machine. On a tape with a density of 800 characters per inch, an 80 character record is 1/10 of an inch long. If the IRG is 3/4 of an inch, most of the tape is blank. To make more efficient use of the tape, several records are often written in groups called *blocks*. Figure 12.4 depicts a tape with five records in a block. If a tape is blocked, the IRG is often referred to as an IBG (interblock gap).

Figure 12.4   A Blocked Tape

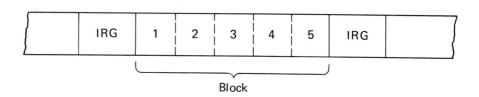

Block

The tape drive also determines the patterns in which the characters are written. Some machines use 9 tracks in which to code the characters. A track on a tape corresponds to a row on a card. (Each card contains 12 rows and the placement of the punches in different rows determines a character.) Other tape drives write 7 track tapes. Figure 1.10 of Chapter 1 shows the character representation on a 7 track tape. Contrast that with the diagram in

Figure 12.5   Character Representation on a 9 Track Tape

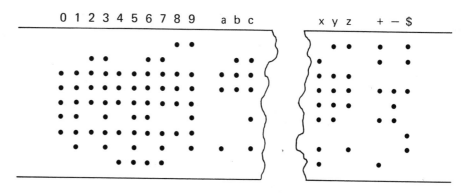

Figure 12.5 which shows a 9 track tape. Also notice in Figure 12.5 that there is always an odd number of spots making up a character; this is called *odd parity*. Some tape drives work with *even parity* tape in which each character is represented with an even number of magnetized spots. Figure 1.10 shows an even parity tape. As a tape is read or written each character is checked to see if it has the correct parity. If it does not, we say that the tape has a parity error. Sometimes dust on the tape may cause a parity error. Rereading that portion of the tape may remove the dust and thereby correct the error. The tape drive reports a parity error, but must rely on a program to tell it to reread the tape. Similarly if a tape is to be blocked, a program must give the commands to do the blocking.

Normally each record in a file is the same length; these records are called *fixed-length* records. They may be 80 characters long like a card, 60 characters, 200 characters, or almost any length. The maximum length record for a tape is not standard, so be sure to check with your installation. Sometimes a file may have records of different lengths; these are called *variable-length* records. For example, the file at a department store may have in a credit record all the items purchased by one charge account. Some accounts may have purchased only one item, others may have purchased many items. The size of the record depends upon the number of purchases made.

A tape file is a *sequential* file because all records are processed in the order in which they are written. It is impossible to go directly to the fifth record unless we have read the first, second, third, and fourth records first. This is one of the disadvantages of using tape. If we need just a portion of the data on the tape, we still must read through the tape until we get to that data. However, if all we want is to process the entire contents of the tape, we find that tape provides a faster means of input than cards. Still faster than tape is the disk.

12.3 Disk

A disk file is in many ways similar to a tape file. Its records may be blocked; they may be fixed-length or variable-length. The file may have header or trailer labels. Like a tape file, it may be a sequential file. But, because of the way the disk is built, the records may be accessed in any order.

A disk is a thin, round piece of metal coated on both sides with a magnetic oxide. Several disks may be mounted as a *disk pack* on a vertical shaft which revolves. On some disk drives the packs are removable, and thus they become a convenient way for storing data or transferring it from one place to another.

Each disk surface contains many tracks on which data may be recorded. The *tracks* are concentric circles and are numbered so the computer will know exactly where to write information or to read it. See Figure 12.6. Each

Figure 12.6   Tracks on a Disk

Tracks 000–200

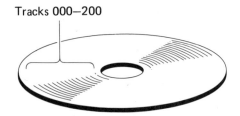

disk surface uses the same number for its tracks. For example, there is a track 50 on each surface. The diagram in Figure 12.7 shows a disk drive with ten surfaces and ten read/write heads. A read/write head is a mechanism which can electromagnetically read data or record data on the surface. The heads are located on arms which can move in and out over the disk and can reach any track. All the arms move together. Therefore, if we want to write something on track 63, all the read/write heads are positioned to track 63. Each set of tracks with the same number is called a *cylinder*, so the 10 tracks numbered 63 form a cylinder. Frequently a disk file is stored on one or more neighboring cylinders, because there is less movement involved to access parts of the file. The arm movement is mechanical and is very slow compared

Figure 12.7 Diagram of Disk
Read/Write Heads

Read/Write Heads

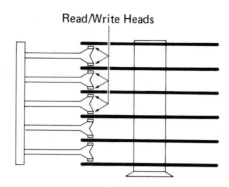

to the speed at which the disk can read or write data. Even though there is a read/write head for each disk surface, only one may operate at a time. Each head can read and write, but it cannot do both operations simultaneously. Because the arms move in and out over the surface, the disk records may be processed in any order. They do not have to be read in the same sequence in which they were written, as on a tape file. With tape, if we want to read the 300th record, we must read through the first 299 records. On disk, the heads can be moved directly to the 300th record. A file whose records are processed in an order different from the one in which they are written is called a *random access* file.

Many benefits result from using disk files instead of tape files. They are faster than tape. They may be sequential access or random access files while tape can be only a sequential file. However, the disk drive is more expensive than a tape drive. To compromise between speed and cost, most installations have tape and disk drives, reserving the disk for high priority jobs.

A disk can store so much information that it is called a *mass storage device*. The actual capacity varies from model to model. Another example of a mass storage device is a drum, which consists of a cylinder rotating at a constant speed. Its outer surface is coated with a magnetic oxide so that any area may be magnetized. Like the disk there are tracks on the surface, but each track has its own read/write head. The drum is extremely fast (and expensive) because the heads do not need to be moved from one track to another. This makes the drum a much faster device than the disk.

Figure 12.8 Disk Pack

If a file on a mass storage device is a sequential file, then we may think of it in the same way we picture a card, tape, or printer file. The differences in the flowchart and the PROCEDURE DIVISION are negligible. The main differences are in the ENVIRONMENT DIVISION.

12.4 The ENVIRONMENT DIVISION

In the ENVIRONMENT DIVISION a COBOL programmer specifies the particular device to which each file is assigned. If the file is on tape or on disk, additional items must be specified in the SELECT statement. An optional paragraph is I-O-CONTROL. If used, it can save space by allowing several files to share the same area in memory. The general form of the ENVIRONMENT DIVISION is given below.[1] Phrases which have not been discussed previously will be explained. Table 12.1 lists names particular to specific computers commonly used.

[1] We have included only the most frequently used options. For a complete version consult your manufacturer's reference manual.

ENVIRONMENT DIVISION.
CONFIGURATION SECTION.
SOURCE-COMPUTER. computer-name.
OBJECT-COMPUTER. computer-name.
[SPECIAL-NAMES. forms-control IS mnemonic-name . . .] .
INPUT-OUTPUT SECTION.
FILE-CONTROL. {SELECT file-name ASSIGN TO [integer]
input-or-output-device-1 [input-or-output-device-2] . . .
[FOR MULTIPLE REEL]
[ACCESS MODE IS SEQUENTIAL]
[PROCESSING MODE IS SEQUENTIAL].} . . .
[I-O-CONTROL. [SAME AREA FOR file-name-1 file-name-2 . . .] . . . .]

File-Control

1. Each file in the program must have its own SELECT statement.
2. Each file selected must be described in the FILE SECTION.
3. The integer is the number of input or output devices assigned to a particular file. It is used when the file is on tape and more than one tape drive is assigned.
4. If the file is a sort file, only the ASSIGN phrase may be used. (See Chapter 13.)
5. The MULTIPLE REEL phrase must be included if the number of tape drives assigned is less than the number of reels in the file. This means that the file is a multi-reel file and the same tape drive is used to process more than one reel. When it has finished with one reel, an operator removes the first from the tape drive and puts on another one.
6. Both the ACCESS and PROCESSING MODE phrases must be included for a mass storage file. ACCESS MODE IS SEQUENTIAL means that the mass storage records are obtained or placed sequentially; PROCESSING MODE IS SEQUENTIAL says that the records will be processed in the order in which they are read.

I-O-Control

1. This paragraph is optional and may be omitted.
2. The SAME clause specifies that two or more files will share the same memory area during execution. It is not possible to have more than one of the files open at the same time.
3. A sort file-name may not appear in the SAME clause. (Refer to Chapter 13.)
4. More than one SAME clause may be included in the program, but the same file-name may not appear in more than one SAME AREA clause.

Table 12.1   ENVIRONMENT DIVISION
Elements for Specific Computers

Computer	Computer-name	Input-or-output-device	Meaning
BURROUGHS 5500	B-5500	READER	card reader
		READERS	card reader
		CARD-READERS	card reader
		PRINTER	line printer
		PRINTERS	line printer
		TAPE	tape drive
		TAPES	tape drive
		SORT-TAPES	sort tape
		PUNCH	card punch
		CARD-PUNCH	card punch

Computer	Computer-name	Input-or-output-device	Meaning
		KEYBOARD	console
		MESSAGE-PRINTER	console
		DISK	disk
		PAPER-TAPE-READER	paper tape reader
		PAPER-TAPE-PUNCH	paper tape punch
		SORT-DISK	sort disk
		MERGE	disk
CONTROL DATA 6400, 6500, 6600	$\begin{Bmatrix} 6400 \\ 6500 \\ 6600 \end{Bmatrix}$	INPUT	card reader
		OUTPUT	printer
		PUNCH	card punch
		any name beginning with a letter, 1–7 characters long, containing only letters and numbers	disk or tape file
IBM 1130	IBM-1130	RD-1442	1442 model 6 or 7 used for reading only
		PU-1442	model 6 or 7 used for punching only
		RP-1442	model 6 or 7 used for reading and punching
		PO-1442	model 5
		RD-2501	card reader
		PR-1132	printer with no carriage control used
		PR-1132-C	printer when carriage control used
		PR-1403	printer when no carriage control used
		PR-1403-C	printer when carriage control used
		$DF\text{-}\begin{Bmatrix} file \\ number \end{Bmatrix}\text{-}\begin{Bmatrix} number \\ of \\ records \end{Bmatrix}\text{-}[\text{-}X]$ file-number between 1 and 32767 no. of records between 1 and 32767 -X means that a file will have its own buffer; otherwise it shares a buffer	disk file
IBM S/360	IBM-360	$SYSnnn\text{-}UR\text{-}\begin{Bmatrix} device \\ number \end{Bmatrix}\text{-}S$ nnn is a number between 000 and 221 device number:	card and printer
		2540R	card reader
		2501	card reader
		2540P	card punch
		1403	printer
		SYSnnn-UT-2400-S	tape drive
		$SYSnnn\text{-}DA\text{-}\begin{Bmatrix} device \\ number \end{Bmatrix}\text{-}\begin{Bmatrix} S \\ A \\ D \\ U \\ W \\ I \end{Bmatrix}$ device number: 2311 2314 2321 S—sequential file	disk

Computer	Computer-name	Input-or-output-device	Meaning
RCA Spectra 70	RCA-SPECTRA [model-number]	SYSIN SYSIPT	system input device (card reader or tape)
		SYSOUT SYSLST	system listing device (printer or tape)
		SYSPUNCH SYSOPT	system output device (card punch or tape)
		'SYSnnn' $\begin{Bmatrix} \text{UTILITY} \\ \text{UNIT-RECORD} \end{Bmatrix}$ device number UNIT[S] nnn—3 digit number between 004 and 254 device number:	any other device
		UNIT-RECORD: M70-234	card punch
		M70-236	card punch
		M70-237	card reader
		M70-242	printer
		M70-243	printer
		UTILITY: M70-432	magnetic tape
		M70-442	magnetic tape
		M70-445	magnetic tape
		M70-564	disk
		M70-565	drum
		M70-568	mass storage
UNIVAC 1108	UNIVAC-1108	CARD-READER-EIGHTY CARD-PUNCH-EIGHTY PRINTER UNISERVO MASS-STORAGE	tape

Example 1

To assign the card file PAYROLL-DATA on Burroughs 5500 computer we would write

SELECT PAYROLL-DATA ASSIGN TO READER.

Example 2

To assign a multi-reel file named MASTER-ACCOUNTS for the IBM 360 computer we would say

SELECT MASTER-ACCOUNTS ASSIGN TO SYS007-UT-2400-S
  MULTIPLE REEL.

Example 3

To assign the file CURRENT-INVENTORY to the RCA Spectra 70 disk we write

SELECT CURRENT-INVENTORY ASSIGN TO 'SYS008' UTILITY
  M70-564 ACCESS MODE IS SEQUENTIAL PROCESSING IS
  SEQUENTIAL.

Example 4

If a program first uses the MONTHLY-RECORDS file to generate a report and then uses CURRENT-TRANSACTIONS for a second report, both files may share the same memory area. The I-O-CONTROL paragraph would be

I-O-CONTROL. SAME AREA FOR MONTHLY-RECORDS
CURRENT-TRANSACTIONS.

However, both files may *not* be processed at the same time. The program works with one file, closes it, opens the other file, and then works with it. The PROCEDURE DIVISION commands are the same ones that would be used if the files did not share the area.

12.5 The DATA DIVISION

The DATA DIVISION contains specific information about each file. The File Description (FD) entry tells whether or not the file has a label; it names the records in the file, and tells whether or not the records are blocked. On some computers the FD may state the contents of the label; on other computers the label information is given in the control cards. If your tape or disk file has a label, check with the manufacturer's reference manual for details. The general form of the FD follows.

FD   file-name

$$\left[\underline{BLOCK} \text{ CONTAINS integer-1} \left\{ \begin{array}{l} \text{RECORDS} \\ \text{CHARACTERS} \end{array} \right\} \right]$$

$$\underline{DATA} \left\{ \begin{array}{l} \text{RECORD IS} \\ \text{RECORDS ARE} \end{array} \right\} \text{record-name [record-name . . .]}$$

$$\underline{LABEL} \left\{ \begin{array}{l} \text{RECORD IS} \\ \text{RECORDS ARE} \end{array} \right\} \left\{ \begin{array}{l} \text{STANDARD} \\ \text{OMITTED} \end{array} \right\}$$

[$\underline{RECORD}$ CONTAINS [integer-2 $\underline{TO}$] integer-3 CHARACTERS]

[$\underline{VALUE}$ OF data-name-1 IS literal-1 [data-name-2 IS
literal-2] . . .] .

Rules for the File Description (FD)

1. The clauses which follow the file-name may be included in any order.
2. All integers used must be positive.
3. If the file's records are blocked, the BLOCK clause is required. All the steps necessary to process a blocked file are taken care of automatically when this one clause is included.
4. Each record-name must be described with the level number 01.
5. The records of a file are described in detail using level numbers of 01 and higher, as necessary, following the FD for the file. The records do not have to have the same description and the order in which they are listed is not important.
6. Each file has one area in memory which may hold the contents of a record. A file which has several 01 record descriptions still has one area in memory, which all the records share. If the records are of different lengths, the size of the memory area is equal to the size of the longest record.
7. The RECORD clause is not necessary because the size of each record is determined by its description. If only integer-3 is used in the RECORD

clause, the compiler assumes that the records are of fixed-length. If both integer-2 and integer-3 are used, integer-2 must be the size of the smallest record and integer-3 the size of the largest.

8. The VALUE clause may be used to describe items in the label record. Data-name-1, data-name-2, and so on are fixed names which are specified by individual manufacturers. On some computers all label information is given in the control cards and the VALUE clause would be omitted.

Example 1

To describe a printer file QUARTERLY-REPORT with records named TITLE-LINE, COL-HEADINGS, and REPORT-LINE we would write the following. The order in which we describe the records is not important.

```
FD    QUARTERLY-REPORT DATA RECORDS TITLE-LINE
      COL-HEADINGS REPORT-LINE.
01    REPORT-LINE.
      03    FILLER    PIC X(20).
      .
      .
      .
01    TITLE-LINE.
      03    MARGIN    PIC X(10).
      .
      .
      .
01    COL-HEADINGS.
      .
      .
      .
```

Example 2

The File Description of a tape file named CENSUS-DATA with standard labels and whose records are written 10 to a block would be the following.

```
FD    CENSUS-DATA BLOCK CONTAINS 10 RECORDS
      LABEL RECORDS STANDARD
      DATA RECORD TRACT-INFO.
01    TRACT-INFO.
      .
      .
      .
```

12.6 The PROCEDURE DIVISION

COBOL uses the same instructions to process tape files, disk files, card files, or printer files. The instructions automatically take care of blocking, handling errors, and label processing as required by the files. In the ENVIRONMENT and DATA divisions we define the physical attributes of the file. This determines how the PROCEDURE DIVISION instructions work with the file. If a file has header labels, the OPEN statement checks the label. If a file has no labels, the OPEN statement does not do any label processing. If a file is blocked, the compiler inserts additional instructions which enable the computer to work with blocked records. Let us now discuss the OPEN, READ, WRITE, and CLOSE commands in that order. We will give the general form and rules for using each instruction.

OPEN

The OPEN statement initiates the processing of files. It performs the checking and/or writing of labels and other input and output operations. Its general form is the following.

$$\text{OPEN} \begin{Bmatrix} \underline{\text{INPUT}} \\ \underline{\text{OUTPUT}} \\ \underline{\text{I-O}} \end{Bmatrix} \text{file-name [file-name} \ldots \text{]} .$$

Rules for the OPEN Statement

1. INPUT means that the file will be read; OUTPUT means that the file will be written; I-O is only for mass storage files and means that the file may be read and/or written.
2. An OPEN statement must be executed before the first READ or WRITE command for the file.
3. A file which is open may not be opened a second time. However, an open file may be closed and then opened.
4. If the file is assigned to a device which may be rewound (e.g. tape or mass storage), the OPEN statement positions the file at its beginning.
5. If the file is an input file with a label, the OPEN statement checks the label. If the file is an output file and should have a label, the OPEN statement writes the label.
6. Sort files should not be opened. (See Chapter 13.)
7. A mass storage file may be opened as an I-O file only if it is already in existence; the I-O option may not be used if the file is being created.

   A credit card company's master account file is an example of an I-O file. On disk they store the card number, name, address, and credit limit of each card holder. If a person moves, his address on the file must be changed. To do this a program would have to read the person's record, make sure it was the correct account to change, and then write the new address on the disk. An I-O file is one which can be read or written.

Example

The following commands will get the SALES-RECEIPTS and INVENTORY files ready to be read and LEDGER ready to be written.

```
OPEN INPUT SALES-RECEIPTS INVENTORY.
OPEN OUTPUT LEDGER.
```

READ

The READ statement transfers one record from the file into the computer's memory. If the file's records are blocked, the first READ statement causes an entire block to be read, but the program has access to only the first record. The other records are saved in a different portion of memory called a *buffer*. When the computer executes the READ statement a second time, the second record in the block is transferred from the buffer into the file's record area. The computer can save time because it doesn't have to read data from the input device with each READ statement. When all of the records in the buffer have been used, the computer reads another block of records into the buffer and places the first one in the file's record area. This process is called *deblocking* because it allows us to work with one record at a time from the block. The READ statement automatically takes care of deblocking records from any file whose description includes the BLOCK CONTAINS clause.

The general form of the READ statement for non-mass storage files and for mass storage files in sequential access and process mode is

<u>READ</u> file-name RECORD AT <u>END</u> imperative-statement. . . .

Rules for the READ Statement

1. The file must be OPEN before the first READ statement is executed.
2. After the computer has read the last record in the file and the program commands it to read another record, the file is in its AT END condition. The last record is no longer available in the record area and the computer executes the imperative-statement or statements following the AT END phrase.

   An imperative statement is any of the following statements.

   ACCEPT, ADD[2], ALTER, CLOSE, COMPUTE[2], DISPLAY, DIVIDE[2], EXAMINE, EXIT, GENERATE, GO TO, INITIATE, MOVE MULTIPLY[2], OPEN, PERFORM, RELEASE, SET, SORT, STOP, SUBTRACT[2], TERMINATE, WRITE[3].

3. The program must not try to read any more records from a file in its AT END condition. If the file can be rewound, it may be closed, then opened and reread.
4. When a file contains more than one 01 record description, all records automatically share the same storage area. When one record is read, it is placed in that area and no attention is paid to the record descriptions. Then, as parts of the record are referenced by MOVE, ADD, SUBTRACT, or other commands, the computer consults the record description to know which fields are being accessed. At this time it also knows whether the contents of the field should be numeric, alphabetic, or alphanumeric.
5. At any particular time the file's record area holds the contents of only one record. Each time a READ statement is executed, the previous record's data is replaced by the new record's. Therefore, we must use the information from each record immediately after reading it or save the data in WORKING-STORAGE.
6. When the computer comes to the end of a tape reel (or a mass storage unit) and there is another reel (or unit) to process, the READ statement checks the ending reel (or unit) label when necessary. After an operator has put a new reel on the tape drive (or a new disk pack on the disk), the READ statement processes the beginning label, if present, and transfers the first data record into memory.

Example

The following statement reads one record from the file UPDATE-ACCOUNTS and if there is no record to read, it writes the message "no records to update" and transfers to paragraph END-IT.

[2] Without the SIZE ERROR option.
[3] Without the INVALID KEY option.

READ UPDATE-ACCOUNTS AT END
  DISPLAY 'NO RECORDS TO UPDATE'
  GO TO END-IT.

WRITE

The WRITE command releases a record stored in memory to an output device. It also can be used for vertical spacing on the printer. There are two general forms of the WRITE statement. The first one is for non-mass storage files; the second one for mass storage files.

Form 1: <u>WRITE</u> record-name $\left[\begin{Bmatrix} \text{BEFORE} \\ \text{AFTER} \end{Bmatrix} \text{ADVANCING integer } \underline{\text{LINES}} \right]$.

Form 2: <u>WRITE</u> record-name <u>INVALID KEY</u> imperative-statement. . . .

Rules for the WRITE Statement

1. The file must be OPEN before writing the first record.
2. The record-name must be the name of a record belonging to a file which is not a sort file. (See Chapter 13.)
3. The record is no longer available to the program after it is written.
4. If the ADVANCING option is not used on a printer file, there will be automatic single spacing. If used, the ADVANCING option will advance the printer the number of lines specified. The BEFORE phrase specifies that the line will be printed before the spacing occurs; the AFTER phrase specifies that the spacing will take place and then the line will be written.
5. The WRITE statement processes ending labels if included at the end of a reel or at the end of a mass storage file contained on more than one unit. After an operator gets the next reel or unit ready, the WRITE statement (if requested) places the beginning label on the file.
6. The INVALID KEY option on a sequential mass storage file opened for output checks to see if the end of the area assigned to the file has been reached. If it has, the computer executes the statement (or statements) following the INVALID KEY phrase.
7. The WRITE statement on an I-O mass storage file is used mainly to change records on the file, to replace an old record with its corrected version. This process is known as *updating* and is an important part of business programming problems.

It is relatively easy to update an I-O file because we do not need to rewrite the entire file. We merely need to write over the old records and keep everything else the same. However, if we were working with tape, we would need to make a new tape since a tape file cannot be an I-O file. The new tape would contain the unchanged records and the corrected ones. Most businesses do not update every day because it is too costly to create a new tape just to correct a few records. Therefore, a file is only as current as its last update date. A credit card company which sends statements containing only last month's purchases is a month behind in its updating. People who complain about receiving computer-produced bills showing a zero balance are probably the victims of a poor billing and updating system. No one thought to have the program check for a zero balance. No one thought of including a way to mark a zero balance "paid." And therefore, the individual continues to receive bills, final notices, and threatening letters. He lays the blame on the computer, when it really should be directed toward the system's designers.

Example

To double space before writing TOTAL-LINE, the command is

WRITE TOTAL-LINE AFTER ADVANCING 2 LINES.

CLOSE

The CLOSE statement terminates the processing of files. Its general form is the following.

CLOSE file-name [file-name . . .] .

Rules for the CLOSE Statement

1. If the file is at its end, the CLOSE statement processes (if present) the label of an input file. For an output file, the CLOSE statement writes a label, if the file contains labels.
2. If an input file is not at its end, there is no label processing.
3. The file-name may not be the name of a sort file. (See Chapter 13.)
4. The CLOSE statement rewinds tape or mass storage files.

Example

We may close the files STANDARD-SALES, SALES-REPORT, and SUBSCRIPTIONS in one statement.

CLOSE STANDARD-SALES SALES-REPORT SUBSCRIPTIONS.

Programs

The following program assignments illustrate many of the different uses of files. The ones marked with an asterisk (*) are suitable for term projects. They are somewhat more detailed than the other programs. Any one of the following programs may be modified so that it works with a different type of file than the one specified. For example, a disk file may be specified instead of a tape file, or a tape file could be specified instead of cards.

1. Write a program which will read a deck of cards and will create a tape with 10 records in a block. The program should copy to the tape all the data exactly as it is punched on the cards.

2. Write a program which will print the first record in each block of a tape. This list will be used to check the contents of a tape which contains 12 records to a block. Each record is 90 characters long and should be printed exactly the ways it appears on the tape.

3. The complete inventory of an automobile parts warehouse is stored on a disk file. Each record contains the following information:

part number   cols. 1–7   (alphanumeric)
part description   8–25

price	26–30	xxx.xx
number on hand	31–33	
reorder point	34–36	

To update the inventory, the warehouse needs a program which will process sales and stocking. Changes in the inventory are recorded on cards in the following format:

part number	cols. 1–7	
quantity	11–13	
code	15	(1—sales; 2—new shipment)
customer's name	17–35	
customer's street address	36–55	
customer's city and state	56–75	

The items sold should be subtracted from the quantity on hand and the new shipments should be added to the inventory.

You may assume that the disk and card files are ordered by part number (ascending order). The output of the program should be a listing of the updated inventory as it appears on the disk. As a check, the programmer may wish to print the original inventory and the card file.

Some considerations: what if more items are sold than are on hand? what if a part number on a card is not found in the disk file? does it matter if the files were not in any particular order?

* 4. Use the data in program 3, update the inventory, and print invoices. Include the customer's name, address, part number, part description, quantity sold, unit price, total price. Design your own format for the invoices. The program should be able to handle an order for a larger quantity than on hand. It should also handle incorrect part numbers.

* 5. This program is a variation of programs 3 and 4. Assume that there may be more than one card from each customer and that the cards are ordered first by customer name. Then within a group of cards for one customer, the items are in ascending order. The program should produce one invoice for each customer.

* 6. Change program 3 (or 4 or 5) so that it will keep track of various totals: number of items sold, total amount sold, net worth of inventory, and so on. Use your imagination to vary any of these programs.

7. The Morgan County Tax Collector has a card for each taxpayer in the county. Each card contains the following information:

last name	cols. 1–15	
first name	16–25	
street address	26–40	
city	41–55	
zip code	56–60	
property tax	61–67	xxxxx.xx
P (if tax has been paid)	70	

If no tax has been paid, column 70 will be blank. Write a program which will process the tax file. Assume that the records are in alphabetical

order by town and that within each town the people's names are alphabetized. The output should be a listing by town of the people's names,
addresses, and an amount which is either the tax paid or the tax due.
To make the output readable include a separate column for each amount.
Therefore, the printout should look something like the following.

NAME	ADDRESS	PAID	DUE
BAMSON ABE	110 ELM	$140.00	
MILDS ROSE	1936 PALM		$379.76
_____	_____	_____	
_____	_____	_____	
_____	_____		_____

At the end of each city print the total amount paid and the total
amount owed. Also, at the conclusion of the report print the total
amount paid to the county and the total amount owed.

* 8. The master checking account records are stored on disk. Each record
  contains the following information:

account number	cols. 1–6	
name	7–30	
street address	31–50	
city and state	51–75	
ending balance for last mo.	75–80	xxxx.xx

The disk records are sorted in ascending order by account number. On
a tape, the bank has accumulated each account's transactions for the
month. These records are sorted by account number (ascending order).
Each account's records are arranged by date and for each day all deposits
come before any checks. There are 20 records to a block and the format
of the record is as follows.

account number	cols. 1–6	
amount	7–12	xxxx.xx
code	13	(1—deposit; 2—check)
date	14–19	mo da yr

Write a program which will produce monthly statements for each
customer. Design your own format, but make the statements as realistic
as possible. They might include such items as a list of checks, dates, and
deposits, beginning balance, ending balance, number of deposits, and
number of checks.

The program should penalize a person $2.00 for each overdrawn
check and a service charge of $.50 plus $.08 a check. If the account's
balance *never* falls below $150.00, there is no service charge. Try to
make the program as true to life as possible. It should be able to handle
incorrect account numbers on the tape and accounts which had no
transactions during the month.

9. The master records at the First Federal Savings and Loan are stored on
   a tape. Each record contains the following information:

```
account number    cols.  1–7
name(s)                  9–37
street address           38–57
city                     58–72
state                    73–74
zip code                 75–79
type of account            80
    1—regular passbook
    2—savings certificate
    3—trust
```

The Savings and Loan wants a program which will update their master tape once a month. Any changes required will be on cards in the following format:

```
account number    cols.  1–7
code                       8
new information          9–80
```

The code will determine which change should be made to the account's master information. The codes are:

1 new account; to be added to master file
2 closed account; to be deleted from master file
3 change in name
4 change in street address
5 change in city
6 change in state
7 change in zip code
8 change in type of account

The new information will be left-adjusted in columns 9–80. For example, if the code is 7, the zip code will be punched in columns 9–13.

Both files, tape and cards, are in ascending order on account number. The new tape should be created so that it keeps the same order.

*10. Some of the codes in program 9 were not realistic because it is possible that a person could change name and street address at one time. Or, a change in city would mean a change in zip code. One way to fix this would be to have one card for each change. But then the program would need to decide when to write the record on the new tape. Devise a system and write a program to handle these and other similar cases.

*11. The payroll records of Maxwell Construction Company are stored on a tape. Each record contains the following information:

```
social security number    cols.  1–9
name                             10–30
salary code                         31    (1—salaried; 2—hourly rate)
salary information               32–36
number of dependents             37–38
```

The salary information is of the form xxx.xx if a person is salaried. If a person is paid by the hour, the number of hours worked is in columns 32-33 and the hourly rate is in columns 34–36 (x.xx).

Write a program to compute the payroll for the company. Pay each non-salaried employee time and a half for any hours worked over 40. Deduct 5.85% for social security. Also calculate the amount of income tax deduction based on the number of dependents. Consult the Internal Revenue Service to find out how this is calculated.

The output should include a listing of social security numbers, names, gross salary, deduction, and net salary. If desired, the output may be in the form of a check to each employee.

Special Terms

1. *IRG*
2. *load point*
3. *leader*
4. *end of tape mark*
5. *end of file mark*
6. *multi-volume file*
7. *multi-file reel*
8. *label*
9. *density*
10. *block*
11. *deblocking*
12. *odd parity*
13. *even parity*
14. *track*
15. *IBG*
16. *read/write head*
17. *sequential file*
18. *random access file*
19. *mass storage device*
20. *drum*
21. *buffer*
22. *I-O file*
23. *updating*
24. *bpi*
25. *cylinder*

Chapter 13

Sorting

13.1 Introduction

Frequently data is kept in a particular order to facilitate looking up an item or making changes to the data. Employees' payroll records are often alphabetized or arranged by social security number. In a company which has several departments, the records may be sorted by department keeping the names within each department in alphabetical order. The particular item which determines how the file is ordered is called a *key*. If the file is in alphabetical order by name, then the key is the name field. It is possible to have several keys which determine the order. For example, a plant manager may keep his records arranged by department and within each department are the section records. In this case the two keys are department and section. The department key is the more important one because each department is a group containing several sections. Since there are only two keys, we may speak of the more important one as being the *major key* and the less important one as the *minor key*.

Arranging data in a specific order may be done in a COBOL program with the SORT command. The process of sorting is extremely complex, yet just one COBOL statement will take care of the entire sorting operation. This is different from most situations in which the programmer must write many instructions to accomplish a single task such as producing a payroll or printing a report. Sorting data is such a common occurrence and one which is rather hard to program that most installations have a general purpose sorting routine. This is a program which will arrange data in any order using any number of keys. When the compiler encounters a SORT command in a COBOL program, it gets a copy of the sorting routine, adapts it for the sort requested in the program, and attaches it to the machine language version of the COBOL program. (Normally the sorting routine is already in machine language.) The sorting program uses a lot of memory and therefore some installations may not have machines which are capable of handling the COBOL SORT. Consult your computer center to see if the SORT command may be used. If not, this chapter may be omitted.

In section 13.2 we will compare two programs which show alternate ways of applying the COBOL SORT command. Section 13.3 discusses the rules of sorting. Before we begin to look at the examples, let us discuss what happens when data is sorted. This process involves three steps:

1. the data to be sorted is transferred to a file called the sort file
2. the data on the sort file is arranged in the requested order
3. the sorted data may be read and used from the sort file or it may be transferred to a separate file.

When the sorting takes place, the programmer has the option of transferring his data to the sort file or letting the SORT statement do it. He also has the option of either allowing the SORT to put the sorted information on a new file or using the data directly from the sort file. If the programmer does his own input and output for the SORT, he has a great deal of flexibility. He may take data from WORKING-STORAGE; he may calculate items and have them sorted; or he may take the sorted data and either write a report or place it in WORKING-STORAGE. If the SORT command does the input and output, it works with files. It copies data from the input file onto the sort file, and when the data is sorted, it copies the data onto an output file. Of course the programmer may do his own input and let the SORT write the output or vice versa. The sort file and output file are usually disk files because they are faster than tape files.

13.2 An Introductory Sort Program

Our input file consists of payroll cards for the employees of the Acme Brush Company. Each card contains the following information:

last name	cols. 1–10	
first name	11–20	
social security number	21–29	
pay per hour	31–33	(x.xx)
hours worked per week	34–35	
year to date gross pay	41–47	(xxxxx.xx)

The problem is to produce an alphabetical listing of the employees and their social security numbers.

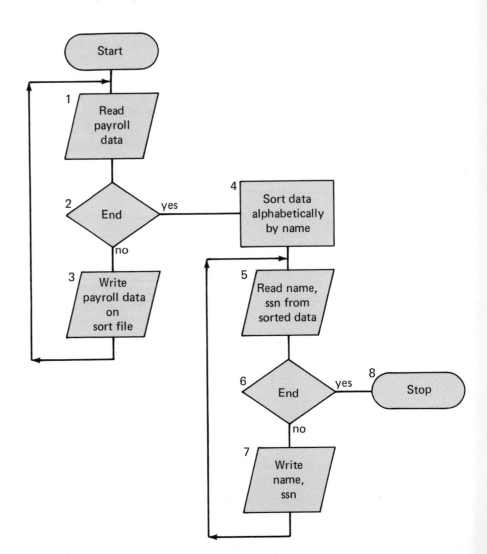

As we write our flowchart we realize that there are three steps: get the data, sort it, and print it. Boxes 1–3 in the preceding flowchart transfer the data to the sort file; box 4 says to sort the data; and boxes 5–8 print the listing of the sorted data.

We will now give two programs which will solve the problem. Program 13.1 lets SORT do the input and output. Boxes 1–3 are taken care of by the phrase USING PAYROLL in the SORT command. After the sorting takes place the information is placed on the file named IN-ORDER. This is determined by the phrase GIVING IN-ORDER in the SORT statement.

Program 13.2 does its own input and output. There is no need for the IN-ORDER file since this program gets the data directly from the sort file SFILE. Notice the new commands RELEASE and RETURN. RELEASE transfers data from memory onto the sort file; RETURN takes data from the sort file and places it in memory. In other words, RELEASE works like a WRITE statement and RETURN like a READ, but these are special commands which work only with sort files.

Also notice that the sort file is described with an SD (Sort Description) in the FILE SECTION. The differences between Programs 13.1 and 13.2 are in boldface type for easy identification.

Program 13.1	Program 13.2

IDENTIFICATION DIVISION.
PROGRAM-ID.   SORT-BY-NAME.
ENVIRONMENT DIVISION.
CONFIGURATION SECTION.
SOURCE-COMPUTER.   IBM-360.
OBJECT-COMPUTER.   IBM-360.
INPUT-OUTPUT SECTION.
FILE-CONTROL.
    SELECT PAYROLL ASSIGN TO
        SYS005-UR-2540R-S.
    SELECT SFILE ASSIGN TO
        SYS006-DA-2311-S.
    SELECT IN-ORDER ASSIGN TO
        SYS007-DA-2311-S OR
        SYS008-DA-2311-S.
    SELECT LISTING ASSIGN TO
        SYS009-UR-1403-S.
DATA DIVISION.
FILE SECTION.
FD   PAYROLL
    DATA RECORD PY-EMP
    LABEL RECORD OMITTED.
01   PY-EMP   PIC X(80).
SD   SFILE DATA RECORD SF-EMP.
01   SF-EMP.
    03   SF-NAME   PIC A(20).
    03   FILLER   PIC X(60).
FD   IN-ORDER
    DATA RECORD IO-EMP
    LABEL RECORDS OMITTED.
01   IO-EMP.
    03   IO-NAME   PIC A(20).
    03   IO-SS   PIC 9(9).
    03   FILLER   PIC X(51).
FD   LISTING
    DATA RECORD LS-LINE
    LABEL RECORDS OMITTED.
01   LS-LINE.
    03   FILLER   PIC X(46).
	IDENTIFICATION DIVISION.
	PROGRAM-ID. SORT-BY-NAME.
	ENVIRONMENT DIVISION.
	CONFIGURATION SECTION.
	SOURCE-COMPUTER. IBM-360.
	OBJECT-COMPUTER. IBM-360.
	INPUT-OUTPUT SECTION.
	FILE-CONTROL.
	    SELECT PAYROLL ASSIGN TO
	        SYS005-UR-2540R-S.
	    SELECT SFILE ASSIGN TO
	        SYS006-DA-2311-S.
	
	    SELECT LISTING ASSIGN TO
	        SYS009-UR-1403-S.
	DATA DIVISION.
	FILE SECTION.
	FD PAYROLL
	    DATA RECORD PY-EMP
	    LABEL RECORDS OMITTED.
	01 PY-EMP PIC X(80).
	SD SFILE DATA RECORD SF-EMP.
	01 SF-EMP.
	    03 SF-NAME PIC A(20).
	    03 SF-SS PIC 9(9).
	
	FD LISTING
	    DATA RECORD LS-LINE
	    LABEL RECORDS OMITTED.
	01 LS-LINE.
	    03 FILLER PIC X(46).

Program 13.1	Program 13.2

```
    03    LS-NAME    PIC A(20).
    03    FILLER     PIC X(11).
    03    LS-SS      PIC 9(9).
    03    FILLER     PIC X(46).
PROCEDURE DIVISION.
SORTING SECTION.
SORT-CARDS.    SORT SFILE
    ASCENDING SF-NAME
    USING PAYROLL
    GIVING IN-ORDER.




REPORT-IT SECTION.
READY-FILES.
    OPEN INPUT IN-ORDER.
    OPEN OUTPUT LISTING.
    MOVE SPACE TO LS-LINE.
WRITE-LISTING.
    READ IN-ORDER
    AT END GO TO CLOSE-F.
    MOVE IO-NAME TO LS-NAME.
    MOVE IO-SS TO LS-SS.
    WRITE LS-LINE.
    GO TO WRITE-LISTING.
CLOSE-F.
    CLOSE IN-ORDER LISTING.
    STOP RUN.
```

```
    03    LS-NAME    PIC A(20).
    03    FILLER     PIC X(11).
    03    LS-SS      PIC 9(9).
    03    FILLER     PIC X(46).
PROCEDURE DIVISION.
SORTING SECTION.
SORT-CARDS.    SORT SFILE
    ASCENDING SF-NAME
    INPUT PROCEDURE READ-CARDS
    OUTPUT PROCEDURE REPORT-IT.
    STOP RUN.
READ-CARDS SECTION.
OPEN-FILE.    OPEN INPUT PAYROLL.
READ-LOOP.    READ PAYROLL AT END
    GO TO CLOSE-FILE.
    MOVE PY-EMP TO SF-EMP.
    RELEASE SF-EMP.
    GO TO READ-LOOP.
CLOSE-FILE.    CLOSE PAYROLL.
REPORT-IT SECTION.
READY-FILES.

    OPEN OUTPUT LISTING.
    MOVE SPACE TO LS-LINE.
WRITE-LISTING.
    RETURN SFILE
    AT END GO TO CLOSE-F.
    MOVE SF-NAME TO LS-NAME.
    MOVE SF-SS TO LS-SS.
    WRITE LS-LINE.
    GO TO WRITE-LISTING.
CLOSE-F.
    CLOSE LISTING.
```

Now that we have given the complete programs let us go back and explain the differences:

1. Program 13.1 has four files; program 13.2 has only three since it does not place the sorted data on a separate file (IN-ORDER). Program 13.2 reads the data directly from the sort file.

2. The sort file cannot have any labels, so the entire LABEL RECORD clause is omitted from the Sort Description (SD).

3. In the SFILE in program 13.1 we describe only the items which will be sort keys. Underneath the IN-ORDER file we name all the items which we wish to report. However, in program 13.2 we name as part of SFILE the sort keys *and* all the items we wish to use from the sorted data. Since our instructions transfer the data to SFILE, the record SF-EMP can be any size. In program 13.1 the size of the records PY-EMP, SF-EMP, and IO-EMP must be the same.

4. SFILE is the name of the file to be sorted and must be described with an SD entry in the FILE SECTION.

5. In the SORT command the word ASCENDING also means alphabetical since on most computers the letter A is defined to be less than the letter B which is less than a C and so on. Check with your computer installation to be sure.

6. The phrase USING PAYROLL in the SORT command of program 13.1 says that the file named PAYROLL will be input to the sort. Before the actual sorting takes place, the PAYROLL file is opened, copied onto SFILE, and then closed. All these operations are automatically taken care of by the

SORT program. The COBOL programmer needs no OPEN or CLOSE statements for the PAYROLL file.

7. The SORT command in program 13.2 tells the computer that the program is doing its own input and output for the SORT and that these are in the sections READ-CARDS and REPORT-IT respectively. When the computer begins to execute the SORT command, the first thing it does is to perform the READ-CARDS SECTION. This section begins with the header READ-CARDS SECTION and ends with the last line before the REPORT-IT SECTION. In this section the program reads the payroll cards and transfers only the data needed for the report (name and social security number) to the sort file. Since the name and social security number were punched in the first 29 columns of the card, we do not need to describe the separate fields in PY-EMP. However, if the format of the card were different, we would need to break down PY-EMP into 03 levels. The command RELEASE SF-EMP writes the contents of SF-EMP onto the disk area assigned to SFILE. When the computer finishes executing the READ-CARDS SECTION, it returns to the SORT command and sorts the data released to SFILE.

8. The phrase GIVING IN-ORDER in the SORT command of program 13.1 specifies the name of the file on which the sorted information will go. SORT automatically opens this file before writing it and closes it when finished.

9. When the computer finishes sorting the information on the sort file in program 13.2, it performs the REPORT-IT SECTION. At the conclusion of the REPORT-IT SECTION the computer returns to the statement (STOP RUN) following the SORT (and stops).

The REPORT-IT SECTION reads the sort file and prints a list of names and social security numbers. The sort file does not have to be opened; the programmer merely needs to give the command RETURN SFILE AT END GO TO CLOSE-F. This instructs the sort file to transfer one record from disk to memory. When the end of the file is reached, the computer proceeds to paragraph CLOSE-F. RETURN is a command used only with sort files; the AT END phrase must always be included.

10. In program 13.1 after the SORT instruction has been executed, our output is on the IN-ORDER file. To print it we must read the file, move the data to the printer file LISTING, and write the report. All these commands are in the REPORT-IT SECTION. Program 13.1 does not really need to have the PROCEDURE DIVISION divided into sections; paragraphs would be sufficient. However, sections were included to make the two programs more similar.

The file IN-ORDER was closed by the SORT and must be opened before it can be read. At the conclusion of the program all files are closed and execution stopped.

13.3 Rules for Sorting

In this section we will discuss the portions of COBOL which are used exclusively with sorting. These include FILE-CONTROL, SD, SORT, RE-LEASE, and RETURN. They will be covered in this section in the same order in which they are used in a program.

ENVIRONMENT DIVISION: FILE-CONTROL

Form 1: FILE-CONTROL. SELECT file-name ASSIGN TO [integer]
input-or-output-device-1 [input-or-output-device-2] . . . .

Form 2: FILE-CONTROL. SELECT file-name ASSIGN TO
output-device-1 [output-device-2] . . . OR output-device-3

[output-device-4] . . . $\left[\text{FOR } \underline{\text{MULTIPLE}} \left\{ \begin{array}{c} \underline{\text{REEL}} \\ \underline{\text{UNIT}} \end{array} \right\} \right]$.

The first form must be used for the sort file. The second form can be used only for the output file specified by the GIVING option of the SORT statement. The OR option says that the output file will be on one device (set of devices) or another. When sorting is concluded, the computer will indicate which device (devices) contain the file.

DATA DIVISION: Sort Description

The sort file is described with an SD (Sort Description) entry in the FILE SECTION. The SD is similar to the FD and is followed by a description of all the records in the file. Its general form follows. Notice that there is no LABEL RECORDS clause.

$$
\underline{\text{SD}} \quad \text{file-name } \underline{\text{DATA}} \begin{Bmatrix} \underline{\text{RECORD}} \text{ IS} \\ \underline{\text{RECORDS}} \text{ ARE} \end{Bmatrix} \text{ record-name}
$$

$$
\text{[record-name . . .] } [\underline{\text{RECORD}} \text{ CONTAINS [integer-1 } \underline{\text{TO}}]
$$

$$
\text{integer-2 CHARACTERS].}
$$

The SD contains many of the same clauses as the FD. Each clause in the SD has the same meaning as it does in the FD and therefore will not be explained here. Refer to section 12.5 for more details.

PROCEDURE DIVISION: SORT

The general form of the SORT statement is the following.

$$
\underline{\text{SORT}} \text{ file-name-1 ON } \begin{Bmatrix} \underline{\text{DESCENDING}} \\ \underline{\text{ASCENDING}} \end{Bmatrix} \text{ KEY data-name-1}
$$

$$
\text{[data-name-2] . . .}
$$

$$
\left[\text{ON } \begin{Bmatrix} \underline{\text{DESCENDING}} \\ \underline{\text{ASCENDING}} \end{Bmatrix} \text{ KEY data-name-3 [data-name-4] . . . } \right] . . .
$$

$$
\begin{Bmatrix} \underline{\text{INPUT PROCEDURE}} \text{ IS section-name-1 [}\underline{\text{THRU}} \text{ section-name-2]} \\ \underline{\text{USING}} \text{ file-name-2} \end{Bmatrix}
$$

$$
\begin{Bmatrix} \underline{\text{OUTPUT PROCEDURE}} \text{ IS section-name-3 [}\underline{\text{THRU}} \text{ section-name-4]} \\ \underline{\text{GIVING}} \text{ file-name-3} \end{Bmatrix} .
$$

Rules of the SORT Statement

1. File-name-1 must be described with an SD entry in the FILE SECTION. File-name-1 is called the *sort file*.
2. Each data-name must be described as part of the sort file.
3. File-names 2 and 3, if used, must be described with FD entries in the FILE SECTION.
4. The records in file-name-1, -2, and -3 must be the same size.
5. The data-names following the word KEY must be listed in their order of importance with the major key coming first, followed by the next most important key, and so on. Standard COBOL does not specify the number of keys permitted, so check with your computer installation. The records will be arranged in order according to the major key. Thus any records having the same value for the first key will be grouped together. Within each group the data will be arranged according to the second key. If there is a third key, it determines how the data is ordered

in a group whose values for the first and second keys are the same. In a similar manner the order of the rest of the keys determine the way the data is sorted. See example 5 below.

6. The KEY items may not be subscripted.
7. The input procedure, if present, must consist of one or more sections which are written consecutively in the program and are not part of any output procedure. Also, the input procedure must contain a RELEASE statement in order to transfer records to the sort file. It must not contain the SORT statement. Nor may the procedure transfer control through a GO TO, PERFORM, or ALTER statement to a portion of the program outside of the input procedure.
8. If the input procedure is specified, it is executed as the first part of the SORT statement. After the last statement of the input procedure is executed, the data is sorted.
9. The output procedure, if present, must consist of one or more sections written consecutively in the program. The sections may not be part of the input procedure. The output procedure must include a RETURN statement to take records from the sorted file. It must not contain the SORT statement nor any transfer of control through a GO TO, PERFORM, or ALTER statement to a place in the program outside of the output procedure.
10. If the output procedure is specified, it is executed after the data is sorted. When the output procedure is completed, the computer returns to the statement following the SORT.
11. If the USING option is present, file-name-2 is opened, its records are transferred to the sort file (file-name-1) and then file-name-2 is closed.
12. If GIVING is used, the computer opens file-name-3 (the output file), writes all records in their sorted order from the sort file onto file-name-3, and then closes file-name-3.

Example 1

To arrange the data from the file WORKERS from oldest to youngest we would use the following SORT instruction. The sorted data is placed on a file named RANKED-BY-AGE and WA-AGE is the name of the age field in the sort file WORK-AREA.

```
SORT WORK-AREA DESCENDING WA-AGE USING WORKERS
    GIVING RANKED-BY-AGE.
```

Example 2

To arrange the file MEMBERS alphabetically we may write the following. Our sort file is called ARRANGE and contains the names AR-LAST (the last name field), AR-FIRST (the first name field), and AR-MID (the middle name field). See also example 3.

```
SORT ARRANGE ASCENDING AR-LAST ASCENDING AR-FIRST
    ASCENDING AR-MID USING MEMBERS OUTPUT
    PROCEDURE DIRECTORY.
```

Example 3

The SORT instruction in example 2 may be shortened since all the keys are to be arranged in ascending order. Writing ASCENDING once says that the keys following it are all in ascending order.

SORT ARRANGE ASCENDING AR-LAST AR-FIRST AR-MID
USING MEMBERS OUTPUT PROCEDURE DIRECTORY.

Example 4

ASCENDING and DESCENDING may be used in the same SORT statement. The following one says that the people will be grouped in descending order by GS-GRADE and that those with the same GS-GRADE will be alphabetized. Can you give an example of the way the data would be arranged?

SORT SRT-FILE DESCENDING GS-GRADE ASCENDING NAME
USING GOV-WORKERS OUTPUT PROCEDURE SUMMARY.

Example 5

The following example illustrates the way sorting takes place. Notice that all the data in each record remain the same. Sorting changes only the order of the records.

Suppose we have data on the foremen at a company's three plants. The data contains plant number, department number, foreman's name, and number of men supervised by the foreman.

Plant	Department	Foreman		Number of Men
10	12	JONES	MACK	20
20	3	WATSON	BILL	15
30	8	FARMER	SAM	17
10	22	WOODS	MARK	17
20	33	BLUE	HANK	20
30	8	COOPER	LYLE	19
10	12	KNAPP	MARY	15
20	3	BROWN	LARRY	20
30	4	STERN	JOE	12
10	22	CONNOR	MATT	14
20	3	SMITH	TOM	16
30	4	SKYE	LUCY	20

If we arranged the data in ascending order using only plant number for the sort key, then we would have the following.

Plant	Department	Foreman		Number of Men
10	12	JONES	MACK	20
10	22	WOODS	MARK	17
10	12	KNAPP	MARY	15
10	22	CONNOR	MATT	14
20	3	WATSON	BILL	15
20	33	BLUE	HANK	20
20	3	BROWN	LARRY	20
20	3	SMITH	TOM	16
30	8	FARMER	SAM	17
30	8	COOPER	LYLE	19
30	4	STERN	JOE	12
30	4	SKYE	LUCY	20

Notice that there are three distinct groups: plant 10's data, plant 20's data, and plant 30's data. To be more useful and easy to read, the data should be sorted in ascending order by plant number and within each plant in ascending order by department. Then we should have the foremen alphabetized within each department. This means that we have three keys: plant number, department, and name. The most important is plant number; the least important is name. When the sorting is completed we would have the data in the following order.

Plant	Department	Foreman		Number of Men
10	12	JONES	MACK	20
10	12	KNAPP	MARY	15
10	22	CONNOR	MATT	14
10	22	WOODS	MARK	17
20	3	BROWN	LARRY	20
20	3	SMITH	TOM	16
20	3	WATSON	BILL	15
20	33	BLUE	HANK	20
30	4	SKYE	LUCY	20
30	4	STERN	JOE	12
30	8	COOPER	LYLE	19
30	8	FARMER	SAM	17

PROCEDURE DIVISION: RELEASE

The RELEASE statement transfers a record from memory onto the sort file. Its general form is the following.

<u>RELEASE</u> record-name.

Rules for the RELEASE Statement

1. RELEASE may be used only in the input procedure section associated with a SORT statement.
2. The record-name must be a record in the sort file.
3. The sort file consists of all the records transferred to it when the RELEASE statement is executed.

Example

When the sort file is described in the following way, the following statements move data into the sort record and release it to the sort file.

```
SD    ORDER-FILE    DATA RECORD OF-ACCOUNT.
01    OF-ACCOUNT.
      03    OF-NUM    PIC 9(6).
      03    OF-ITEM   PIC X(4).
      03    OF-QTY    PIC 999.
      03    OF-DESC   PIC X(20).
        .
        .
        .
```

PROCESS-ACCOUNTS SECTION.
.
.
MOVE IN-NUM TO OF-NUM.
MOVE IN-ITEM TO OF-ITEM.
MOVE IN-QTY TO OF-QTY.
MOVE IN-DESC TO OF-DESC.
RELEASE OF-ACCOUNT.

PROCEDURE DIVISION: RETURN

The RETURN statement removes data from the sort file and places it in memory so that it may be printed, used in calculation, or processed in any way. The general form of the RETURN statement is

RETURN file-name RECORD AT END imperative-statement.

Rules for the RETURN Statement

1. The file-name must be described with an SD in the FILE SECTION.
2. RETURN may be used only in an output procedure associated with a SORT command for the file mentioned in the RETURN.
3. Each time the RETURN statement is executed, the computer gets one record from the sort file. The records are returned in the order in which they have been arranged on the sort file.
4. When all records have been returned from the sort file, the computer executes the statement (or statements) following the AT END phrase.

Example

With the following sort description the RETURN statement below will read one record from the sort file and will place it in the memory area MF-RECORD.

```
SD    MASTER-FILE DATA RECORD MF-RECORD.
01    MF-RECORD.
      03    MF-ACCT    PIC  X(10).
      03    MF-NAME    PIC  X(20).
      03    MF-ADRS    PIC  X(30).
      03    MF-BAL     PIC  999V99.
      .
      .
      .

PROCESS-OUTPUT SECTION.
      .
      .
      .
      RETURN MASTER-FILE AT END GO TO TERM.
```

Exercises

1. If we want to sort some data in WORKING-STORAGE should we use the INPUT PROCEDURE option or the USING option?

2. How many files does sorting involve? List the purpose of each file.

3. The letters SD stand for the words _____ _____ and are used in the _____ Division.

4. Give an example of the type of output which would be produced by the following SORT. The NAME is a person's name and AGE is a number which is the person's age.

   SORT S-FILE DESCENDING AGE ASCENDING NAME
       USING AFILE GIVING BFILE.

5. From the following SORT command tell
   a. which file is the data to be sorted
   b. which file is the sort file
   c. which file contains the sorted data
   d. which file is described in an SD
   e. the name of a sort key

   SORT DISK-FILE DESCENDING SCORE
       USING STUDENT-CARDS GIVING ORD.

6. What is the difference between the following instructions?

   SORT WAREA ASCENDING VERBAL USING INFO GIVING STD.
   SORT WAREA DESCENDING VERBAL USING INFO GIVING STD.

7. What is the difference between the following instructions?

   SORT DISK-AREA ASCENDING SS USING STU-INFO GIVING
       ORDERED-STU.
   SORT DISK-AREA ASCENDING SS INPUT PROCEDURE GET-DATA
       OUTPUT PROCEDURE MAKE-ROSTER.

8. If the data is punched in the following format and we wish to alphabetize the names should we describe one field for the name or two fields—one for the first name and one for the last name?

last name	cols.	1–15
first name		16–30
other data		31–80

9. Use the following description to answer the question in exercise 8.

first name	cols.	1–15
last name		16–30
other data		31–80

10. What would have to be changed in program 13.2 so that we could sort the data in descending order according to salary (pay per hour × hours worked per week)? Could we make the modifications on program 13.1?

Programs

1. Write a program to produce a list of the employees at the Machine Manufacturing Company. First list the males in alphabetical order and then list the females in alphabetical order. There is one card for each employee in the following format:

name	cols. 10–33	
sex	40	(M—male; F—female)

For output include the names and sexes of the employees. Begin the list of males on a new page and the list of females on a new page.

2. As an administrative programmer at Westover State University you are asked to produce a schedule of courses. For input each card contains:

department name code	cols. 1–3
course number	6–8
section number	11
course title	13–30
meeting time:	
period number	33
days	34–38

Design your own output, but make it easy to read.

3. Basketball Coach Huey has accumulated data from his team's most recently completed season and wishes to summarize it. For each game the following information was punched on a card about each player.

school played	cols. 1–30
player's name	31–40
points scored (blank if not played)	41–42

The coach wants the information sorted with school as the major key. Within each school sort on the number of points scored by a player so that the player scoring the most points comes first. If any players score the same amount of points put the names in alphabetical order.

Write the output in the following format:

$$
\begin{array}{ccc}
 & \text{Title} & \\
\text{school}_1 & \text{points}_1 & \text{player}_1 \\
 & \text{points}_2 & \text{player}_2 \\
 & . & . \\
 & . & . \\
\text{school}_2 & \text{points}_1 & \text{player}_1 \\
 & . & . \\
 & . & . \\
 & . & . \\
\end{array}
$$

4. Paxton Overstreet Thompson, Inc. has obtained quarterly sales information on each of its salesmen and needs a report written. The report should be broken down by department, listing each department's salesmen in alphabetical order. Along with each salesman's name should be his sales for the quarter. The department's total sales should be listed at the end of each department.

The input is on cards in the following format:

last name	cols. 1–15	
first name	16–25	
sales amount	31–37	xxxxx.xx
department number	41–42	

Design your own output for the report.

5. A card is punched for the number of beds in each hospital of the United States. The input file contains the following information:

date	cols.	1–6
state		7–8
county		10–25
city		26–40
hospital number		41–43
number of beds		46–50

Sort the data cards alphabetically in the following sequence: state, county, city. Prepare a report in a format of your own choice. Include totals such as number of beds per city, county, or state if desired.

6. The Bertram, Craig, and Masters Advertising Agency has given an aptitude test to each of its employees. The results are punched on cards with each card containing the following information:

social security number	cols.	1–9
last name		11–25
first name		31–40
verbal test score		41–43
graphics test score		45–47

Write a program which will produce a list of the test results ranking the employees on the basis of total score which is equal to verbal score plus graphics score. The list should be arranged from high score to low score and if several people make the same score, their names should be alphabetized. On the output include the employee's name, verbal, graphics, and total score.

Special Terms

1. *key*
2. *major key*
3. *minor key*
4. *sort file*

Appendix A

COBOL Reserved Word List

The words marked with an asterisk (*) are not ANS COBOL reserved words, but are reserved words for the major computer manufacturers. To write programs suitable for different computers, do not use any of the following reserved words for programmer-supplied names.

ABOUT*	CODE	DECIMAL
ACCEPT	COLUMN	DECIMAL-POINT
ACCESS	COM-REG*	DECLARATIVES
ACTUAL	COMMA	DEFINE*
ADD	COMMON-STORAGE*	DELETE*
ADDRESS	COMP	DENSITY*
ADVANCING	COMP-1*	DEPENDING
AFTER	COMP-2*	DESCENDING
ALL	COMP-3*	DETAIL
ALPHABETIC	COMPASS*	DIGIT*
ALPHANUMERIC*	COMPUTATIONAL	DIGITS*
ALTER	COMPUTATIONAL-1*	DISP*
ALTERNATE	COMPUTATIONAL-2*	DISPLAY
AN*	COMPUTATIONAL-3*	DISPLAY-ST*
AND	COMPUTE	DIVIDE
APPLY*	CONFIGURATION	DIVIDED*
ARE	CONSOLE*	DIVISION
AREA	CONSTANT*	DOLLAR*
AREAS	CONTAINS	DOWN
ASCENDING	CONTROL	
ASSIGN	CONTROLS	EDITION-NUMBER
AT	CONVERSION*	EJECT*
AUTHOR	COPY	ELSE
	CORE-INDEX*	END
BASIS*	CORR	END-OF-PAGE*
BEFORE	CORRESPONDING	ENDING
BEGINNING	CSP*	ENDING-FILE-LABEL*
BEGINNING-FILE-	CURRENCY	ENDING-TAPE-
LABEL*	CURRENT-DATE*	LABEL*
BEGINNING-TAPE-	CYL-INDEX*	ENDING-TAPE-
LABEL*	CYL-OVERFLOW*	LABEL-IDENTIFIER*
BINARY*	C01*	ENTER
BITS*	C02*	ENTRY*
BLANK	C03*	ENVIRONMENT
BLOCK	C04*	EOP*
BWZ*	C05*	EQ*
BY	C06*	EQUAL
	C07*	EQUALS*
CALL*	C08*	ERROR
CF	C09*	EVERY
CH	C10*	EXAMINE
CHANGED*	C11*	EXCEEDS*
CHARACTER*	C12*	EXHIBIT*
CHARACTERS		EXIT
CHECK*	DATA	EXPONENTIATED*
CLASS*	DATE-COMPILED	EXTENDED-SEARCH*
CLOCK-UNITS	DATE-WRITTEN	
CLOSE	DE	FD
COBOL	DEBUG*	FILE

FILE-CONTROL
FILE-LABEL*
FILE-LIMIT
FILE-LIMITS
FILLER
FIRST
FLOAT*
FOOTING
FOR
FORMAT
FORTRAN-R*
FORTRAN-X*
FROM

GOBACK*
GQ*
GR*
GREATER
GREATER-EQUAL*
GROUP

HASHED*
HEADING
HIGH*
HIGH-O
HIGH-O-CONTROL
HIGH-VALUE
HIGH-VALUES
HOLD*
HYPER*

ID*
IDENTIFICATION
INCLUDE*
INDEX
INDEXED
INDICATE*
INITIATE
INPUT
INPUT-OUTPUT
INSERT*
INSTALLATION
INTO
INVALID
I-O*
I-O-CONTROL*

JUST
JUSTIFIED

KEY
KEYS

LABEL
LABEL-RETURN
LAST
LEADING
LEAVE*
LEAVING*
LEFT
LESS
LESS-EQUAL*
LIBRARY*
LIMIT
LIMITS
LINAGE*
LINAGE-COUNTER*
LINE
LINE-COUNTER
LINES
LINKAGE*
LOCATION*
LOCK
LOW*
LOW-VALUE
LOW-VALUES
LOWER-BOUND*
LOWER-BOUNDS*
LQ*
LS*

MASTER-INDEX*
MEMORY
MINUS*
MODE
MODULES
MORE-LABELS*
MOVE
MULTIPLE
MULTIPLIED*
MULTIPLY

NAMED*
NEGATIVE
NEXT
NGR*
NLS*
NOMINAL*
NOT
NOTE
NQ*
NSTD-REELS*
NUMBER
NUMERIC

OBJECT-COMPUTER
OBJECT-PROGRAM*
OCCURS
OH*
OMITTED

OPEN
OPTIONAL
ORGANIZATION*
OTHERWISE*
OV*
OVERFLOW*

PAGE
PAGE-COUNTER
PERFORM
PF
PH
PIC
PICTURE
PLACES*
PLUS
POINT*
POSITION
POSITIONING*
POSITIVE
PREPARED*
PRINT-SWITCH*
PRIORITY*
PROCEDURE
PROCEDURES*
PROCEED
PROCESS*
PROCESSING
PROGRAM*
PROGRAM-ID
PROTECT*
PUNCH*
PUNCHB*

QUOTE
QUOTES

RANDOM
RANGE*
RD
READ
READY*
RECORD
RECORD-MARK*
RECORD-OVERFLOW*
RECORDING*
RECORDS
REDEFINES
REEL
REEL-NUMBER*
RELEASE
REMAINDER*
REMARKS
RENAMES
RENAMING*
REORG-CRITERIA*
REPLACING

REPORT
REPORTING
REPORTS
REREAD*
RERUN
RESERVE
RESET
RETENTION-CYCLE*
RETURN
RETURN-CODE*
REVERSED
REWIND
REWRITE*
RF
RH
RIGHT
ROUNDED
RUN

SA*
SAME
SD
SEARCH
SECTION
SECURITY
SEEK
SEGMENT-LIMIT
SELECT
SELECTED*
SENTENCE
SEQUENCED*
SEQUENTIAL
SET
SIGN
SIGNED*
SIZE
SKIP1*
SKIP2*
SKIP3*
SORT
SORT-CORE-SIZE
SORT-FILE-SIZE
SORT-MODE-SIZE

SORT-RETURN
SOURCE
SOURCE-COMPUTER
SPACE
SPACES
SPECIAL-NAMES
STANDARD
START*
STATUS
STOP
SUBTRACT
SUM
SUPERVISOR*
SUPPRESS*
SWITCH*
SYMBOLIC*
SYNC
SYNCHRONIZED
SYSIN*
SYSIPT*
SYSLST*
SYSOUT*
SYSPCH*
SYSPUNCH*
S01*
S02*

TALLY
TALLYING
TAPE
TAPE-LABEL*
TERMINAL*
TERMINATE
THAN
THEN*
THROUGH
THRU
TIME-OF-DAY*
TIMES
TO
TOTALED*
TOTALING*
TRACE*

TRACK*
TRACK-AREA*
TRACK-LIMIT*
TRACKS*
TRANSFORM*
TYPE*

UNEQUAL*
UNIT
UNTIL
UP
UP*
UPON
UPPER-BOUND*
UPPER-BOUNDS*
UPSI-0*
UPSI-1*
UPSI-2*
UPSI-3*
UPSI-4*
UPSI-5*
UPSI-6*
UPSI-7*
USAGE
USE
USING

VALUE
VALUES
VARYING

WHEN
WITH
WORDS
WORKING-STORAGE
WRITE
WRITE-ONLY*
WRITE-VERIFY*

ZERO
ZEROES
ZEROS

Appendix B

Quick Reference

This appendix contains a quick reference to the complete skeleton outline of all the COBOL statements discussed in the text. Options are marked high level or low level as defined by American National Standard COBOL (bulletin X3.23-1968). One column in the outline is set aside so that the student may mark the particular items applicable at his computer installation. Another column gives page references to the discussion of the statements. Ample room is left so that the student may write in the ENVIRONMENT DIVISION entries which apply to his computer. Preceding the skeleton outline is a brief summary of rules on punctuation, programmer-supplied names, literals, and figurative constants.

Rules for Punctuation

1. COBOL statements must be punched in the following format.
   - cols. 1–6 sequence number (optional); checked for ascending order
   - 7 contains a hyphen if the card contains the remainder of a word or literal which is continued from the previous card. See rules 2 and 3.
   - 8 the A margin; starts a DIVISION name, SECTION name, paragraph name, File Description (FD), Sort Description (SD), Report Description (RD), record description level number (01), or level number 77
   - 12–72 the B margin; contains data descriptions, commands, or continuation of commands
   - 73–80 alphanumeric identification (optional)
2. If it is not possible to complete a word before column 72 on a card, place a hyphen (-) in column 7 of the next card and begin in column 12 to write the remainder of the word. In low level COBOL words may not be broken between cards.
3. If a non-numeric literal cannot be completed before column 72 of a card, place a hyphen (-) in column 7 of the next card, a literal mark (') in column 12 and continue the literal in column 13. All together there will be three literal marks: one at the beginning and end of the literal and one in column 12. Any spaces between the first literal mark and column 72 will be included in the literal.
4. It is not necessary to end every statement in column 72. To avoid splitting a word or a literal between two cards, just begin the word or literal on the next card.
5. DIVISION and SECTION names are followed by a period, and the remainder of the line is blank.
6. A level number must be followed by at least one blank and the data name.
7. A paragraph name is followed by a period and at least one blank before the text begins. A paragraph name may appear by itself on a card.
8. The first sentence in a paragraph begins in or after column 12. Spaces or blank cards may be used freely to make the program more readable.
9. If a period follows a word, it must be placed immediately after the word, with no space in between.

10. There must be at least one space after every period.
11. A space must be included before and after the $+$ $-$ $*$ or $/$ symbols.
12. A space must be included before every left parenthesis.
13. When using two or three subscripts with a data name, the subscripts must be separated by commas with no comma after the last subscript. After each comma must be a space.

Rules for Programmer-Supplied Names

1. A name may contain the digits 0–9, the letters A–Z, and the hyphen (-).
2. A name may be from 1 to 30 characters in length.
3. A name may *not* contain blanks.
4. A hyphen may not be the first or last character of a name. Hyphens may not be used consecutively.
5. Paragraph and section names may be entirely numeric. All other names must contain at least one letter. In low level COBOL, the letter must be at the beginning of the name.
6. A name may not be one of the COBOL reserved words in Appendix A.
7. In low level COBOL each data name must be unique. High level COBOL data names may be qualified. Refer to section 10.8 on qualification.

Rules for Literals

1. A *non-numeric* literal is enclosed in single quotation (literal) marks (') and may contain a maximum of 120 characters. Any combination of characters may be used within the quote marks.
2. A *numeric* literal is a number which is not enclosed in quote marks. It may be written with a leftmost plus ($+$) or minus ($-$) sign. A numeric literal with no sign is positive. The literal may contain a decimal point, but the decimal may not be the rightmost character. Its maximum size is 18 digits.

Figurative Constants

Low level	Alternate spellings for high level only	Meaning
ZERO	ZEROS, ZEROES	the value 0 or the character 0
SPACE	SPACES	one or more blanks
HIGH-VALUE	HIGH-VALUES	one or more occurrences of the character which has the highest value on the computer
LOW-VALUE	LOW-VALUES	one or more occurrences of the character which has the lowest value on the computer
QUOTE	QUOTES	one or more occurrences of the quote (literal) mark; may not be used in place of the literal marks enclosing a non-numeric literal

not available	ALL literal	one or more occurrences of the programmer-supplied literal, which may be a non-numeric literal or one of the figurative constants above

Notation Used in Skeleton Outline

1. Any underlined word must be included unless it is in brackets.
2. Any capitalized word that is not underlined is optional.
3. A phrase in brackets, [ ], is optional. However, if the phrase is included, any underlined words it contains must be used.
4. From all the items in braces, { }, one and only one must be included in the program.
5. Any word not capitalized is to be supplied by the programmer. It must follow the rules for programmer-supplied names.
6. A phrase immediately preceding the ellipsis marks, . . . , may be repeated as required by the programmer.

COBOL Skeleton Outline

Low level	High level	Available on computer		Page reference
x	x		IDENTIFICATION DIVISION.	23, 25
x	x		PROGRAM-ID. program-name.	25, 33
x	x		[AUTHOR. sentence . . .]	23
x	x		[INSTALLATION. sentence . . .]	23
x	x		[DATE-WRITTEN. sentence . . .]	23
	x		[DATE-COMPILED. sentence . . .]	23
x	x		[SECURITY. sentence . . .]	23
x	x		[REMARKS. sentence . . .]	31, 33
x	x		ENVIRONMENT DIVISION.	23, 25, 211, 215
x	x		CONFIGURATION SECTION.	23
x	x		SOURCE-COMPUTER. computer-name.	25, 32
x	x		OBJECT-COMPUTER. computer-name.	26
x	x		[SPECIAL-NAMES. forms-control IS mnemonic-name . . .].	61, 69, 216
x	x		[INPUT-OUTPUT SECTION.]	26
x	x		FILE-CONTROL. {SELECT file-name ASSIGN TO [integer] input-or-output-device-1 [input-or-output-device-2] . . .	26, 216, 233
x	x		[FOR MULTIPLE REEL]	216, 233
x	x		[ACCESS MODE IS SEQUENTIAL]	216
x	x		[PROCESSING MODE IS SEQUENTIAL].} . . .	216
x	x		[I-O-CONTROL. [SAME AREA FOR file-name-1 file-name-2 . . .]. . . .]	216

ENVIRONMENT DIVISION SPECIFICS:

Low level	High level	Available on computer		Page reference
x	x		DATA DIVISION.	23, 27, 35
x	x		FILE SECTION.[1]	23, 35, 40

[1] This entire section may be omitted.

Low level	High level	Available on computer		Page reference
x	x		FD file-name	204, 219
x	x		[BLOCK CONTAINS integer-1 {RECORDS / CHARACTERS}]	219
x	x		DATA {RECORD IS / RECORDS ARE} record-name [record-name . . .]	40, 219
x	x		{LABEL {RECORD IS / RECORDS ARE} {STANDARD / OMITTED} }	40, 219
			{REPORT / REPORTS} report-name [report-name . . .]}	204
x	x		[RECORD CONTAINS [integer-2 TO] integer-3 CHARACTERS]	219, 220
x	x		[VALUE OF data-name-1 IS literal-1 [data-name-2 IS literal-2] . . .].	219, 220
x	x		level-number {data-name / FILLER} [{PICTURE / PIC} IS picture-string]	37–39 28, 37, 70 27, 36–37, 47–54, 123–125, 126
x	x		[OCCURS integer TIMES].[2]	133–135, 138–146, 184–186
	x		88 condition-name {VALUE IS / VALUES ARE} literal-1 [THRU literal-2] [literal-3 [THRU literal-4] . . .].[3]	115–116
	x		SD file-name DATA {RECORD IS / RECORDS ARE} record-name [record-name . . .] [RECORD CONTAINS [integer-1 TO] integer-2 CHARACTERS].	234
x	x		WORKING-STORAGE SECTION.[4]	23, 35, 36, 41, 70
x	x		77 data-name [{PICTURE / PIC} IS picture-string] [VALUE IS literal].	39
x	x		level-number data-name [{PICTURE / PIC} IS picture-string] [OCCURS integer TIMES][5] [VALUE IS literal].	27, 36–37, 47–54, 123–126 133–135, 138–146, 184–186 39–40, 70 25, 246
	x		REPORT SECTION.[6]	35, 204
	x		RD report-name [{CONTROL IS / CONTROLS ARE} {FINAL / data-name . . . / FINAL data-name . . .}]	205–208 204–208
	x		[PAGE {LIMIT IS / LIMITS ARE} integer {LINE / LINES}]	196, 199
	x		[HEADING integer] [FIRST DETAIL integer]	199, 199
	x		[LAST DETAIL integer] [FOOTING integer].	199, 200

---

[2] May not be used at the 01 level.

[3] May be used in WORKING-STORAGE SECTION.

[4] This entire section may be omitted.

[5] OCCURS may not be used at the 01 level. An item containing or subordinate to an OCCURS clause may not contain the VALUE phrase.

[6] This entire section may be omitted.

Low level	High level	Available on computer		Page reference
	x		01 [data-name] TYPE IS { REPORT HEADING / RH }	200
			PAGE HEADING / PH	200, 202
			{ CONTROL HEADING / CH } { data-name / FINAL }	200, 204–208
			DETAIL / DE	200
			{ CONTROL FOOTING / CF } { data-name / FINAL }	200, 204–208
			PAGE FOOTING / PF	200, 202
			REPORT FOOTING / RF	200
	x		[LINE NUMBER { integer / PLUS integer / NEXT PAGE }]	201
			[NEXT GROUP IS { integer / PLUS integer / NEXT PAGE }].	201, 202
	x		nn [data-name] [COLUMN NUMBER IS integer]	201
			[LINE NUMBER IS { integer / PLUS integer / NEXT PAGE }]	201
			[{ SOURCE IS { data-name / LINE-COUNTER / PAGE-COUNTER } / SUM data-name }]	197, 202 / 208
			[VALUE IS literal]	39–40, 70
			[{ PICTURE / PIC } IS picture-string].	36–37, 47–54, 123–126
x	x		PROCEDURE DIVISION.	24, 28, 56–57
x	x		ACCEPT data-name.	172
	x		ACCEPT data-name [FROM mnemonic-name].	172
x	x		ADD { data-name / literal } [{ data-name / literal } ...] TO data-name-n	71, 74–78
x	x		[ROUNDED] [ON SIZE ERROR statement ...].	
x	x		ADD { data-name / literal } { data-name / literal } ... GIVING data-name-n	74–78
			[ROUNDED] [ON SIZE ERROR statement ...].	
	x		ADD { CORRESPONDING / CORR } data-name-1 TO data-name-2	188
			[ROUNDED] [ON SIZE ERROR statement ...].	
x	x		ALTER procedure-name-1 TO [PROCEED TO] procedure-name-2.	181
x	x		CLOSE file-name [file-name ...].	58, 224
	x		COMPUTE data-name [ROUNDED] = { literal / arithmetic expression / data-name }	90, 96
			[ON SIZE ERROR statement ...].	
x	x		DISPLAY { data-name / literal } [{ data-name / literal } ...].	128, 173–174
	x		DISPLAY { data-name / literal } [{ data-name / literal } ...] [UPON mnemonic-name].	

Low level	High level	Available on computer		Page reference
x	x		DIVIDE {data-name-1 / literal} INTO data-name-2 [ROUNDED] [ON SIZE ERROR statement ...].	84–86
x	x		DIVIDE {data-name-1 / literal-1} {INTO / BY} {data-name-2 / literal-2} GIVING data-name-3 [ROUNDED] [ON SIZE ERROR statement ...].	71, 84–86
x	x		EXAMINE data-name {TALLYING {UNTIL FIRST / ALL / LEADING} literal-1 [REPLACING BY literal-2] / REPLACING {ALL / LEADING / [UNTIL] FIRST} literal-3 BY literal-4}.	177–179
x	x		EXIT.	163–164
	x		GENERATE data-name.	197–198, 203
x	x		GO TO procedure-name.	29, 64
x	x		GO TO procedure-name-1 [procedure-name-2] ... procedure-name-n DEPENDING ON data-name.	179–180
x	x		IF test {statement ... / NEXT SENTENCE} [{ELSE statement ... / ELSE NEXT SENTENCE}]. where test may be:	101–104, 113–116
x	x		{data-name / literal} {IS [NOT] GREATER THAN / IS [NOT] LESS THAN / IS [NOT] EQUAL TO} {data-name / literal}	
x	x		data-name IS [NOT] {NUMERIC / ALPHABETIC}	104–105
	x		{data-name / literal / arithmetic-exp.} {IS [NOT] GREATER THAN / IS [NOT] > / IS [NOT] LESS THAN / IS [NOT] < / IS [NOT] EQUAL TO / IS [NOT] =} {data-name / literal / arithmetic-exp.}	114
	x		{data-name / arithmetic-expression} IS [NOT] {POSITIVE / NEGATIVE / ZERO}	114–115
	x		[NOT] condition-name	115–116
	x		INITIATE report-name [report-name ...].	198, 202–203
x	x		MOVE {data-name / literal} TO data-name [data-name ...].	28, 61–63
	x		MOVE {CORRESPONDING / CORR} data-name-1 TO data-name-2.	188
x	x		MULTIPLY {data-name-1 / literal} BY data-name-2 [ROUNDED] [ON SIZE ERROR statement ...].	82–84
x	x		MULTIPLY {data-name / literal} BY {data-name / literal} GIVING data-name-3 [ROUNDED] [ON SIZE ERROR statement ...].	51, 73–74, 82–84
x	x		NOTE sentence. [sentence] ...	175–176
x	x		OPEN {INPUT / OUTPUT / I-O} file-name [file-name ...].	23, 57–58, 221
x	x		paragraph-name. sentence [sentence ...]	28, 56–57

Low level	High level	Available on computer		Page reference
x	x		PERFORM procedure-name [THRU procedure-name].	155–169
x	x		PERFORM procedure-name [THRU procedure-name] $\begin{Bmatrix} \text{data-name} \\ \text{integer} \end{Bmatrix}$ TIMES.	154–169
	x		PERFORM procedure-name [THRU procedure-name] VARYING data-name FROM $\begin{Bmatrix} \text{literal-1} \\ \text{data-name-1} \end{Bmatrix}$ BY $\begin{Bmatrix} \text{literal-2} \\ \text{data-name-2} \end{Bmatrix}$ UNTIL condition.	154–169
x	x		READ file-name RECORD AT END imperative-statement.	28, 58–60, 221–222
	x		RELEASE record-name.	231, 233, 237
	x		RETURN file-name RECORD AT END imperative-statement.	231, 233, 238
x	x		section-name SECTION.	56–57
			paragraph-name. sentence. [sentence . . .]	28, 56–57
	x		SORT file-name-1 ON $\begin{Bmatrix} \text{DESCENDING} \\ \text{ASCENDING} \end{Bmatrix}$ KEY data-name-1 [data-name-2] . . . $\left[\text{ON} \begin{Bmatrix} \text{DESCENDING} \\ \text{ASCENDING} \end{Bmatrix} \text{KEY data-name-3 [data-name-4] . . .} \right]$ . . . $\begin{Bmatrix} \text{INPUT PROCEDURE IS section-name-1 [THRU section-name-2]} \\ \text{USING file-name-2} \\ \text{OUTPUT PROCEDURE IS section-name-3 [THRU section-name-4]} \\ \text{GIVING file-name-3} \end{Bmatrix}$.	229–234
x	x		STOP RUN.	64
x	x		SUBTRACT $\begin{Bmatrix} \text{data-name} \\ \text{literal} \end{Bmatrix} \left[\begin{Bmatrix} \text{data-name} \\ \text{literal} \end{Bmatrix} \right]$ . . . FROM data-name-n [ROUNDED] [ON SIZE ERROR statement . . .].	78–82
x	x		SUBTRACT $\begin{Bmatrix} \text{data-name} \\ \text{literal} \end{Bmatrix} \left[\begin{Bmatrix} \text{data-name} \\ \text{literal} \end{Bmatrix} \right]$ . . . FROM data-name-m GIVING data-name-n [ROUNDED] [ON SIZE ERROR statement . . .].	78–82
	x		SUBTRACT $\begin{Bmatrix} \text{CORRESPONDING} \\ \text{CORR} \end{Bmatrix}$ data-name-1 FROM data-name-2 [ROUNDED] [ON SIZE ERROR statement . . .].	188
	x		TERMINATE report-name [report-name . . .].	198, 203
x	x		WRITE record-name $\left[\begin{Bmatrix} \text{BEFORE} \\ \text{AFTER} \end{Bmatrix} \text{ADVANCING integer LINES} \right]$.	29, 60–61, 223–224
x	x		WRITE record-name INVALID KEY imperative-statement.	223

Appendix C

Operating the IBM 29 Card Punch

The card punch, or key punch as it frequently is called, is a device for punching cards. It has a keyboard very similar to a typewriter (see Figure C.1) and will print characters on the cards as well as punch the holes which represent them. Normally the card punch is in alphabetic mode, so pressing the keys will punch letters and other characters which are printed on the lower portions of the keys. All letters are capitalized; there are no lower case letters. To punch numbers or other characters in the upper positions of the keys, we must keep the NUMERIC key depressed. The comma and period may be punched in either alphabetic or numeric mode.

Figure C.1 Keyboard of IBM 29
Card Punch

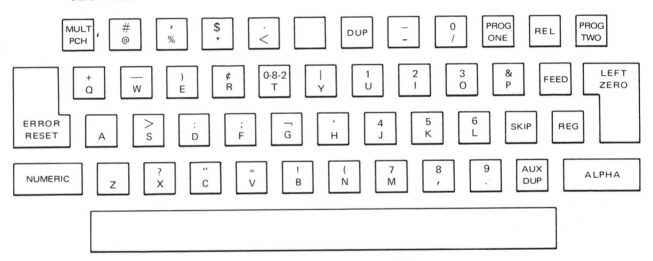

Source: Laura G. Cooper and Marilyn Z. Smith, *Standard FORTRAN: A Problem-Solving Approach* (Boston:
Houghton Mifflin Co., 1973), Figure 4.5, p. 31.

For the beginner, there are a few basic steps to follow and several important keys to remember (DUP, BACKSPACE, AUTO FEED). For the advanced student who already knows how to punch cards, we recommend learning how to use the drum control card. This card acts like the tab on a typewriter and allows us to set our own margins. It can also define fields in either alphabetic or numeric mode so that it may not be necessary to keep the NUMERIC key depressed. Therefore, this appendix contains two sections: elementary card punch instructions and drum control card operations. For better understanding the student should be seated at a card punch so he can verify the operations.

Basic Operating Instructions

1. Be sure there are enough unpunched cards in the card hopper. If not, get some and fill the card hopper.
2. Make certain the card punch is on. The main switch is located underneath the table on the front of the machine.
3. Turn off the AUTO FEED and AUTO DUP switches. (You may wish to use AUTO FEED if you have many cards to punch. For instructions in its use see below.)
4. Press the FEED key to feed a card from the card hopper into the punch area.

Figure C.2 Close-up View of IBM 29
Card Punch

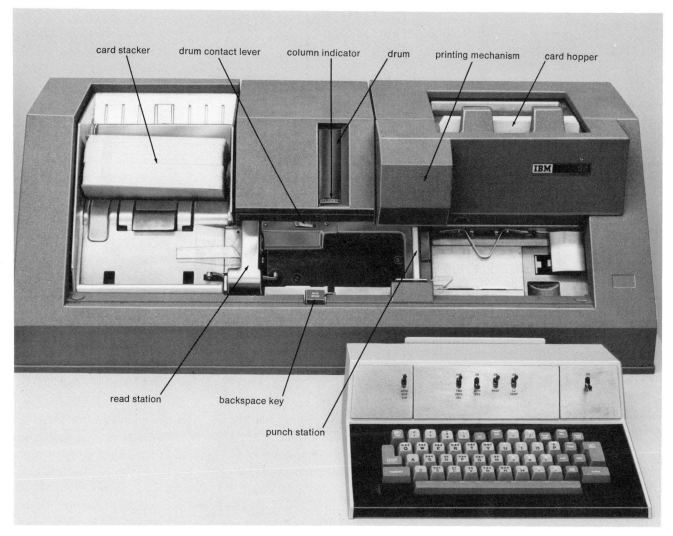

Source: Laura G. Cooper and Marilyn Z. Smith, *Standard FORTRAN: A Problem-Solving Approach* (Boston: Houghton Mifflin Co., 1973), Figure 4.6, p. 32.

5. Press the REG key to register the card. Notice that the card moves over so that its left edge is underneath the punch station.

6. You are now ready to begin punching the card. To leave a column blank, press the space bar. If you space too far, use the backspace key. The column indicator located at the bottom of the drum window points to the column which the machine is ready to punch and helps you punch information in the correct columns.

7. When you have finished with one card, press the REL key to release the card and move it into the read station.

8. After releasing one card, you may feed another card and punch it. The card in the read station will not affect the card in the punch station unless the DUP key is pressed. (See the DUP key description.) Releasing the second card will cause the first to move over and the second to move into the read area. Pressing the REG key will cause the first card to move into the card stacker. To punch more cards return to step 4.

9. To move all cards into the stacker, keep pressing the REL and REG keys

alternately until all cards are in the stacker. An easier way is to flip the CLEAR switch.

10. Remove cards from the stacker and proofread them. To correct cards use the DUP key described below. Throw away any incorrect cards and leave the table of the card punch empty.

Important Keys

Some keys of special importance are the following.

DUP Key. The DUP (duplicate) key can help when correcting cards. If a card contains a mistake, there is no way to correct the card and no need to punch it a second time. We may duplicate the correct portions onto a new card and punch only where we have made mistakes. To do this, place the incorrect card in the read station, feed and register a blank card in the punch station. Hold down the DUP key until you reach an incorrect column. Punch the corrections and duplicate some more if necessary. If there is no card in the read station, you can use the DUP key for rapid spacing.

BACKSPACE Key and Column Indicator. The backspace key will cause the card punch to move the card to the right as long as the key is held down. To determine the correct column in which to stop, refer to the column indicator. It moves forward as the card is punched and backward whenever the backspace key is depressed. The column indicator always points to the column which is ready *to be punched*.

MULT PCH Key. Depressing the MULT PCH (multi-punch) key keeps the card punch from advancing to the next column. As a result several punches will appear in one column. This key is useful when you need a special combination of punches which determine a character not on the keyboard. For example, the CDC 6000 series computers use a 6 7 8 9 card for their end of data. This card contains the numbers 6, 7, 8, and 9 multi-punched in column 1. When using the MULT PCH key, the card punch is automatically in numeric mode.

AUTO FEED Switch. This switch is useful if you have many cards to punch. The basic steps to follow are given below.

1. Turn on the AUTO FEED switch.
2. Press the FEED key twice. There will be two cards in the punch station. One is registered and ready to be punched; the other is waiting.
3. Punch the first card. When finished, press the REL key. The punched card moves to the read station; the card which was waiting is now registered and ready to be punched; and the card punch automatically feeds down a new card.
4. Continue punching cards, pressing REL when necessary to feed another card. When finished, flip the CLEAR switch to remove all cards into the card stacker.

Instructions for Using the Drum Control Card

Using a drum control card can increase the speed of punching because it allows a person to specify the format of his cards. He can set margins, define numeric areas, skip fields, and automatically duplicate other fields. If a field is numeric, it is not necessary to depress the NUMERIC key when punching characters in the upper positions of the keys. Setting margins no longer requires us to space over to get to a certain column. Instead, pressing the SKIP key can move the card there instantly. For the student who is just beginning we recommend that he become more familiar with card punch operations before learning to use the drum control card.

To use a drum control card decide upon the format of the cards you will be punching. Then, using the special codes discussed below, punch a card which shows the format column by column. This card is the drum control card and must be placed on the keypunch's cylindrical drum to activate the machine. The best way to learn how to attach the card is from a personal demonstration. Therefore, in this text we will not attempt to explain the mechanics of putting the card on the drum. Instead, let us discuss the codes for the drum card. The IBM 29 card punch has two codes: program one which uses the 12, 11, 0, 1, and blank punches and program two which uses the 4, 5, 6, 7, and blank punches. The use of these codes is similar; and there is a switch on the key punch to tell it whether you are using program one or program two codes on the drum control card. If one card contains two programs, we can use the switch to go from one card format to the other. The codes are of two types:

1. ones for the beginning column of a field
2. ones for the remaining columns of a field

The meaning of the codes are given in Tables C.1 and C.2. Remember that a slash (/) punch is a 0 1 multipunched in a column, and that an A punch is a 12 1 multipunch.

Table C.1   Punches to Indicate the Beginning of a Field

Program 1	Meaning	Program 2
1 punch	Begin alphanumeric field	7 punch
blank	Begin numeric field	blank
11 punch*	Begin skip field	5 punch
/ punch	Begin automatic duplication of an alphanumeric field	6 7 multipunch
0 punch	Begin automatic duplication of a numeric field	6 punch

*A minus sign is an 11 punch.

Table C.2   Punches to Indicate the Remainder of the Field

Program 1	Meaning	Program 2
A	Alphanumeric field	4 7 multipunch
12 punch*	Numeric field	4 punch

*On most keypunches the ampersand (&) key produces a 12 punch; on others the plus sign (+) is a 12 punch.

Example of Drum Control Card (Program 1) for COBOL Program

b&&&&&&1AAA1AAAAAAAAAAAAAAAAAAAAAAAAAAAAAAAAAAAAAAAAAAAAAAAAAAAAAAAAAAAAA–&&&&&&

columns 1–7 indicate a numeric field (the b represents a blank)
8 indicates the A margin
9–11 continuation of the statement begun in the A margin
12 marks the B margin
13–72 continuation of a statement
73–80 skip field (nothing will be punched here)

If we wanted to skip columns 1–7 and not punch a sequence number on the card, we would begin the control card with –&&&&&& punches. If we wanted to punch something in columns 73–80 for identification, we would end the card with 1AAAAAAA punches. To create additional fields for indenting level numbers past column 12, or for marking the beginning of the PICTURE field we could include more ones on the drum card.

Example of Drum Control Card (Program 2) for Punching Data

Suppose we wish to punch data in the following format.

Then our drum card is the following.

$$b4444444457\frac{4444444444444}{7777777777777}7\frac{4444444444444}{7777777777777}54444444444444444444444444444444444446\frac{6666}{7777}$$

The $\frac{4}{7}$ denotes that the 4 and 7 are multipunched in the same column; the $\frac{6}{7}$ denotes a 6 and a 7 multipunch.

Since the 5 in column 10 is followed by the beginning of a new field, only one column is skipped.

The automatic duplication field in columns 76–80 indicates that whatever is in those columns on the card in the read station will be duplicated onto the card being punched. If we are punching the second data card, it will contain a duplicate of columns 76–80 of the first card. In order to get the cycle going for the first card, we must punch the desired characters on a separate card, place it in the read station, and then feed and register our first card.

Instructions for Use of the Drum Control Card

1. Punch a drum control card according to the format desired.
2. Remove the drum from the keypunch. Be sure the star wheels are raised before removing it. The drum contact lever located below and to the left of the drum window controls the height of the star wheels.

Figure C.3   Drum Control Card in Place on Card Punch

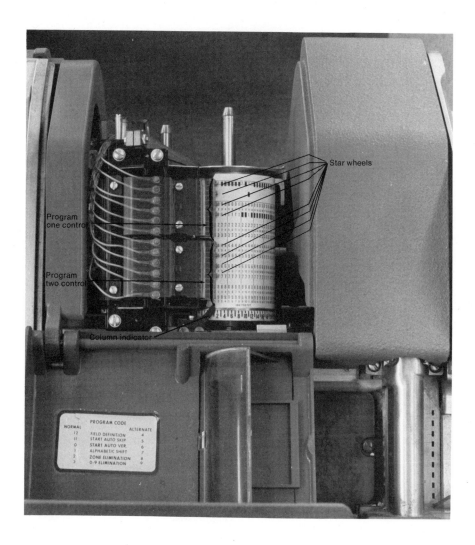

3. Fit the drum control card snugly on the drum. A loose card may not work properly.
4. Replace the drum on the keypunch and lower the star wheels.
5. Turn on the AUTO SKIP DUP (automatic skip and duplicate) switch.
6. Begin punching cards. You may wish to use AUTO FEED to speed up the card feeding process. If the drum card contains an automatic duplicate field, punch a card to begin the cycle and place it in the read station before feeding any cards. (See the second example above for an explanation.)
7. Raising the contacts will disengage the action of the control card.
8. Pressing the DUP key once will duplicate the remainder of an entire field from the card in the read station onto the card in the punch station.
9. Depressing the NUM key or the ALPHA key will override the mode specified on the drum control card.

Index